INJURY

INJURY

The Politics of Product Design and Safety Law
in the United States

Sarah S. Lochlann Jain

PRINCETON UNIVERSITY PRESS
PRINCETON AND OXFORD

Copyright © 2006 by Princeton University Press
Published by Princeton University Press, 41 William Street,
Princeton, New Jersey 08540
In the United Kingdom: Princeton University Press, 3 Market Place,
Woodstock, Oxfordshire OX20 1SY

Library of Congress Cataloging-in-Publication Data

Jain, Sarah S. Lochlann, 1967–
Injury : the politics of product design and safety law
in the United States / Sarah S. Lochlann Jain.
p. cm.

Includes bibliographical references and index.

ISBN-13: 978-0-691-11907-6 (cloth : alk. paper)—ISBN-13: 978-0-691-11908-3
(pbk. : alk. paper)
ISBN-10: 0-691-11907-4 (cloth : alk. paper)—ISBN-10: 0-691-11908-2 (pbk. : alk. paper)

1. Personal injuries—United States. 2. Product safety—Social aspects—United States.
3. Wounds and injuries—Social aspects—United States. I. Title.

KF1257.J35 2006
346.7303'23—dc22   2005054464

British Library Cataloging-in-Publication Data is available

This book has been composed in Palatino

Printed on acid-free paper. ∞

pup.princeton.edu

Printed in the United States of America

10 9 8 7 6 5 4 3 2 1

TO MY PARENTS
Evelyn and Sudhir Jain

Contents

Preface

A few years ago, at a seminar on the typewriter and the material production of literature, I remarked on the way that typewriters had been the primary means by which women entered the labor force. The response was silence. Even more intriguing was a colleague's comment on litigation stemming from keyboard-induced injuries. This latter comment gnawed at me as I made the long commute home over the Santa Cruz mountains. Suing? Over a repetitive strain injury? By reputation I knew that Americans sued each other. And having lived in the United States for a year I had by that time seen several news stories on the phenomenon. Though they tended to dismiss such lawsuits as frivolous, I became curious about the logic that must have rendered them legible within some larger legal and social system.

The more I inspected injury lawsuits, the more intrigued I became. First, there were the stories themselves: the seemingly endless number of ways that human sentience came under siege through everyday products. Then there were the various narratives employed to make sets of arguments about the agency of objects and people in the law: how could it not matter that someone was *drunk* when his door handle malfunctioned as his car hit the median? How could a particular Wal-Mart parking lot be defectively designed when it looked like every other suburban parking lot? How could a damage award against a huge corporation, intended to be punitive in virtually every statement and theory of tort law, be reduced to a paltry sum because it infringed on a corporation's constitutional rights to due process?

Then there always seemed to be an edge of investigative reporting to this research. Newspapers invariably got the facts wrong, misreported crucial details, or squashed the legal analysis into a space that required the amputation of all the interesting parts. In a sense, injury law—this central site of American culture making—was invisible through its overrepresentation in popular culture.

But most important, recorded opinions and archived complaints provide an astonishing testament to the ingenuity of plaintiffs who were in so many ways the losers to the technologies that "progress" tendered. In 1905 after ten-year-old Branch Lewis Jr. was hit and killed by an automobile on an Atlanta street, his mother brought a potentially revolutionary complaint. She sued Mr. Amorous, the owner of the vehicle, for allowing an unlicensed young man to drive his car, which she described as "a large and heavy machine, capable of going at a great rate of speed." This was the mark she left. We know nothing else about her—whether she was white or black, rich or poor, whether she had other children, where her husband was, or whose idea it had been to bring the complaint. Yet the complaint, and the legal opinion that dismissed it, articulate the competing interests of American industry and commodity ownership of the period. Social and technical forces collaborated to render a nearly inevitable ruling against Lewis. But the complaint registers a possibility that things might have been otherwise—that an alternative world that recognized the dangers posed by automobiles was once imaginable. In *Lewis v. Amorous*, had the judge, the court, or the logic been otherwise—had responsibility for the dangers of autos been placed with owners in the way that Lewis was suggesting—the United States would be a very different place. The legal archive is filled with such imagined other worlds.

As my research continued, I also began to note on the one hand a high political content, one that can at times seem to verge on an arbitrary application of logic and rules. This effect is what Duncan Kennedy has termed the "bad faith" of law. On the other hand, Americans still believe—albeit amid great cynicism—that there is such a thing as "the law" and in its inherent justness, finality, and ultimately, transparency. This was indicated to me in the response I received to a funding application to analyze tobacco trials, in which a reviewer wrote, "[T]his issue is already being resolved through legal channels," as if those legal channels themselves were beyond scrutiny. This faith in the transparency of the law, despite its frequent demonstrable bad faith, infuses everyday life in America.

Anthropologists write about strange cultural phenomena, and the American culture of litigation certainly fits this mandate. At cocktail parties it became clear to me that Americans, too, find it a bizarre cultural practice. Everyone has a story to add, some deadly serious, some funny: relatives with long, drawn-out deaths from cancer and emphysema; friends killed in and by sport utility vehicles; bizarre warning labels on recent purchases; grandparents undergoing needless surgery. Injury, causation, and agency are central to personal agendas, consumptive behaviors, and life in America.

Then, as I was writing, a strange thing began to happen—Canadians began suing each other in greater numbers. They began both literally suing each other and using litigation as a convenient device to explain why certain things were happening—why playgrounds were being torn down in Toronto, or why school trips were being phased out in Vancouver. In real civil questions—such as what kind of warnings should be placed in outdoor nature parks or what would be appropriate supervision on school trips—litigation (or fear of litigation) has become the vernacular explanation for a series of decisions that may have more straightforward, predictable, or democratic arenas for debate. And so what are Canadians and, increasingly, Europeans importing? I believe that in importing American injury law, other countries import more than a simple logic, more than a commonsense way of understanding and explaining. Injury law presents an entire infrastructure for thinking about social relations. More, it provides a powerful index of the defensive responses to privatization of interests in health and welfare.

Finally, as I studied design process in more detail, it became clear that the American world of commodities is produced in highly speculative contexts in which designers imagine potential users—from their size to how they might take up new products. Corporations control budgets and imagine various bottom lines (including one for potential lawsuits). These are always approximations. As approximations, with built-in sets of agencies structuring what they can and cannot do, objects can only ever simulate a full consumer fantasy. An airbag inspires the notion that it will increase safety for all consumers, but, in fact, it will "work" better for some people and actually pose a threat to others, depending on human factors such as height. Thus, injury provides a way to analyze the social discrepancies inherent to material culture and often missing from anthropological and science studies theories of human and object interaction.

In a nation committed to consumerism as a means of expressing economic and social citizenship, injury provides both a shocking moment of disjuncture and a predictable outcome of design and market systems. Any culture will have to address the problem of what to do when its members are physically wounded and to what extent health for its own sake will be a goal of the society. But in the United States, a country with no universal national health care and yet a well-developed rhetoric of individual well-being, injury law has a unique valance. It offers people not only an opportunity to tell their stories and have their day in court, but for some, a means of survival. It also poses as a highly rational and formalized arena for sanitizing and then adjudicating the messy and contradictory sets of goals, ideals, and desires of commodity culture. The location of injury and its distribution powerfully bring into view the dynamics of contemporary American culture as it undergoes further privatization in the arenas of welfare and health care.

The number of people who have talked to me about this project and shared their expertise in the many areas this research has required are too numerous to mention. I was inordinately lucky to meet so many people along the way who shared, indulged, or forbore my work.

Quite simply, the book would have taken a different and lesser form without the sustained critical readings of a number of colleagues and friends: Aneesh Aneesh, Nick Blomley, Erica Bornstein, Deborah Bright, Wendy Brown, Victor Buchli, Nancy Chen, Elizabeth Churchill, Jim Clifford, Kris Cohen, Jane Collier, Ruth Schwartz Cowan, Angela Davis, Rozita Dimova, Paula Findlen, Michael Fischer, Carla Freccero, Janet Halley, Donna Haraway, Caren Kaplan, Matthew Kohrman, Jake Kosek, Steve Kurzman, Celia Lowe, Samara Marion, Bill Maurer, Catherine Newman, Joy Parr, Jason Patton, Alain Pottage, Elizabeth Povinelli, Matt Price, Hugh Raffles, Teemu Ruskola, Jeffrey Schnapp, Derek Simons, Mimi Sheller, Vivian Sobchack, Lucy Suchman, Anne Stott, Marilyn Strathern, Neferti Tadiar, Miriam Ticktin, James Todd, Sherrie Tucker, Martha Umphrey, Nina Wakeford, Ann Weinstone, and Sarah Whatmore.

Still others have offered mentorship, granted extensive interviews, offered invitations for talks, and provided the kind of lively debate and support that makes academic research not only possible but, for so much of the time, outright enjoyable: Ann Annagnost, Bettina Aptheker, Adam Arms, Lee Balefsky, Frank Bardacke, Stephane Barnes, Sharron Beamer, Genevieve Bell, Carolyn Bledsoe, Susan Boyd, Ruth Buchanan, Judith Butler, Ermalinda Campani, Jamie Cassells, Ellen Christensen, Andrew Coburn, Deborah Cohler, Shelly Coughlan, George Collier, Marianne Constable, Fosca d'Acierno, Cletus Daniel, Carol Delaney, Gina Dent, Joe Dumit, Kathy Durcan, Paulla Ebron, Donna Evens-Kesef, Dana Frank, Marge Frantz, Estelle Freedman, Margot Geary, Angelica Glass, Jennifer Gonzales, Leif Granberg, Victoria de Grazia, Akhil Gupta, Cindy Hahamovitch, Dixie and Richard Hayduck, Marty Glick, David Hess, Rajeev Kelkar, Anita Jain, Kamini Jain, Luis Jaramillo, Maurice Jourdane, Ann Katten, Chris Kelty, Audrey Kobayashi, Hannah Landegger, Michael and Hannah Laurence, Linda Layne, Cynthia Leighton, Michael MacNabb, Dick Maltzman, Purnima Mankekar, Chris Marion, Jacques Marion, Wayne McCready, Ramah McKay, Donna Medley, Michael Millner, Jennifer Mnookin, Michael Montoya, Mike Mueter, Benji Newman, Maureen O'Malley, Leonard Ortolano, Nelly Oudshoorn, Colleen Pearl, Jane Perna, Kay Peterson, Adriana Petryna, Sheila Peuse, Steven Phillips, Jo Plante, Richard Pollay, Laura Punnett, Robert Rabin, Daniel Reilly, David Rempel, Rick Robinson, Hector de la Rosa, Renato Rosaldo, Becki Ross, Asher Rubin, Michael Rucka, Megan Sanderson, Austin Sarat, Lea Scarpelli, Mimi Sheller, Stephen Sheller, John Sherry, Ann Stoler, Anne Stott, Florentine Strzelczyk, Charles Taylor, David Thompson, Ellen Timberlake, Victoria Vesna, Don Villarejo, Barb Voss, Wendy Waters, David Watson, Robert Weems, Miriam Wells, Jim Willson, Eric Wright, Claire Young, and Earnie Susan Zieff, among others too many to name.

Thanks also to my editors at Princeton, Mary Murrell and Fred Appel, as well as my two reviewers, Elizabeth Povinelli and Michael Fischer, who provided critical, encouraging, and insightful feedback as the manuscript expanded to what I could no longer in good conscience ask colleagues to read.

For research funding, I gratefully acknowledge the Program on Urban Studies, Stanford University; Marilyn Yalom Research Fellowship; Killam Foundation Postdoctoral Fellowship; Social Sciences and Humanities Research Council of Canada Postdoctoral Award; the American Association of University Women; the History of Consciousness Department; a National Science Foundation Grant; and the Chicano/Latino Research Center at University of California—Santa Cruz.

INJURY

FIGURE 1. Joel Pett, CWS / CartoonArts International.

Introduction

Injury in U.S. Risk Culture

REFERRING TO A class action in which several black youths sued Mc-
Donald's for the injury of obesity, this political cartoon spoofs the
American turn to litigation as a means of solving economic and social
issues.[1] By juxtaposing one of the plaintiffs in what became known
simply as the "McDonald's obesity suit" against third world famine,
the cartoon poses a rich set of paradoxes: a large American with a bag
of food set against a malnourished subaltern with an empty bowl offering the naïve advice to use an already suspect litigation strategy in the
face of the "genuine" complexity of poverty. Furthermore, the astro-
naut-like precision of the U.S. flag hints at a past American greatness
besmirched by the impropriety and ubiquity of injury lawsuits—a once
great nation now littered with empty soda cups. The satire, then, parodies the misplaced confidence of this woman and her black vernacular appeal to litigation.[2] Can litigation be the answer to the web of
problems that includes obesity, famine, and global politics? Is obesity
not the only one of these issues that can at least be attributed to personal responsibility? To consume is American. To sue is American. In
the interstices of these positions lies a culture of injury only hinted at
in the layers of this cartoon. Herein lies the central theme of this book.

For parents of an infant injured by a poorly designed baby carrier,
for someone who loses a spouse after a door lock failure, or even for
someone who wants to lay blame for accidental pregnancy after
spreading contraceptive jelly on toast, tort law is an obligatory passage
point. It is the place one must go to have injuries recognized, health
care bills paid, and moral outrage salved. The arena gives form, if only
in a highly structured and artificial way, to deep-seated anxieties about
the body, technology, consumption, agency, and injury.[3] In this way,
throughout the twentieth century injury law has held a critical place
in the United States to a degree unmatched in any other country, and
it remains a key infrastructure for negotiating the responsibilities that
manufacturers should have in product design, given the ease with
which human flesh is injured.

In many ways, as legal theorists such as Laura Nader and Richard
Abel have argued, tort law offers a radical potential for social justice.[4]
Waves of cases, typified recently by a group of litigants whose children

were accidentally killed by guns, result from frustration with federal regulation of industry and attempt to enforce the development of safer designs through litigation. Similarly, resource-intensive lawsuits have had striking success in bringing attention to cigarettes, asbestos, Agent Orange, and the Dalkon Shield where other methods of regulation have failed. These cases demand careful consideration because they take seriously—and assert—the right that injury law promises: the right of consumers not to be injured by mass-produced consumer objects. These cases raise the politics of design through issues such as how easily features such as safety locks and ballistics fingerprinting could have been and could yet be integrated into handgun designs or how guns are purposely made attractive to young children or to those with potentially criminal intent. Indeed, groups such as the National Rifle Association and the tobacco industry have lobbied hard to ensure that their products have been exempt from the regulatory reach of federal agencies. Furthermore, specificities of American culture such as the high cost of medical care and a regulatory system open to political suasion, as well as a tort system that unlike in Canada or Europe allows for high punitive damages, has led several tort theorists to argue that after bad accidents many Americans have no choice but to litigate.[5] In these "activist" senses, tort law can be understood as a back door, private way of regulating dangerous products when the government refuses to do so.[6]

While injury law demands to be understood in the context of a battery of civil rights advocacy strategies, this activist standpoint has also obviated a more thorough analysis of the cultural politics of injury and the ways that injury law and product design produce American subjects. The famous American tort cases, as well as the more modest ones I examine closely in this book, illustrate that the law does far more than recognize, measure, and compensate injuries. It does the political and social work of determining what will count as an injury and, ultimately, how it will be distributed through product designs.

In these ways, close and contextualized readings of legal texts can lead us beyond the question of efficacy in realizing the stated goals of the institutions addressed to the problem of injury and toward an analysis of how physical injuries are made material (made to count), how they circulate, and how their distribution creates the material conditions of everyday life. This shift in analysis, in which I interrogate not only how the law adjudicates claims of product defect and personal injury, but how legal entities (guns, consumers, injuries, defects) are constituted allows us to better examine how the law is deeply political in ways that are central to and constitutive of American citizenship, consumerism, wounding, and the distribution of responsibility. These central cultural and political questions are merely glossed over by these laws; they determine who pays for and what counts as national progress. But further, they sustain the separation and individuation of the consumer as the very basic tenet of consumer capitalism, allowing for the liberal chooser who rationally selects the items he consumes. This allows for the logical step of understanding injury as a by-product, not central to production and consumption.

Injury laws pervade American consciousness as a central and unique drama, one whose complexities are often posed in the media and blockbuster films as parodies of pure good meeting pure evil. The form of the trial pits private citizen against huge institution, with law structured as a neutral seeker of the facts and objective adjudicator. It so well captures—and structures—an American framing of right and wrong that fact-based suits are played out again and again in films such as *A Civil Action* and *Erin Brockovitch*. Tort laws "make sense" to Americans in a way that tends to mystify Canadians and Europeans. Tort laws hold a peculiarly vital place in the United States, given—undoubtedly as a result of—the lack of universal health care coverage, the dearth of regulatory bodies (and so the hint that bodies are used as guinea pigs or canaries), and the particular qualities of money, which can mutate in purpose from compensation to punishment, while so easily mutating again through desire and greed. These laws also fit within an individualized notion of American citizenship, understanding injury not as a structural premise of capitalism and a condition of its possibility but as an accidental side effect—a problem that can be rectified at the level of the individual and the particular facts of her case. Nevertheless, American injury culture is produced and consumed in a global economy, one in which injury and risk can also be outsourced to poorer nations who are willing to use pesticides or child labor.[7]

In its vernacular reiteration in popular domains such as film and media, the law is a powerfully interpellative discourse, posing crosscutting narratives of the "small guy" versus the "vast corporation," and the "valid" versus the "frivolous" case.[8] Both of these accounts indicate that though appealed to as an objective adjudicator of facts, legal institutions addressed to the law of personal injury offer powerful social technologies for deciding how (and which) human wounding will carry political, economic, and social weight. These two narrative axes also begin to hint at the complexities of popular understandings of injury law. As Elizabeth Povinelli argues in the context of state recognition of race and rights in Australia, the difficulty of law as a primary conduit for politics is that "moral obligation—moral sensibility— is exactly where critical rationality is not."[9] Since institutions addressed to injury law pose as both moral *and* rational, they remain susceptible to political manipulation. This is evidenced by well-publicized iconic cases such as the "McDonald's hot coffee case," in which an elderly woman was burned by a cup of hot coffee and sued McDonalds.[10] The misinformation campaign that followed this case, *Leibeck v. McDonald's Restaurants*, and the related pathologization of the "ambulance chaser" demonstrate the high stakes in conditioning how this form of private judicial activism will be understood by the American public.[11] Individuated injury claims, while providing an outlet for private justice, can be picked up and ridiculed in formats easily translated into sound bites by parties interested in conservative tort reform, whereas the complicated stories that lead to complaints such as *Leibeck* do not tend to translate so well. Further pitfalls of assuming the validity and efficacy of the stated goals of the law include an erasure of the problematic case-law approach, which enables single judges to make far-reaching and value-laden precedents. Other issues lie with legal assumptions that injuries can be narrowly traced to single products and incidents and that large punitive awards serve as sufficient deterrents.

Despite their central role in the production of American culture, in themselves these laws provide us with only an emaciated language with which to understand the material world and its relations with human sentience, or corporate capitalism and its human costs. In this book, then, I step outside of the questions of frivolous cases and junk science to offer an examination of how injury laws determine how human wounding and risk subjectivities are distributed both prior to and through litigation.[12] As I will analyze and argue in detail, legal trials structure narratives about injuries and differences; they are a key site at which a common sense about object use, design, and consumer expectations is both constituted and articulated. They are central to the valuation and reproduction of consumer culture.[13]

Injury takes seriously the ways that commodity design harbors assumptions about sociality, behavior, and human action. This observation has been well noted in recent work in material culture studies, which has recognized that objects "acquire their full significance only if one takes account of their double role in both the 'practical' order, which includes social arrangements for maintaining life, and the 'expressive' order, which creates hierarchies of honour and status, and which enjoys priority over the former."[14] What this dichotomy glosses over too quickly is the way in which human and nonhuman actors always act in themselves only partially and always within fields of distributed agency. Thus in the chapters that follow, I trace the ways in which humans and non-humans act among one another, implicating each other to constitute safe or dangerous passages through everyday life. In these passages, wellness and wounding will always be at play within various cross-cutting hierarchies.

Injury law inserts itself into these fluid relations, separating out the terms through which agents will be understood, responsibility distributed, and inequalities recalibrated. In assuming that injury is always incidental to American culture, tort law and its promise of reparable harms redistribute human wounding—already distributed through the prior machinations of consumption and capitalism—with vast implications of whose bodies the costs of progress fall into. This insertion is constitutive: should cars, or certain kinds of cars, be crashworthy by definition in a 45 to 0 miles-per-hour side-impact crash? For what size person?[15] What if the driver was drunk or not wearing a seatbelt? What if she slipped under the airbag? Should she have done more research before buying the car, or should she have depended on the automaker or the agencies in charge of auto safety? What if the vehicle was advertised as being safe for everyone, but what if each car had a warning sign that stated that people under five feet tall should not sit in the front seat?

In one sense, wounding itself brings a mode of attention to objects into being. Heidegger noted this point with his famous example of the carpenter's tools, in which objects only emerge as separate from the craftsperson when something goes wrong.[16] But injury law furthers this distinction—one depended on also in consumer capitalism. Injury laws provide a discourse through which the fluidity of everyday interactions are stilled, and thus they allow the analyst to understand how its categories are made sensical. Thus, these laws can be understood as a mechanism for maintaining, reproducing, and challenging unequal social relations—continually setting and resetting the acceptable relations between markets and bodies—isolating the body as an atemporal artifact from the temporality, the process, of the acculturated self. Injury laws present a moment through which to understand how bodies, products, and their agencies are consolidated and attributed and, through time, how regulations recursively enable the coding of these assumptions through product design.

The cartoon at the beginning of this chapter presents one example in its illustration, albeit in crude terms, of the recursivity of bodies consolidated through consumption. A group of young, racially marked individuals were either targeted or otherwise vulnerable to the consumption of certain products, which in this case, they claim, made them fat and unhealthy. They then attempted to stabilize this identity—as fat and unhealthy—at a place from which they could claim to be "injured," and assert their rights to citizenship vis-à-vis claims to the right *not* to have been injured. The court, on the other hand, understood these teenagers to have been freely choosing agents who partook too liberally in an everyday part of American culture. As the wide debates about obesity, health, and mass-produced food that this case spurred demonstrates, the law itself—as a process, a body of rules, an administration, a group of people—is ill-equipped to handle the grand social questions about markets and human wounding that are presented to it.

The Book

As a legal term of art, "injury" is structured by a concept of rights. Deriving from the Latin "in" meaning against, and "jus," meaning something done against the right of another person, injury was described by Blackstone in 1768 as an "infringement of private rights."[17] This is the basic structure that the term has held through the centuries, with the crucial difference that now each person holds the rights to his or her own body (rather than in the early century, say, when a husband held the rights to his wife's body).[18]

Legal theorists seek to balance how the importance of the body will be weighed in terms of economic and technological notions of progress and profit, such that manufacturers will ensure that their products are reasonably safe. They do this in a variety of ways that vary from cost-benefit "tests" to theories based on insurance models, as I will outline later in this chapter. When these equations have caused "unjust" losses, reallocation takes place through compensatory damages, which cover the costs of the injury (medical, loss of consortium, pain and suffering, and so on). In the case of egregious misconduct, such as premarket knowledge of a serious defect or fraudulent advertising, a court may decide to award punitive damages as way of literally "punishing" a company. The injury law requires the physical body to come to the table as a preceding artifact being reclaimed after having been unjustly altered. This reclamation is an act of citizenship both in the individuated terms of literally reclaiming the body through compensation and in the ways referred to by certain tort scholars as fulfilling one's social duty to keep corporations honest. Thus the physical body serves as the collateral for the "justness" of that culture such that certain practices— child labor, dumping toxic waste—become morally reprehensible or unacceptable. (The necessity for these can be outsourced to other areas of the global economy.)

But if we take the body—wounded or well—as a material repository of culture on every level of the onion, from language to gender to health to education and behaviors, the political and economic sense of such claims makes less sense. If this is the case, who or what is the preceding subject that does the work of claiming, and what is being claimed? A consumer culture will have palpable interests in maintaining a strict division between subjects and objects, for the distinction does the work of maintaining the liberal framework of the free consumer-chooser.[19] But if we understand these distinctions between subjects and objects as far from self-evident, as problematic temporal and discursive formations, we will be better able to consider how injury laws themselves—including their human (lawyers, plaintiffs, judges, clerks) and nonhuman participants (amicus briefs, complaints, texts, restatements)—are key actors in the cultural reproduction of material difference.

This paradox of the acculturated body, or the ways that state and corporate power negotiate physical bodies, entitlement, costs, and progress, can be approached through a recollection of the importance of materiality to governmentality. In his explication of governmentality, Michel Foucault traces the way in which power gains its influence through subject formation. Control over a contemporary citizenry is gained not through repression and punishment, as it once was, but through the subject's own interpellation into regimes of conduct. He further focuses on the capacity of the material world to distribute power as an instrument of governmentality: "one governs *things*. . . . The things, in this sense, with which government is to be concerned are in fact men, but men in their relations, their links, their imbrication with those things that are wealth, resources, means of subsistence, the territory with its specific qualities . . . and finally men in their relation to those still other things that might be accidents and misfortunes such as famine, epidemics, death, and so on."[20] As the subsequent chapters of this book demonstrate, what will count as rational conduct or what is taken as common sense privileges certain forms of behavior and modes of citizenship. This book is not about whether or not a person "truly" was injured or hurt, but presents a fine-grained analysis of the specifics of several injury claims in light of their roles in governmentality.

The legal infrastructure for adjudicating injury brings us back to the Durkheimian paradox. Americans are required to examine and explain each injury accident in isolation—as an event that could have not happened. As Durkheim writes in *Suicide*, although we cannot know in advance how many people will commit suicide each year, we can predict with tremendous accuracy that several thousand people will. The paradox, then, to which I return below, is that while injury laws tend to understand each wound as an avoidable side effect of American economics—and can sometimes be translated into a legal injury deserving of compensation—they miss the structural ways that wounding is central to American society. Approximately 45,000 people will die—violently—in car crashes this year, no matter how avoidable each of those crashes may retroactively be understood to have been. Thus, in this book I take this effect seriously to ask how, if we understand human wounding to be a central feature of capitalism, the "accident" or "side effect" lens of injury laws affects how suffering is both distributed and made legible.

In the chapters that follow, I focus on elucidating different aspects of this argument through an analysis of several different objects, injuries, and legal struggles. In the remainder of this chapter, I examine more fully the ways in which injury laws have circumscribed and addressed the rise of consumer technologies and human wounding. In chapter 1 I lay out in further detail the paradoxes of what I am calling American injury culture. I work out what I understand to be some of the key consequences of this specifically American way of understanding injury. To do this I juxtapose the "rhetorical effect" of law—or the way in which it sets out injury as the exception to normal exchange patterns—and the "inequality effect" of material culture—by which I mean the ways in which fields of production and consumption are simultaneously wounding *and* enabling. Furthermore, injury itself is a productive force. In chapters 2, 3, and 4, I analyze, respectively, the short-handled hoe and its attendant back injuries suffered primarily by Mexican American laborers; the computer keyboard and repetitive strain injuries suffered by typists; and mentholated cigarettes and the injuries suffered by African American smokers.

The chapters that follow are not intended to be case studies; they do not set about to prove or reiterate the arguments I lay out here. Read as a collection, each illustrates different facets of what I have called injury culture. Read individually, each documents a history of the present, or a genealogy of how particular injuries and objects have come to be understood at particular moments.

Terminating Accounts

In some ways, a radical assumption inherent to product liability law is one that has been strongly stated in science and technology studies— that nonhumans are, as Bruno Latour argues in many contexts, "nothing more than discourse, totally expressible in other media."[21] The Berlin key is one of several examples Latour uses to demonstrate this point. As a key with a peculiar design, the Berlin key fits into a specialized lock. This lock can be programmed by a building manager so that on one setting, after the key is extricated the lock will remain locked on both sides, and on another setting, the lock will remain unlocked on one side. In that sense, argues Latour, the key does nothing except "carry, transport, shift, incarnate, express, reify, objectify, reflect, the meaning of the phrase: 'lock the door behind you during the night, and never during the day.'"[22] For Latour, in this case, design is a transparent translation process.[23] The key materially inscribes the demand's compliance such that the human factor is removed: the manager will no longer have to post directions as to how the door should be left and depend on tenants to obey. The key, then, inhabits and expresses the door-locking agency. In an historical analysis of airline accident investigation, historian Peter Galison makes a similar point. Through tracing the ways that accident reconstruction explains cause, Galison concludes that "there is an instability between accounts terminating in *persons* and those ending with *things*. . . . It is *always* possible to trade a human action for a technological one: failure to notice can be swapped against a system of failure to make noticeable."[24] These arguments help us understand how agency is encoded in the design of objects: the lock and key that *itself decides* whether it will be left locked or unlocked, or the fluorescent dye that *did not make itself* adequately seen thus causing the pilot not to notice a mechanical failure. However, the transfers of agency and responsibility are not as straightforward as these explanations suggest, for they do not provide analysis of how designs and legal infrastructures in decoding, or translating agency, draw on and produce various kinds of inequities.

Injury law accepts, even predicates, the Latourian contention that objects are "full of people." Galison's suggestion that the premise that "actors" or sets of agencies can be stabilized as an end point for explanation is also inherent to this mode of adjudication. A legal defense team aims to tell a story in which objects are self-evident—the manufacturer has built a product that has been properly made and that must be responsibly used. The defense seeks to erase any misfit between the object and its life world and foreground the users as bad actors. Plaintiffs, on the other hand, foreground an object as an actor that embodies manufacturer carelessness or malevolence.[25]

These projects require acts of translation whereby the intentions of and expectations for human and nonhuman actors are made to correspond. Jacques Derrida put this quandary of translation in a way that could be used to further unpack the moral problem of human and nonhuman agents: "To address oneself to the other in the language of the other is, it seems, the condition of all possible justice, but apparently, in all rigor, it is not only impossible (since I cannot speak the language of the other except to the extent that I appropriate it and assimilate it according to the law of an implicit third) but even excluded by justice

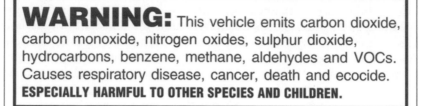

FIGURE 2. Produced by World Carfree Network, http://www.worldcarfree.net

as law . . . inasmuch as justice as right seems to imply an element of universality."[26] At issue, then, is not only what objects say but who gets to translate that "voice" and how. What are the terms for the object's intelligibility? Like any translation, this is an ethical issue.

Whether the plaintiff's behavior or the corporate mediated object will be held "responsible" for a given wound (will the wound translate into an injury?) constitutes the most basic question of injury law. The initial premise of injury law is based in this commonsense assumption that objects can be separated from and judged against behaviors. Therefore, plaintiffs' lawyers tend not to believe in accidents or acts of god—they locate the person who made a decision to save some money and make the tunnel too narrow, resulting in a client's paralysis; or someone (or an institution) who decided not to warn about or add a coloring to a poisonous gas, resulting in a client's chronic asthma; or someone who carelessly replaced a brake pad, resulting in a fatal car accident. The plaintiff's job is to show precisely how messages of danger "should" have been encoded into products and how the consequences of materialized decisions were visited on specific, real people and not statistical futures. In other words, the various theorizations of personal injury law offer different moral codings of how agency in design will be determined and accepted.

But further analysis shows that this retroactive storytelling is misleading, since the physical and behavioral "fit" between any one object and any particular person is only one of many factors that go into design in a market economy.

Designers and engineers—builders of the material world—make assumptions about users. As FXPal designer Elizabeth Churchill says, "We simulate." Designers approximate users and possible worlds in the process of materially intervening in the future through their distribution networks. This is a simple idea at the outset. But in a mass market, a designer will have multiple and contradictory interests at play in the creation of these simulations. For one thing, even if safety and ergonomics were high on a list of important design components, a mass market will require catering to averages. To take a well-known example, drivers are assumed to be between 5'6" and 6'4" and a driver seat and airbag will be designed accordingly. In this case, drivers' height becomes a category of risk distribution. Or, in other design decisions having nothing to do with safety, a particular color or shape will be thought to harbor the desires of the imagined consumer. Or, as tobacco companies found in the 1950s, a cigarette will be found to sell better when it contains more nicotine.

So within this vast pool of design and marketing concerns, the imagined users and their activities will be approximated, simulated, and, through a successful product, to some extent, effected. Similarly, the "corporation" (as a set of individuals acting within a body of economically and legally proscribed interests) will add its own limits and desires to the process in accordance with profit motives and regulation. The airbag may have to have, according to the National Highway Traffic Safety Administration (NHTSA), two speeds for faster or slower crashes; the seatbelt buzz may be purposely annoying to try to prevent further regulation (the buzz says, "Look what we had to do *to you* in order to comply with the last crazy set of regulations"); or the assumptions about the size of occupants may need to be altered in response to an outcry about children's deaths. Marketers will add their narratives to the object: they may teach consumers how to use it (no ice in beer, please), or lend imaginative worlds to the product (people will make space for your SUV), or educate potential users (you will be safer with your airbag). These strategies may be based on expensive niche market research.[27] Furthermore, as design historians such as Ruth Schwartz Cowan, Adrian Forty, Joy Parr, and Ellen Lupton have shown in detail, designs will often narrow and fix possible worlds based on banal or pernicious stereotypes.[28] Ultimately, designs embody possible worlds and distribute potentials on multiple levels for social and physical enabling and wounding.

Similarly on the consumptive side, consumers conjure through their purchases (for themselves and other around them) the promises of material and semiotic worlds. One short driver may attempt to simulate safety when she decides to purchase a particular car, while another, having slipped below the inflated bag, may find that she did not fit the designers' correlates for imagined safety and thus die in a low-speed crash. A cyclist may find that the cars around her move faster when their drivers feel that they are safer with their new airbags. In short, consumption harbors fantasies about the self in particular social and physical roles, always in a network of assumptions, ideals, desires, and fears. Bodies assume designs and designs assume bodies. Through these assumptions and simulations, safe or dangerous passages through everyday life evolve.

In this product design perspective, injury (in both the legal and vernacular sense) is precisely that place at which the approximations of some combination of these actors have predictably and unpredictably not "fit" and the human part of the equation has absorbed that misfit. As an inevitable consequence of inexact processes of simulation, injury provides a moment of disjuncture in which object expectations are breached. It potentially threatens, in the most radical way, the entire basis of economic rhetoric that insists that production and consumption take place in the interests of the common social good, and therefore produces a need for a rational logic of determining compensation: this trope of compensation is continually renegotiated through the various theories of injury law, as I will explain later in this chapter. Within this trope the isolation of the subject is, in legal logic, what allows for an injury to be counted in market terms such that the injury can in some sense be, as Elaine Scarry writes, "undone" through the monetary award that will in a rough sense "buy back" what it has taken.[29] The spectre or the trope of compensation stands at the far opposite end of the potential profitability of production, and there sticks its ideal of deterrence.

As a counter to this threat to economic rhetoric, product liability law offers only two sites of explanation and blame within this slippery network of design and use: person or thing. Thus, struggles over what will count as "good" design also harbor assumptions about what will count as rational behaviors.[30] A trial in the business of determining if a hamburger or stepladder was negligently or dangerously designed will also need to figure out if the product was eaten in moderation or climbed when the user was sober. One way for defendants to protect themselves through this translation exercise is to write their intentions clearly on the product; this directive is known as the product warning, and it remains the easiest and cheapest way to alter a product's "design" to try to avoid the injurious misfit.

Consumers in the United States who began smoking before 1965, when warnings were introduced in small print on one side of the package, have had considerably greater success than plaintiffs who began smoking later. This success tends to show that the warning, "Caution: Cigarette Smoking May Be Hazardous to Your Health," has been understood by juries as sufficient to give consumers adequate information and to leave open the possibility of rational choice. Each lawsuit, as it builds on others through the system of precedent, focuses assumptions such as these about reasonable behaviors, further consolidating

FIGURE 3. Canadian cigarette package warnings.

what will count as rational behaviors and whose interests these will privilege.[31] As I will demonstrate in detail in the following chapters, enormous amounts of discursive energy frame and consolidate what will count as rational behaviors and whose interests these will privilege. This ability to create the norms of rational behavior constitutes the cumulative built-in ethics of injury law. Further, the cumulative effect of these judgments recursively stabilizes design in ways that literally allow for the creation of certain material worlds over others. That car owners or manufacturers were never consistently held accountable for design in pedestrian injuries and deaths, for example, meant the deaths of hundreds of thousands of pedestrians through the century were "accidental," though avoidable.

The legal question, then, reflects the kinds of anthropological concerns raised by the Berlin key and the airline crash explanations raised by Latour and Galison: what kinds of intentions fill objects—are they pernicious or benign? This question is at base about the co-constitution of humans and nonhumans and first, who should bear responsibility

for the ostensibly intractable qualities of each, and second, who gets
to devise the explanations about responsibility. But if one takes, as serious play, Latour's contention that there exists no logical division between subjects and objects, how would an object such as a cigarette,
like the Berlin key, be "totally expressible in other media"? How might
the cigarette "translate" to English? Most certainly, "Please give RJR
(and by extension its employees, employees' gardeners, employees'
children's teachers, and the 'economy' more generally) a little money
each day for as long as you live." Again, quite clearly, "I need a home
for particles that disintegrate as I am smoked, and your mouth, throat,
and lungs, will do the job nicely." These concepts are materially inscribed in the commodity form of the cigarette as an object whose social function is to be smoked. But the cigarette itself would not express
its terms in the moral language of injury, as in "I want to 'hurt' you,"
or "My presence in your lung will cause grief to those around you."
Rather, the cigarette through its own agency causes a series of reactions
that then bring the smoker into new social and material relations: hospitals, experimental cancer treatments, sociological studies on smoking, litigation. Counterreactions in this case included targeting less educated groups for its products, covering up medical evidence of
product failure, halting research of "safe cigarettes," and establishing
its own channels to publicize false medical research.

But the cigarette itself does not care to injure. Even the industry, for
all its duplicity and counter to its actual actions, would not *want* to
wound, let alone kill, a consumer. Rather—if a corporation could have
its own desires—it would want to keep consumers returning to the
product. That the corporation could not stop wounding as a matter of
course was merely an unfortunate side effect of its main aim, which
was to make money for its shareholders. We might also say that the
cigarette does not itself precisely injure (in the legal sense). Rather a
relation of its particles and a human lung will likely result in the
growth of another entity: a cancer. This cancer will change the way that
the human is noticed in social networks. Some of these networks will
now interpellate the human as a potential member of a class for a class
action, understand her as a site for experimentation for new cancer
drugs, or perceive him as a bad investment for a life insurance policy.
Another social network will notice the capacity of that cancer to take
from its host friendship, consortium, and labor power, and may attempt to locate a site for compensation against this loss.[32] Thus to have
a wound or an accident translate to an injury and thus a set of responsibilities requires this lineup of recognitions and intelligibilities. The legal
"injury" (if the company loses the suit) is not per se the cancer, but
a legal attribution. In the 1980s and 1990s, no one doubted that Rose

Cipollone's cancer was caused by tobacco smoke. Nevertheless, courts wrangled over whether or not the tobacco companies should be responsible for her death. The legal question was one of interpretation: should the responsibility for the wounding she suffered by smoking convert through the courts to an infracted right not to have been injured? To make the wound intelligible, the law demands a convincing enrollment of the terms of injury itself, and often these terms are contingent. Before the activism of MADD popularized the notion that drunk driving was legal homicide, drunk driving deaths were just accidents; before *Unsafe at Any Speed* and the regulation of windshield glass, car occupants regularly (and accidentally) were beheaded in low-speed crashes in what was popularly called the "glass guillotine."[33]

Injury is a project of translation through which the co-constitutive effects of agency are interpreted and distinguished. This translation exceeds the terms of responsibility (object or person) itself and thus the political charge to the translation project. Through the process of litigation, the cigarette can potentially be socially registered as a new form of actor in the world that not only needs to be transported, marketed, held in a certain way, kept dry—but also one that injures. Precisely this movement in the 1990s allowed parties to cohere under categories such as those injured by smoking, those unaware of smoking's dangers, those vulnerable to or targeted for more dangerous cigarettes, and those who suffered from secondhand smoke.[34] These laws are part of the network through which the cigarette—as an object that both can and cannot be traced back solely to the corporation—becomes a political actor in the world and spawns stakes in its economic, injuring, and sociopolitical meanings.[35] Thus if objects and laws are standardized and if people and objects are always only partial—implicating each other in day-to-day life—the wounded people who come to the law for compensation are different in layered ways that identity and subordination theories cannot capture. To get at this, we need to go beyond Latour.[36]

The legal framework is an actor, or merely an adjudicator, in the injury drama. As Francois Ewald writes, "[T]he fact that bodily damage can . . . be transformed into a cash price may lead an insured person to speculate on his or her pain, injury, disease or death, so as to extract the maximum profit from them."[37] This profit motive is only one of a number of possible intentions a plaintiff may have in launching a suit. Others include a desire for public recognition that a person has been "wronged" or a desire to make similar injuries less likely in the future. Furthermore, the existence of the equation to begin with may encourage new behaviors, thus undermining the purported goals of injury law itself. Thus, the suit itself is a primary actor in the injury drama—as much as it mediates, it constitutes how injury is understood. As an actor, a lawsuit isolates certain moments within injury culture and defines those as key in framing what injury will mean.

Attempts to terminate accounts in persons or things shift with varying understandings of material and rhetorical articulations of the product on the body. A potential plaintiff may be at different times (or at the same time) a defensive smoker and an outraged litigator, or he may move among positions of choosing, addicted, medical, and legal subject. Each of these will work within promises, fantasies, or attempts to gain various abilities, freedoms, communities, and rewards. But when subjects shift so fluidly among agentive moments—liberal chooser, wounded consumer, ill citizen with or without a health insurance plan, injured litigant—who and where is the preceding subject? Which of these positions are descriptive, and which are constitutive of the legal positioning? Where and from whom is the injury of, say obesity, to be claimed? Is it poverty, poor health and physical education, bad parenting? Who is at fault? Parents, the McDonald's Corporation, Ronald McDonald, the state, the food industry, the public health system, the American Medical Association for its continuing lobby against socialized medicine? Are increasing obesity- and fast food-related diseases simply to be accepted as a result of so-called American lifestyles and choices, and to be distributed invariably among poor communities of color? The point here is precisely that explanations can*not* interchangeably terminate in persons or things. Human and nonhuman agencies are not parallel and interchangeable in some larger system, but affect the quality and potential of civil action and the material quality of human action. As subjects are constituted through and by objects, the legal institutions addressed to the law of personal injury separate and articulate distinctions just long enough to interpret what the stakes are in maintaining these boundaries. Lawsuits act rather than arbitrate, consolidate contestants rather than solve health and design questions, trade rather than decipher.

In one of the few accounts that critically investigates the product liability trial, Elaine Scarry uses grander claims for the political ramifications of termination points of explanation. For Scarry, the stakes lie in the very nature of the human body and the nature of the artifice.[38] Injury law confronts the most basic political and economic questions in a culture that bases most of its indices of success on increasing the production and consumption of "goods." The question scholars such as Latour, Galison, and Scarry leave us with is this: what does the location of cause tell us about power relations, and how do these attributions recursively make material worlds?

Agentive moments mutate as easily as bodies, but which ones "count" and which bodies matter? How are different facets of injury (race, gender, defective design) stabilized? Subjects and objects are continually remade through practice. Thus, concepts such as harm, work, and race are contingent and change over time and space. In this project I trace specific histories and phenomenologies of contingent interactions to analyze how, through these interactions, inequality is projected onto and absorbed by others in product design and consumption, and then how this interaction is picked up again by those who want to redefine it (advocacy groups, lawyers, lawmakers, capitalists, lung tissues, scientific studies) in the courtroom—this time as injury.

Because each of the issues I take up in subsequent chapters could easily overflow the bounds of a book, I have limited the arguments in each carefully. Nevertheless, each offers both a particularity and universalism that I intentionally leave open for now. For example, the cigarette, it has been claimed, is a unique product in that it injures as a matter of course when used as intended and, furthermore, that nicotine is addictive exactly contravenes the definition of rational behavior. Eve Sedgwick takes this paradox a step further, beyond the cigarette and to "the present discursive constructions of consumer capitalism," in which "the powers of our 'free will' are always already vitiated by the 'truth' of compulsion, while the powers attaching to an acknowledged compulsion are always already vitiated by the 'truth' of our free will."[39] In this locution, one that as an open question will underwrite the analysis posed in this book, the cigarette is not unique. It writes large the addictive underpinnings of consumption in the United States,[40] and the fetished commodity separated from the conditions of its production and consumption.

Recursive Objects

Critical commentators on the injury problem in capitalism have tended to focus on the productive side of the equation. Marxist interpretations of injury try to determine how much labor power, for example, can be "taken" from the always already injured worker. In these accounts, the problem of commodity production is one of injury produced by production itself. For example, Adam Smith recounts in his famous pin factory analogy how a laborer working at one of a number of total procedures available in machinic culture "generally becomes as stupid and ignorant as it is possible for a human creature to become."[41] This necessary wounding of the worker is required by the growth of social wealth and, indeed, according to Smith, operates in the worker's favor as he emerges from the process as the well-heeled consumer.[42] Smith weighs injury against the benefits of increased production and finds the trade-off worthwhile.

On the other hand, Elaine Scarry locates class difference in the materiality of the physical body: "[T]he problem of the haves and have nots is inadequate to express its [class's] concussiveness unless it is understood that what is had and had not is the human body."[43] In this tradition of thought, one that I will expand on, inequity is materially grounded in the body itself. In this sense, wounding and inequality are inextricable: the former an expression of the latter. In thinking about production, as Scarry is describing Marx's ruminations on capitalist production, the problem of wounding emerges as one of physical takings through labor: the workers' compensation laws instigated after Marx's death might be read as an attempt to codify how much of a worker's physical body may be spent in the process of production. "Excess" wounding will count as injury.

Workers' compensation schemes and product liability laws share the same basis in torts, though the former has followed a different historical trajectory. It is well known that the accident rates in early industrialism were unbelievably high. In 1913 there were 25,000 industrial fatalities and 700,000 injuries resulting in more than four weeks of disability among the 38 million workers in the United States. To put this another way, between 1907 and 1912, ten percent of male deaths were caused by industrial accidents.[44] Still, injured workers had little success in obtaining compensation for five key reasons. First, laborers had to be able to hire experts to show proof of proximate cause. Second, the "fellow servant rule" provided that if an accident was caused by another employee, the employer could not be blamed. Third, it was understood that the worker assumed any risks associated with the job by accepting employment. Fourth, the employer could avoid liability if he could show any contributory negligence on the part of the worker.[45] Finally, employees could be fired for bringing a suit.[46]

Between 1885 and 1910, most states enacted employer liability laws that considerably weakened the previous barriers to the tort system. The new availability of legal redress to workers hastened the development of a workers' compensation system in the 1910s, and between 1913 and 1920 all but eight states passed workers' compensation laws.[47] In a detailed historical study, Anthony Bale outlines the ways in which the passage of state workers' compensation laws in the 1910s resulted from the interplay of four factors. In addition to the huge number of worker injuries and the activist class politics of the period, the rising and uncertain costs in tort trials made it desirable for companies to drastically lower awards even if it meant paying a higher percentage

of claims. Finally, and crucially, corporations realized that the fault discourse inherent to tort trials was an explicit critique of the morality
of production. The substitution of the explicitly no-fault discourse of
workers' compensation allowed companies to continue a paternalistic
language of worker responsibility and accidents.[48] The Occupational
Safety and Health Act (OSH Act) of 1970 was the first federal regulation to give workers the right to be free from danger, although many
commentators argue that the executive agency in charge of implement-
ing the act, the Occupational Health and Safety Administration
(OSHA), has largely failed to do so.[49]

To give an example of the vast difference between workers' compensation and product liability law, consider a case in which a twenty-five-
year-old worker was severely injured when her arm was pulled into
a six-bladed bolt-making machine. Through a workers' compensation
claim she was eligible for a maximum of $34,600 and was unable to
sue the employer.[50] However, when she brought suit against the manufacturer of the machine for negligent design, the jury awarded her $3.5
million.[51] Thus, vast differences exist between workers' compensation,
which is a no-fault insurance system, and tort law, which is a fault-
based compensatory system based in the assertion of the right not be
injured by the everyday products one uses.[52] As the tort scholar Robert
Rabin writes, the former is "grounded in a collective model emphasizing needs-based benefits for a community of victims," while the other
is "grounded in an individual entitlements model of compensating for
harm on a case-by-case basis."[53]

The extreme difference between compensation and litigation reflects
a difference in social models of what constitutes adequate compensation and how this compensation will be decided.[54] But it might also be
used to examine the different universes of production and consumption. While production has injury embedded in it, consumption is generally not theorized in these terms. Injury is generally figured as being
incidental to, or accidental to, consumption, and the history of injury
law has been led by progressive liberals who have laudably—and
often under great pressure not to do so—wanted to maintain a sem-
blance of consumer autonomy in the face of an increasingly complex
world of objects in which consumer choices were understood as becoming increasingly technical, difficult, and shrouded by puffery.
Compensation for harm, rather than the needs-based benefits of workers' compensation, has meant that awards can include compensation
for costs already paid by medical insurance (collateral goods); compensation for pain, suffering, and other non-fiduciary losses; and, most
potentially lucrative for a plaintiff, punitive damages. Since the legal
job of punitive damages is to punish, and since there is broad latitude

given to juries and judges to set them, these damage awards can run into the millions of dollars where very deep pockets are involved. It is worth noting as more than a caveat that by far the majority of the highly publicized and ridiculed punitive damage awards are in fact reduced by the judge and then further reduced through the appeals process.[55]

Astonishingly, though tort is recognized as a major site for public policy on public health and industrial production, the problem of injury continually overwhelms and overflows the case-by-case approach of the law. Thus, though so many dimensions of human activity collapse into this venue, little rigorous critical thinking exists among tort theoreticians about the cultural ramifications of the case law approach and its methods. For example, tort historian Edward White's comment that tort law's "integrity, and its amorphousness as well, can be linked to the place of injury in American life"[56] may seem unduly tautological. What *is* the place of injury in American life? Certainly more than a link to the place of injury, tort law structures what counts as injury in American life.

Though the details can become quickly overwhelming, the generic features of the law are straightforward. Torts covers civil injury claims as broad as libel and workers' compensation; here I focus on product liability, or the law of defective products. These cases are brought in civil courts by plaintiffs who claim that ordinary products injured them in the course of ordinary use. Plaintiffs' lawyers will not charge an initial fee but will take roughly 30 percent of any settlement or jury award. Thus for plaintiffs' lawyers the hint of a gamble requires a negotiation between bread-and-butter and risky but potentially high-paying cases. Manufacturers will have in-house lawyers or will hire attorneys on a fee basis. Furthermore, claims of loss are tightly circumscribed: a person may sue about her own injury or a spouse's death, but a bid for recovery can often not be made by a gay partner and never by the sandwich maker who loses a customer because of the customer's injury. This latter point is not trivial, for it taps into law's history of distributing and legitimating personal relationships, and thus how suffering can be made to legitimately translate and transfer.[57]

Theories of product liability law abound, and the minutiae threaten to swallow the unsuspecting scholar. The most promising way to read these theories, though, is through the different assumptions that each carries about requirements for responsibility in design and use of products and as attempts at disciplining objects and behaviors through competing notions of responsibility and choice and, more globally, over the human costs of capitalism. Through these assumptions emerge conceptions about what will constitute negligence on the part of either party, how proximate cause will be determined, and what responsibilities inhere to the project of manufacturing. For example, strict liability theories seek to distribute the costs of injury to those most able to pay, as well as to deter the marketing of unsafe products. Therein, the equation implies a distributive claim that responsibility for an injury that may be statistically inevitable (an overstepped ladder) should be shared among those who benefit from a product and negligence in design need not be demonstrated by the injured party. The more recent formulation of "reasonable alternative design" (RAD), on the other hand, switches the responsibility back to the plaintiff to prove that a product could have been made more safely within reasonably similar conditions such as cost. The claim there is that individuals need to more carefully consider their behaviors in industrial culture, and if they do so, individual injuries will be avoidable. Strict liability is plaintiff friendly, while RAD favors the defendant's interests.

The history of product liability law taught in American law schools treks through a fascinating series of cases that offer a genealogy of the core elements of tort: negligence, proximate cause, defect, contracts, and damages. Key cases are relied on to teach the main theories of the law and how they were articulated by judges and taken up by lawyers. Thus, law is taught through precedent in a way analogous to the practice of law itself. It pays particular heed to certain key cases and their mind-boggling and mundane anecdotal details. For example, *MacPherson v. Buick* would be excerpted to demonstrate the extension of a notion of the privity of contract such that an occupant of a defective vehicle can sue a manufacturer. In his recognition that the "reliance [of a consumer] on the skill of the manufacturer was proper and almost inevitable,"[58] Judge Cardozo acknowledged the complex economic relations of industrial production that resulted in the lack of consumer expertise on all the products he or she would buy and use. This noting of the disempowerment of consumers—as products became more specialized and complex and consumers were more dependent on advertising than research—became the seeds of twentieth-century product liability law.

MacPherson would be followed in 1928 by *Palsgraf*, perhaps the most famous of the early tort cases. In this case, a passenger dropped an unmarked package filled with dynamite as he was being assisted by a railway worker. The dynamite exploded, causing a scale to fall on Mrs. Palsgraf's head as she waited at the other end of the station. Reversing the lower court's "but for" (but for the event, Palsgraf would not have been injured) decision, Judge Cardozo ruled that the series of events that resulted in a scale falling on Mrs. Palsgraf's head was simply too distant to allow recovery. For that, *Palsgraf* has taken its place along a series of other cases in tort textbooks as a way of explaining the competing notions of proximate cause and duty, and for his "activist" stance, Cardozo took his place among famous judges who contoured the laws.

A case book such as Franklin and Rabin's *Tort Law and Alternatives* would then move to introduce the concept of strict liability, which made its appearance as a theory in 1944 with *Escola v. Coca-Cola Bottling Co. of Fresno*.[59] In justifying an award to a woman who was injured when a Coca-Cola bottle unexpectedly exploded in her face, California Supreme Court Justice Traynor wrote in his concurrence, "I believe the manufacturer's negligence should no longer be singled out as the basis of a plaintiff's right to recover . . . it should now be recognized that a manufacturer incurs an absolute liability when an article that he has placed on the market . . . proves to have a defect that causes injury to human beings."[60] Here he appealed to the demands of public policy to fix responsibility, even without negligence, "wherever it will most effectively reduce the hazards to life and health inherent in defective products that reach the market."[61]

So, in reading hundreds of these cases and their commentaries, the assiduous law student learns the structure of a legal case. The student learns how to name certain kinds of injuries, defects, expectations, implied and stated warranties, and problems with product warnings, and how to argue these within certain legal logics and theories. A year or two later as a practicing lawyer, she will use the same method of reviewing case history to locate legal theories and decisions to cite as precedent in her own briefs, petitions, and complaints. As a young plaintiff's lawyer she will collect evidence, sometimes sifting through hundreds of boxes, having been drowned in files by a defendant hoping that she may miss something. Doing work for a senior attorney, she may, as Dan Bolton did while working on an early silicone breast implant case, discover the smoking gun and go out on her own and make stacks of money. She will then learn to put together compelling stories about corporate misdeeds and human suffering. One set of these stories will fit into the legal parameters of a complaint (under what legal theory should IBM be responsible for a secretary's repetitive strain injury)? Another set will aim to sway jurors who will be confronted with the contradictions of rational languages of cost-benefit, stunningly disfigured people, huge corporate profits, and desperation.

By filing a suit using one of a variety of product liability legal theories, a plaintiff registers a complaint against the way that injuries have been distributed—specifically, that in this case he was injured—and attempts to claim back an ability to fully partake in civil society— namely, as a consumer. In other words, he seeks a financial settlement.

The right being claimed varies depending on the theory of liability used. A plaintiff might claim that he should not have been injured, period. A drill is easy enough to build properly and no one should be injured by a faulty drill. Or, the plaintiff might argue that since his was the one of the 600 inevitable injuries, he should gain compensation on a cost-spreading theory. The court may argue that 600 burn victims was a fair calculation, and in order to properly spread the costs of these inevitable injuries, compensation would be due. Or the court might argue that 600 injuries was a fair calculation, and given factors such as the cost of the product, compensation will not be due. Or, as in the famous *Grimshaw* case in which Richard Grimshaw was horribly burned in a Ford Pinto, the court may decide that the company's initial calculation of burn deaths was immoral and that with simple design changes there would have been far fewer burn deaths. But regardless of the calculus of morality and efficiency used by the state, the plaintiff claims a vernacular right not to have been injured by an everyday product.

Another message is buried alongside this genealogy of law: what counts as reasonable objects and reasonable behaviors evolves jerkily though the combined logic of many judges' ideas and ideologies—not all of which make internal (let alone collective), logical (let alone moral) sense. In his classic rebuke to the notion that judges simply apply laws, Edward Levi points out that terms such as "negligence" do not emerge in law as fully fledged universal touchstones but rather "must be given meaning by the examples to be included under it."[62] In *An Introduction to Legal Reasoning*, he outlines the example of "inherently dangerous" objects to examine how cases are grouped as similar in order to apply precedent.[63] The category "inherently dangerous" included at one historical moment a loaded gun and an exploding lamp, but not a defective coach, while at another it contained poison, gun powder, and a spring gun, but not an " 'iron wheel . . . although one part may be thicker than another.' "[64] At stake in these categories were assumptions about what a consumer could take for granted: that a loaded gun would not fire willy-nilly, but not that an iron wheel would consistently roll at speed under the weight of a carriage.[65]

These deployments of object expectations in turn categorize human behaviors and the actions of a "reasonable person" or "average man." For example, in the 1921 case *Hynes v. New York Central Railroad Company*, a boy who had been swimming in public waters climbed onto a plank used for diving by neighborhood children and owned by a railroad company. While on the plank, "high tension wires from one of the railroad's poles fell, striking him and flinging him into the river to his death."[66] Was he a trespasser or a bather in public waters? The lower court denied recovery on the basis that he was a trespasser. On appeal, Judge Cardozo "simply redefined the boy's status from that of a trespasser to that of a bather in public waters, thus enabling him to apply the protections accorded to such persons."[67]

Among these categories, each of which disciplines subjects and objects in relation to one another, terms such as "defect," "knowledge," and "inherent" take on different valances in differing judges' approaches. In studying the use and emergence of legal trends through cases, it becomes apparent retrospectively that, as Susan Stewart writes in a different context, "the law hovers."[68] Certainly the law hovers among ideological, moral, and economic predilections. But the fact that cases *could* go either way does not mean that they will arbitrarily do so. Trends in compensatory awards emerge that tend to follow the race, class, and gender interests of judges. For example, early cases of rape were understood to be damage done to a man's property. Similarly, convincing evidence shows that compensation follows lines of difference already structured through race, gender, and class, tending to undercompensate members of suspect classes for comparable injuries.[69] This difference in awards is underwritten by a logic that assumes the "value" of a body is already reflected by its compensation on the labor market—a person making more money will be awarded more money for categories such as lost wages. But it also has to do with a politics of sympathy, how judges and juries empathize with plaintiffs and value their bodies, lives, and work. It can also be about shared knowledge. Consider a 1900 ruling that was made before workers' compensation had emerged from the law of torts. Judge Holmes did not allow a plaintiff to recover when a hatchet fell on him from a defective rack, even though the plaintiff had informed the employer and asked him to change the situation. Holmes's assumption was that the plaintiff had known about—and condoned by virtue of continuing the job—the dangerous circumstance.[70] Not until a new moral framework for understanding workers' injuries—one that resulted from decades of hard and dangerous work of labor activism—did this situation change.

After reading several hundred cases one might conclude with legal scholar Duncan Kennedy that "some part of judicial law making in adjudication is best described as ideological choice carried on in a discourse with a strong convention denying choice, and carried on by actors many of whom are in bad faith."[71] Ideology parading as rational language rings through the product liability tome of opinions. The way that objects and bodies are rhetorically stabilized as meaningful entities on a case-by-case basis embodies assumptions about ideology, empathy, and proper behaviors in different contexts and encodes them in terms of objects. Assumptions about reasonable persons are encoded into technological relations in terms such as "jaywalker" or "negligent manufacturer" in ways that allow a disciplining of these subjects. But a case law approach to disentangling fault and blame in injury accidents has a peculiarity that is not quite covered by Kennedy's charge of bad faith. Consider that while each car accident will be retroactively considered avoidable by law (if the driver had paid more attention to the slippery road, if a manufacturer had properly installed the axle), the number of annual accidents can be accurately forecast. Francois Ewald, writing on insurance, considers this theoretical quandary of accidental happenings and statistical inevitability: "When put in the context of a population, the accident which taken on its own seems both random and avoidable ... can be treated as predictable and calculable."[72] Product liability law, even in its theorizations underwritten by insurance (such as strict liability), is not a structural response to injury. In case law each accident is necessarily understood as a precise set of events that can be traced back to a series of actions and that could, therefore, have turned out differently.[73] Nevertheless, collectively, through thousands of cases by more and less important courts and judges, trends emerge as to what "counts" as injury in law.[74]

Product liability's technocratic understanding of injury mirrors engineering approaches to this process of calculating cost-benefits: the width of Golden Gate Bridge weighs directly against a prediction of how many injuries will occur; a narrower bridge will correlate with more traffic fatalities. The law's job is to patrol these equations and decide that either the engineers did a fine job of calculating and the injury costs will be borne by the injured, or that injury was inevitable but too expensive to foreclose and the cost will by borne by all users of the bridge through the distributive capacity of the engineering company (or that the accident was more directly caused by drunk driving than by the width of the bridge).[75] Any given life is infinitely valuable, but as a future abstraction, the width of the bridge is understood as the necessary economic trade-off.[76]

Integral to this trade-off between lives and progress is a determination of what will count as a product failure, and what will be relegated to the category of side effect. In the court, these decisions are at once central (through the capacity to materialize injury by turning it into a line item in the calculation of a project cost) and pushed to the side, since it is up to the defendant to decide when those costs get too high and to wait to see what happens at trial. Thus, in legal discussions on injury law, a key slippage occurs between what among organizational theorists is called "high reliability" and "normal accident" theories. High reliability theorists, such as Aaron Wildofsky, claim that even in large organizations, if management is good enough (an attainable goal), accidents will not happen. An accident is a result of predictable and reparable failure. Normal accident proponents, such as Charles Perrow and Scott Sagan, claim that accidents are an inevitable contingency of any management system.[77] This debate has been most vociferously broached by political scientists engaged in international security issues; however, it also illuminates the politics of injury in capitalism.

This language of transaction central to product liability roughly poses a superimposition of high reliability and normal accident theory, though individual theorists integrate them differently. Commentators such as Marshall Shapo would argue that the goals of the law are to deter negligence in design through a market theory of injury that makes injurious design too expensive for manufacturers. According to this view, laws also acknowledge that injury will be inexorable (*someone* will overstep the ladder, engineering that would reduce accidental death is just too expensive) and thus put forward the cost-sharing proposition: since injuries are inevitable, those most able to pay for them should do so. This latter supposition basically presents an insurance theory. Guido Calabresi, in his influential 1970 book *The Cost of Accidents*, which was written at the height of the pro-plaintiff locutions of strict liability, proposed that the principal goal of accident law should be to fairly reduce the costs of accidents—the latter both in terms of total accident costs and the costs of prevention.[78]

This approach has come under attack by outspoken critics such as Peter Huber, who rues the overzealous use of law and its difficulty adjudicating what will count as scientific evidence. (To be fair, Huber seems to present a willful caricature of Calabresi's arguments.) He writes, in one of his widely read critiques of what he calls "junk science," "Mainstream science often offers little more than speculation about the true causes of cerebral palsy and other birth defects. . . . What then? Whatever we do (many an overeager Calabresian quickly concludes), we must do *something*. Perhaps the scientist who claims ignorance is just too cautious. The rules must therefore be changed, so that the oxymoronic scientist—the one too cautious to sound a specific alarm quite yet—will not stand in the way of the oxymoronic lawyer— the one whose extreme caution impels him to rush in at once."[79] Huber stops short of calling for increased regulation or study of chemicals before they are widely used, limiting his invective to the misuse of inexact science and law rather than to an understanding of risk or the culture of blame.[80]

It is not my aim here to play very differently oriented commentators against each other, or to examine in any detail the strengths and weaknesses of the diverse pro and con positions on the law. The key point is that tort law, by its very structure, assigns injuries to the status of accidental entailment, inevitable by-product, or statistical cost of the benign activity of capitalist market exchange, production, and consumption.[81]

In its case-by-case approach to injury, tort law attempts to reconstitute adequate market relations where someone has been injured. This assumption underpins product liability theories and tests across the spectrum, from cost-benefit and risk-utility to implied warranty and consumer expectations. These theories accept that the proper role of the law is to compensate individuals for injuries that weighs avoidability in the terms of singular events against the integral and unavoidable costs of the free market. So while product liability (at least in the theories that tend along insurance lines) admirably harbors the dual aim of cost spreading and deterrence, it relies on the key assumption that behaviors of people and objects can (and will) be determined, predicted, and, moreover, retrospectively interpreted. Equally, its mode of compensation assumes that monetary awards can be weighed against sentience, and that from those weights, estimations, and forecasts, product manufacturing decisions can be made. Thus it predicates not only that body parts can be traded, albeit inexactly, in the marketplace (that injuries can be compensated for), but that commodities evenly circulate among sovereign subjects who can—and according to commentators such as Abel and Nader, have a moral imperative to do so—insist on their rights not to be (or not to have been) injured.

Many legal theorists express exasperation over the way that tort law negotiates injuries. The standard set of critiques is as follows. Litigation is resource- and time-intensive; a typical suit takes about five years to resolve. For that reason, the vast majority of product liability cases are settled out of court. However, settlements often seal records and thus the supposed deterrent effect of the law is lost; other potential litigants do not have access to important information. Moreover, when cases do go to court and punitive damages are awarded, they have to be vast to fulfill their punitive impulse when set against large or even mid-sized corporations. Thus, awards may often seem at once tiny in their actual punitive effects (if set at, say, one day's net profit for a particular product) and massive when compared to an individual plaintiff's injury. For that reason tort law has been criticized as creating a lottery, or windfall, justice system in which only a few of the hundreds or thousands injured by, say, Bronco II rollovers will recover an award equivalent to the one significantly reduced from the original $290 million awarded to Juan Romo in 2002.[82] Others will settle out of court for much less, will not have the resources to sue, would sooner just forget it, were killed in similar crashes but will not have qualifying dependents, or will meet unsympathetic courts and juries. But even an apparent windfall can be misleading if defendants claim bankruptcy as they have in many high-profile class action cases, such as the Dalkon Shield case. In addition, the punitive effect of tort (namely as a deterrent) has been edged out by the widespread use of insurance and the limitations on punitive damage awards of some states, as well as the use of cost-benefit to simply factor in the corporate losses that may result from bad design.[83] In Texas, for example, punitive damages cannot account for more than four times the compensatory damage unless actual malice has been found by the jury, and recent rulings by the U.S. Supreme Court have in general instated punitive caps to single-digit multiples of the compensatory awards.[84]

But these valid and longstanding critiques miss the crucial way in which the larger teleology of technical and economic progress at stake assumes that the material body can stand as a sort of gold standard or collateral for an economic exchange system, where in the trial, the body asserts itself in its retroactive claims through law not to have been injured. Thus the trial forces the question of how economic development or progress may proceed in light of its costs for individual citizens. The citizen's body becomes, rhetorically, the placeholder—the limit—for corporate behavior. So on the one hand, in tort, the body is presented as that rhetorical and material entity whose well-being underscores the reason for production and whose injury marks the limits of a system whose profit motive is well understood to clash with public health. This materiality and singularity of the citizen-body contrasts rather markedly with the everywhere and nowhere of the corporation. In the cartoon that initiated this chapter, a bag of French fries stands in for the diverse set of interests that designed, marketed, and sold it. Thus even this cartoon shows how the body and the corporation, or the body and the economy, are simply not equals in the way that the plaintiff v. defendant would have the competition structured. There is no there, there; the corporation works within an economy with its own interests. And so while the corporation is made up of individuals, in itself it is impossible to locate as an agent responsible for injury. Analysis of this problematic will form the kernel of chapter 1. But the further point is that when critics accept this rhetorical positioning of the body from the liberal framework of injury law, as do Nader and Abel, they accept the logic of the law itself and thus adopt the denunciatory framework that accepts a logic of reparable harm. This logic misses the broader role of the injury laws in American culture.

Injury laws' failures are inevitable because unlike corporate marketers, they do not account for the wounding premises of consumption and thus cannot count them within the fold of injury. Thus, I have here shifted the terms by which tort law can be understood. In recognizing that law takes place within and also deeply constitutes injury culture, injury can be understood in less instrumental terms that can perhaps allow for a more radical understanding of things like health and inequality in the United States. American-style tort systems, no matter where they are adopted, hinge on more than just a set of laws; they operate within a whole moral universe for thinking about rights and wrongs in the context of health, progress, economics, and commodity exchange.[85] As other countries begin to adopt piecemeal the American approach to tort law, it is crucial to expose the moralism and the mindless expansion of legalistic appeals, because these take place within a range of specifically American cultural forms that include its unique privatized health care system, its culture of regulation, its legal assumptions about corporate personhood, and its media practices. American law cannot be imported in isolation.[86]

Structure of the Book

Although I have primarily used tort law to set out the parameters of the discussion on injury, the cases I read here articulate injury through a variety of legal venues. In part, then, what the collection of these injuries and objects illustrates is the problematic way in which legal institutions addressed to the law of personal injury force a division among types of product use and the way the resulting injuries will be understood in the domains of civil rights, workers' compensation, or product liability. These overlaps among activities divided into work and leisure have two major consequences. The first is simply that issues of choice, design, and governmentality vastly exceed such preconceived notions as worker- and consumer- (in thinking about workers' compensation and product liability) or race-based injury (in thinking about civil rights claims), even as particular complainants are forced to appeal to one of these. Second, one of injury law's foundational notions, that of the "inherently dangerous" object, remains nearly a nonsensical concept. Justice Traynor of the California Supreme Court noticed that objects in themselves are not dangerous—they can only be considered dangerous when in use. However, plaintiffs with other complaints have not been so lucky. As the chapters will show, inherent danger carries many slippages and is vastly open to rhetorical manipulation. Is McDonald's food only inherently dangerous when eaten? Is the computer keyboard only inherently dangerous in certain work situations? Are airbags inherently dangerous only for certain sized people?

In chapter 1, I expand on the notion of American injury culture. This introduction and chapter 1 are intended to be read together as complementary parts of my argument. In chapter 2, I analyze how the agricultural tool of the short-handled hoe became the pivot point of the struggle for a new recognition of Mexican American farm workers in the late 1960s and early 1970s. Relying on transcripts of the hearings and interviews with lawyers from both sides, I examine the way that Mexican American bodies had been paired with the short hoe as an efficient system and the tool was seen as a natural fit with perceived traits of the Mexican American body. Farm worker and activist Frank Bardacke relates a joke told by whites involved in agribusiness: "What do you get when you cross an octopus and a Mexican? I don't know, but it sure can cut lettuce."[87] This joke plays on possible technological improvements of the Mexican body—always already better at cutting lettuce than a white body—as an instrument of production. This discursive framework was ultimately interrupted through administrative hearings and the California Supreme Court. In chapter 3 I examine the wave of lawsuits about computer keyboard–induced repetitive strain injury (RSI) in the 1990s, and I examine the assumptions on which these complaints were dismissed. In the 1980s RSI emerged as an epidemic that was structured through the configuration of a particular relationship of women's hands at the typewriter, the erasure of women's work as work, and fantasies that imagined the computer as an instrument in the project of thinking and that thus erased the work of computer input altogether.

In chapter 4 I turn to the problem of cigarettes. Evidence reveals that menthol may increase the dangers of cigarettes—and on this basis an African American group sued tobacco corporations claiming discrimination, through target marketing, based on the Civil Rights Act of 1866. This strategy, as opposed to the more ubiquitous use of product liability law, raises a host of crucial issues having to do with niche marketing, product design and innovation, and generic liability. Moreover, it demands that we seriously question assumptions about inclusion and assimilation in commodity culture.

Thus, inequities presented to and through the law are not simply blind spots—the law is not "racist"—but they present occasions to examine assumptions about subjectivity that sometimes fracture along familiar lines of race or gender, and other times require us to broaden the scope of how commodity objects create new kinds of categories of inequity.[88] After all, consumptive decisions not only affect producer and consumer but also shape inhabited worlds.

As these chapters will show, laws force plaintiffs to locate blame in isolated ways, through moralistic claims, from a state that has profound—and shifting—interests in how equations about economic and public health are recognized. Injury claims that cannot be set in sociopolitical contexts but have to be individualized and attenuated to fit legal precedent and formality can make them remarkably easy to dismiss on narrow grounds. Furthermore, these cases help to make evident how the material world constitutes difference, and then how these differences tend to be—but are crucially not always—recursively consolidated through court decisions. Production, consumption, and circulation of objects create and sustain inequality in central ways that cannot be understood, let alone compensated through the moral and material logic of repairable harm premised by injury law.

In fact, given the instability of legal claims, lawyers themselves will try to settle cases rather than take them to court. The grounds for this are complicated, in part because of the unpredictability of juries and the huge work burden and expense of the trial. Both plaintiffs and defendants are often interested in maintaining the privacy of matters— related and unrelated—that risk being aired publicly. These are matters of strategy, but the more pertinent point here, and one that each of the chapters that follows will further examine, is that injury claims can also be very difficult to articulate in legal terms. The courtroom is not a Habermasian ideal speech arena in which complaints can be made and carefully debated, but a highly constrained place in which only certain social relations and motivations can be made to count. Furthermore, through the U.S. legal system's reliance on stare decisis, or the cumulation of previous decisions, both parties are dependent on the political biases of judges and their particular interpretations of legislation, the Constitution, and their self-perceived role in meting out justice. This flexibility of law makes it such a broad and fascinating—if potentially disingenuous—field of play. But in its narrowing of the terms of debate, the law can disempower.

Justice and the law are simply two different concepts: judges come to the table with their own ideas and background; plaintiffs and defendants can have vastly unequal resources; legislation and legal opinions change in ways that often favor those who are already empowered against those who suffer various forms of structural disadvantage.[89] Furthermore, the rhetoric employed to discuss law is infused with a putative morality, making it seem like the law's ultimate work is to allocate justice rather than set the terms for what will constitute justice. Particularly for plaintiffs, who may "truly believe they have a good case" and thereby distinguish themselves from others who launch the frivolous cases that are the stuff of the media, insisting on the law as inherently just can be at once self-serving and disempowering. The expanding appeals to the law, then, often fail to address the layering of differences and inequalities that constitute physical injuries. In that sense, the culture of injury law in the United States ties integrally to a larger American injury culture. *Injury*, therefore, analyzes law's structuring of injury claims, premising that how these claims become legible ultimately affects how material health is understood and distributed. Rather than smoothly and simply resolving the problem of injury, legal equations and practices obfuscate understandings of how objects move and are made meaningful within American cultural politics. I argue that these laws, through the way they force us to locate blame, the way they force us to seek legal expertise, the way they individualize claims, the way they are reported through the lens of frivolous cases or brutal corporations, the way they emerge from a broader and uniquely American culture of injury—in short, the way they narrow our modes of perception and apprehension of injury—make us less able to make the connections and trace the networks of our civil and political lives. They narrow moral and political horizons. Thus, rather than reading product liability for its potential to right the wrongs of bad product design, I believe it can more valuably be understood through an analysis of how it creates and sustains social inequality in its retroactive context of judging design.

But if legal equations and practices obfuscate understandings of how objects move and are made meaningful within American cultural politics, they also solidify them in ways that present an opportunity to better understand the problem of how objects carry agency, how claims about that agency are made, and how the ostensibly objective discourses of injury law understand and distribute these claims.

Chapter 1

American Injury Culture

EVEN AMID OUTCRIES of litigation gone mad and tort reform, an ineluctable optimism weaves through the promises of injury law. If only *in this one instance* the Coke bottle had not shattered. Or had the railroad crossing signal not *this one time* malfunctioned just as a train was passing through. If Ford had not lapsed when it negligently designed *just* the Bronco II with a propensity to roll over. In injury law's discourse, misfortune or catastrophe always seems to be precisely incidental to American capitalism, and the role of law is to, where appropriate, salve injuries through the compensatory award.[90] The law asks of the suffering placed before it, was this caused by an "injury"? Injury means not a vernacular wounding but, quite specifically, the violation of a right with physical wounding as a result.[91] Injury laws determine when an individual's right not to be injured has been infracted by incidents caused by poor design, lack of warnings, or corporate malevolence. Within the case law archive, plenty of slippage exists in how theories, statements, and forms of law are applied in various cases. Nevertheless, together, they can be taken as a measure of how human physical bodies are valued in calculating what will count as "fair" commercial practice in a society in which knowledge of everyday designs are simply beyond the ken of the average consumer. The goal of human well-being, no matter how abstract, must have some rhetorical, if not material, purchase in any social economy that wants to pass as democratic, and thus injury law can be understood as one of the foundational discourses on which American capitalism as an adequate, even "good," basic theory for a political economy depends.

Heated debates exist in the field of tort law as to the specificities of product liability law, but its most basic tenet presumes that producers should not profit from commodities that hurt consumers. Therefore, the law exists to determine, in a case-by-case way, how the capitalist system's physical takings should be distributed and, thus, when the costs of what will be called economic progress should remain with the individual (through her own suffering, medical payments, disability) and when they will be redistributed to the manufacturer of a product (through compensation). Understanding how the law distributes responsibility, both in its theories and in practice—and in any given commodity-consumer interaction and in the larger scheme of how they are understood—can lead to a better understanding of a key preoccupation of anthropologists: how designed objects carry meaning, and how they constitute social positions that can be both consolidated or altered through their social circulation.

In the United States, law is primarily understood as an objective system of adjudication, and yet, as I argued in the introduction, a more accurate appraisal would understand it as one of the infrastructures that calibrates, in highly specific contexts, acceptable relations between persons and things. In this sense, an analysis of injury laws can shed much light on what medical anthropologists have described as social suffering, or how suffering is differently distributed. The facile dismissals of injury law on both the left and the right threaten to obscure the crucial role of injury law itself as primary among precisely those mechanisms that distribute suffering.

Injury offers a particularly rich juncture to study American cultural narratives for the way it negotiates consumption and health, two of the great themes on which American notions of progress and dominance rest, and yet two goals that sit uneasily together. I want to push the analysis of injury further through several material threads that animate what I call American injury culture. These I have gathered in what follows under three headings: economy, body, and citizenship. As a way of contextualizing these issues, in the first section I present a reading of *Grimshaw v. Ford*, the most famous of the cases resulting from the exploding gas tanks of the Ford Pinto. By thinking about, in the second section, how public health and economic health play out against each other in the United States, and in the third section how American bodies might be understood to harbor culture, I want ultimately to think about the problem of citizenship.

The way in which injury law recognizes human wounding forces acknowledgment of a major cultural paradox: law, as a primary means of calibrating what will count as negligent injury production, forces the plaintiff to bring a complaint that takes the form of harm as an exceptional form. Thus, unlike on the production side of American capitalism, which through workers' compensation harbors the means of balancing what will count as acceptable injury, on the consumption side injury is always already exceptional. The compensation system thus brooks attention from both the ways in which consumption injures as a matter of course and the ways in which injury itself is a productive force. Examining the question of design more closely, as I do in the following chapters, allows for a more careful deconstruction of the baselines of equality set out in law that pose as neutral and universal. It thus allows for first, a more subtle analysis of both the ways in which product design harbors difference and enables certain people to count differently as subjects—with more or less agency and political prerogative—and second, the way in which injury law recuperates injury into wholeness, and thus acts within the more fundamental political goals of consumerism. Injury law forces the injured subject into the position of *having* an injury that can be traded in the sphere of law, rather than acknowledging subjects as differently enabled by the material world of consumerism.

This argument turns on what I will call the "rhetorical effect" of law and the "inequality effect" of material culture. I will outline what I mean by the former first.

In weighing the responsibilities of producers and consumers, interpreters of legal doctrine and precedent rely on particular notions of normative "whole" bodies: sovereign choosers of similar body types, with similar abilities to rationally use products. (In each of the following chapters we will see, for example, efforts on the part of defense attorneys to show the bodies in question as uniquely susceptible to hurt and thus lay blame on the bodies rather than the products.) Thus, injury laws tend to accept quite unabashedly the tropes of American consumer culture, which also rely on a distinction between reasonable persons and an array of selectable, consumable objects.[92] The separation between human choosers and inert things is a necessary, even foundational, element of both consumer capitalism and injury law.

In the eyes of injury law, the human body comes to the table to claim its injury as a prelegal artifact. In this way, the plaintiff comes not as a subject made through American education, consumer objects, advertising, and other cultural processes, but as a physical embodiment of a "gold standard" for American capitalism. In this rhetorical sense, the integrity of physical bodies stands in for the hard currency that underlies the "real" value of the system, and when these bodies are ruined the system is, in some small way, called to task through the trope of compensation.

But this rhetoric will always already miss the broader structure of American injury culture, for in requiring this move to litigation on the part of the plaintiff, the law maintains the formal integrity of capitalist exchange in the form of exceptionalism (*if only this one time . . .*). In this sense, the tropes of tort law itself, which adjudicate between rational users and defective products (or product warnings) and irrational users and reasonable designs, and furthermore between punitive damage and individuated financial windfall, radically depend on at least two central categories presented by American consumer culture and, particularly, I will argue, the strong role of corporate interests in American culture. First, both the consumptive and legal systems depend on a belief (at least in rhetoric) in the human ability to master the material world through proper design and proper use, one which I will suggest over the course of the book is highly problematic for many reasons but primarily for the way it forces a distinction between persons and things. Second, compensation becomes the device for reinstalling the conditions for the prior economic agency of both plaintiff and defendant; compensatory awards might be read as the ultimate abstraction of money and the ultimate commodification of the body. Furthermore, the trope of compensation undergoes constant reappraisal. What kinds of—and whose—wounds should be compensated? How many millions of dollars does it take to "punish" a multinational corporation? Or according to a recent Supreme Court decision that severely restricts punitive damage awards, why should punitive damages be limited to single-digit multiples of the compensatory award? Why should a company be held responsible for selling hamburgers when the problems of obesity are so much more complicated than the simple existence of high-fat foods? The constant interrogation of and battle over the purpose and configuration of compensation evidences the rhetorical and material slippage between money and value, hurt and injury, pain and acknowledgment, identity and inequity, behavior and rationality. But moreover, it becomes a key channel for voicing debates about the value of the physical body in the economy, what will count in the calculation of the economic good, and in whose interests these will take place.

Thus, injury law consolidates a rhetoric of, on the one hand, unrelenting agency as the underpinning promise of American consumer capitalism and, on the other, that injury is incidental to American systems of production and consumption—or at the very least (and only among the most liberal strict liability theorists) about equal opportunity injuring. Within this logic, the more injury cases are argued (win or lose), the more strength is gained by interests that are also struggling to maintain distinctions between persons and things that rank the agency of consumers over the co-constitution of citizens and consumers. It is this reflection and consolidation of consumer culture that gathers under the rhetorical effect of law.

I juxtapose this rhetorical effect of the law with another facet of the injury problem, which I call the "inequality effect" of material culture. Bodies and things can never be distinct in the ways coded by the legal infrastructure—they are always entangled and co-constituted. Indeed, subjects come into being only through series of relations with the material world. Further, fields of production and consumption carry within the fold of their practices both wounding *and* enabling. This play between wounding and enabling in its multiple levels produces relations of inequality in at least two ways. First, hierarchy is a central feature of consumptive inducement. Part of the inducement is that it tends to work: the expensive sport utility vehicle does intimidate and endanger other drivers—as advertised. The red lipstick does encourage a certain mode of attention—as advertised.

Second, the distribution of the wounding effects of capitalism is not incidental but is a central feature of an economy in which injury, too, produces economic growth. I am not arguing that enabling and injuring is a zero-sum game, as Ivan Illich does in his classic study of human and automotive energy use, *Energy and Equity*.[93] I am suggesting that this dynamic of enabling and wounding centrally structures, specifically through objects, the dynamic between inequality and injury.[94] Celeste Langan has put a similar point this way: "Capital-intensive technologies of amplification . . . have so altered social being that even the unimpaired (but also assisted) body has the character of a disabled subject."[95]

Thus, in the juncture between the rhetorical effect of law in which the body stands in as the collateral for something called economic progress, and the inequality affect of material culture, in which a spectrum with difference on one end and injury on the other is produced and amplified through the material world, design and law live in an uneasily recursive relationship. Where design that injures people is not noticed, those people come to be defined by their injuries: the farm worker and his gait, the secretary and her hormones, the smoker and his cotanine levels.

A return to the automobile airbag illustrates this point. Women tend to be more at risk of being injured and killed by automobile airbags designed for "average sized males" because they tend to be shorter.[96] This funneling of risk toward shorter people coincides with the way in which people identified as female have been virtually defined, constituted, and subordinated *as women* through relentless cultural and material iterations of the car and its role over a century of American culture. Thus an airbag lawsuit will hinge on two injuries: the social injury of the increased physical risk of subordination carried through the design of airbags (not to mention the loaded identity of a woman driver), and the physical injury of the actual injury or death. Only when this double injury occurs can she, or her estate, sue for this airbag defect. She may be lucky enough to win, and she may even beat the statistical odds of compensation awards that consistently value men's bodies more highly than women's.[97] But the piecemeal basis of the law does not address the fact that auto designers are still overwhelmingly male, that automobile ergonomics are overwhelmingly coded to average male bodies, and thus, statistically, in the same accident a female will be more injured than a male, or that the car has been used systematically in the normalization of a version of heterosexuality through which women tend to be subordinated.[98] This unevenly distributed wounding does not reduce to the categorical terms of race, class, and gender but moves among and within various social distinctions as descriptive, constitutive, and characteristic. It is like a fog over American lives: inner-city horizons full of fast food restaurants, pedestrians required to walk unprotected in front of high radiator grills at speed, and cigarettes and candy marketed specifically to children.

When that disability or identity in the form of subordination (short people, African Americans, pedestrians, and so on) is attached to individual bodies rather than to the physical and social environment that structures it, the coding of bodies by the environment becomes obscured in ways that are only further hidden by institutional discourses such as injury law. Thus I want to think more fully in this chapter about what it might mean in a larger sense to claim the right not to have been injured that is held out as the promise of law. I want to consider the limits to those claims and, further, how they structure the ways that injury is understood. If we accept the injury-producing component as integral to American culture, how do we think about citizenship?

Seen through the inequality effect, injury presents a radical opportunity to better understand how the material world in general—and commodity culture specifically—constitutes identities and distributes injuries. Examining tort law in this context, then, allows us to see not only its own limits but also the ways it has framed discussions of how injury carries meaning. The use of tort as the primary means of understanding injury has had two crucial political consequences. First, it shifts attention away from politics into increasingly individualized stances. This happens even in its own attempts to be critical or to take on activist cases, such as gun litigation. Second, it affirms the distinction between persons and things, thus making a critique of the centrality of liberalism and consumerism to citizenship ever more difficult.

Contrary to the 60 percent of Americans who apparently believe that accidents could be avoided altogether,[99] I argue that accidents and physical injury are social facts. My contention is that legal languages for understanding an epistemology of injury will never capture—and thus never be able to adequately compensate for—the ways that injury circulates on so many parallel levels of the present discursive constructions of consumer capitalism. To illustrate this, I present the argument in three sections. First, I examine the way in which the law is called on to directly and unabashedly adjudicate the interests of individuals and public health against the broader interests of the economy. Second, I examine how physical citizen bodies become repositories of this ambivalent valuation of health as a social goal. Finally, I turn to think more critically about links among consumption, citizenship, and inequality in an economy in which health is at once a foundational rhetoric and at odds with the institutions ostensibly in charge of maintaining that health.

Grimshaw

The notorious *Grimshaw* case well illustrates the problems of injury culture and injury law that I analyze in this book. The key insight that the case and the subsequent legal debates about it demonstrates is the way in which the logic of the case and the terms of the debates were based on the very logic posed by Ford as a way to understand the injuries wrought by the Pinto. This is notable, since the public outrage in the 1970s was precisely about the corporate logic that led Ford to calculate the value of the human lives that would be lost because of the design and to Ford's subsequent decision not to make inexpensive improvements to the design of the gas tank. While Richard Grimshaw won the case, Ford won—and continues to win the battle of defining the composition of the terms of defective design, risk, and consumption.

In May 1972, Lily Grey, age fifty-two, was driving her six-month-old Ford Pinto with her thirteen-year-old neighbor, Richard Grimshaw. The car stalled in the middle lane of Interstate 15 in San Bernardino, California, due to a carburetor malfunction. When it was rear-ended by another car that had slowed to between 28 and 37 miles per hour,[100] the Pinto's fuel tank was pushed forward into the passenger compartment and was punctured by bolts on the way. The Pinto burst into flames. Grey died two days later in the hospital, and Grimshaw received multiple burns that left him horribly and permanently scarred even after seventy rounds of surgery. A jury attributed the injuries to the poor design and placement of the gas tank, and awarded the Grey estate $559,680 for wrongful death and Richard Grimshaw $2,516,000 in compensatory and $125 million in punitive damages. The latter sum was reduced by the court to $3.5 million as a condition for denial of a new trial. These awards were affirmed on appeal and the Supreme Court denied a hearing.[101]

Richard Grimshaw gained a vast eminence compared to the other 500–900 people killed in Pinto fires or half million people killed in car accidents in the United States during the eleven years between his crash and the ultimate appeal decision.[102] The key issue for the public, as for the jury, was the fact that Ford knew—before the Pinto went into production—about its tendency to burst into blames in low-speed rear-end collisions (as low as 25 miles per hour) as well as about a variety

of simple solutions that would have cost between $2 and $11 per car
to implement. A document introduced in the trial gained some publicity in a popular *Mother Jones* exposé. The document illustrated that pre-
production, Ford had calculated the costs of future burn deaths and
injuries. "According to the document, the added safety provided by
the device would have resulted in the avoidance of 180 deaths and
another 180 serious burn injuries. Setting $200,000 as the value of life
and $67,000 as the value of injury avoidance, the document calculated
the total safety benefit at $49.5 million, much less than its $137 million
cost."[103] The design change was deferred—explicitly as a cost-saving
measure.[104]

The late tort scholar Gary Schwartz believed that the near mythic
status of the Ford Pinto case rests on two key exaggerations or miscon-
ceptions that were parleyed by the press. His thinking outlines what
has now become the rational perspective on the case and reflects
widely held assumptions about the role of tort law more generally. The
argument runs as follows. First, he claims that the design deficiency of
the fuel tank was massively overstated. He argues that "when occupant fatalities from all highway causes are considered, the Pinto performed respectably,"[105] although he does agree that cheap design
changes would have made the car much safer. Thus, he says that since
all cars had major design failures that could have been rectified, why
pick on the Pinto? The second public overstatement of the case resided
in Ford's calculation of the worth of human life. The significance of
Ford's cost-benefit report was overrated, he contends. Schwartz considers Ford's figure "within the range of expected and acceptable advocacy."[106] Each of these hesitations is worth considering here, not only
with regard to the Pinto but in light of the auto industry and safety
more generally, for they are at the core of a crucial safety—engineering—business triangulation.

Grimshaw was tried as a consumer expectations case; that is, the jury
was instructed that a product is defective in design if it has failed to
perform as safely as an ordinary consumer would expect when used
as intended. During the trial, another formulation of product liability
law, the risk-benefit test, was announced by the Supreme Court.
Schwartz comes to his analysis of the Pinto case "convinced that risk-
benefit analysis is not only proper, but just about essential."[107] Thus,
he retroactively inspects *Grimshaw*, giving full consideration to a risk-
benefit test, nevertheless realizing that public opinion tends to view
the calculations inherent to risk-benefit as distressing—especially in
the face of badly injured victims facing a jury.

Schwartz first considers the specific problems of demanding product
warnings for complex mechanical commodities such as automobiles,

when consumers would likely be faced with lists of warnings and would not have the specialized knowledge required to make use of them. Taking the Pinto figures seriously in considering a possible risk-benefit analysis of the case, he asks, "[W]hat is the actual significance of, say, a $10 safety figure?" As the beliefs that surround the Pinto case would have it, "all consumers would or should be willing to spend $10 each so that a few deaths might be avoided." But he goes on to show that while this may make sense if many lives are saved, the position becomes analytically weaker when only five lives are saved. In that case, each life would be worth $20 million, and "unless consumers are extremely risk averse, one would expect them to be unhappy with that expenditure."[108] Thus, at a certain point one is forced to consider the "magnitude of the safety gain" and measure it against the costs that will mount as more modifications are considered.

The question, as Schwartz poses it, of how much a life is worth may deserve consideration in its own right. However, it becomes much more useful when considered in the wider context of contemporary automobile design, the safety movement, and government regulation—and this is precisely where Schwartz's analysis becomes problematic. Although public outcry focused on the calculation tables, the controversy of the case was indicative of a broad-reaching frustration about the facility with which automobile companies could consistently make overwhelming profits by making such decisions. For example, Schwartz takes NHTSA as the "public's representative." But regulatory agencies are highly political bodies.[109] In fact, by 1976 NHTSA was virtually hamstrung by the litigation of manufacturers who contested every one of its regulatory attempts. Ford had particularly targeted the fuel integrity standard—one of several standards NHTSA was struggling to mandate at the time—and Ford's monumental lobbying campaign against that standard had already delayed it for six years. NHTSA was so bogged down that finally the standard was mandated by Congress in response to the public outrage over the Pinto.[110] Schwartz furthermore assumes an implicit negotiation between auto consumers and Ford through an implicit risk-benefit decision that manifests in consumer habits. In fact, while Ford could accept an extra $5 in profits, a consumer did not have the opportunity to make the calculations of $5/hundred lives or $10/two lives. To make this argument, then, falsely assumes both that automobile manufacturers have the ability to calculate how consumers will value safety and that other costs such as profit, salaries, and design work can be factored out, calculated, and somehow limited or controlled. These assumptions confuse economic decisions based on stock valuation and social decisions based on social well-being.

The existence of an equation such as risk-utility requires that both risk and utility can be isolated, calculated, and then weighed against one another.[111] Two major problems exist with this assumption, however. First, only certain costs are put in social terms and spread (as risks) while others, such as styling costs, are determined solely on the basis of profit. The risk-benefit "test" has no means of understanding the ways in which costs of risks and profits are distributed and borne.

Second, this is a legal rather than an engineering framing of the question. Put in engineering terms, safety features of a machine are not "added on": in good engineering they are an integral part of the design itself.[112] That cheap changes could have been made to a finalized design to avoid a certain number of traffic deaths was central to *Grimshaw*. The legal debate over the design focused on the addition of piecemeal improvements such as bladders, covered bolt heads, or shifting the tank. But the issues were all of a piece: the poverty of the bumper, which was less substantial than the bumper of any American car produced then or later; the lack of rear reinforcement bars; and the exposed flange and row of exposed bolt heads that were sufficient to puncture the gas tank all colluded with other highway geometries to make a deadly low-speed crash. The formulation of a risk- or cost-benefit equation assumes that safety is something "added" to an auto design retroactively. This is a deeply ingrained but problematic assumption about products more generally.

Therefore, to put the question in terms of a trade-off between safety and cost—or in terms of the additional cost of safety—is to take it from Ford in the way that the company chooses to handle design and engineering questions. Why do some "extra" expenditures count as going to the consumer while others are just part of remodeling the car for profit? Why could it not be accepted as definitive content that a car is something that can be hit at 30 or 50 or 70 miles per hour and will not burst into flames? The court could have more specifically acknowledged NHTSA's inability to set standards and stated that fulfilling NHTSA's standards were not necessarily to be taken as the benchmark for "safe enough" design in a product liability suit. While it essentially acknowledged this by using a consumer expectations test, it might have provided some precedent to foreclose the regulatory intent defense.

But the further problem of the risk-benefit logic is that it suggests a rationalization and a linearity of technology development and trade-offs that simply do not exist. For most of the twentieth century, auto manufacturers have made it clear not only that safety does not fall with their primary goals but that their reasoning behind adding various safety devices is emphatically not one of a simple cost-profit settlement. Recall that in the 1950s, seatbelts were the best-selling optional device in automotive history. Nevertheless, they were not offered for long, and, furthermore, when they were removed, the industry launched one of the most successful misinformation campaigns in U.S. history: safety doesn't sell.[113] Schwartz ultimately misses not only the public investment in this struggle, one that is pivotal to understanding the Ford Pinto case, but also the critical way in which the various legal theories depend on different definitions of and tolerances for injury production. The real myth of the Pinto is that Americans "choose" how safe their automobiles are and that they do so in a context unsullied by car culture itself.

While both the court's and Schwartz's views of *Grimshaw* present radically different ways of understanding how the costs of the crash should be distributed, both still balance terms under which human bodies will carry value; how the body itself will maintain its place as the collateral, the gold standard, of what counts as fair market exchange; and how injury law should set and reset the terms for injury as an economic externality. In what follows, I examine the stakes of this rhetoric of injury law more closely.

Economy

One of the key understandings of product liability law is that a paradox exists between economic growth and human health, and therefore certain checks are required for the kinds of objects that can be put in the marketplace. The Supreme Court opinion denying the FDA's mandate to regulate the tobacco industry offers one recent example that demonstrates how clearly this trade-off has been articulated.[114] The majority opinion in *FDA v. Brown and Williamson* understood cigarette regulation as one of major "economic and political magnitude" and analyzed it as such, even arguing in essence that cigarettes are *too* dangerous to be regulated by the FDA.[115] The majority stated that since cigarette companies never claimed that they were selling a drug, the FDA should not be able to regulate the industry. Furthermore, both willfully ignoring the history of the political finagling of the cigarette industry and dubiously solidifying the "intent" of the state, the court held that the government had explicitly organized a distinct regulatory scheme focusing on labeling and advertising while informing consumers of the dangers of cigarettes, and thus it was never the congressional intent for the FDA to regulate.[116] The dissent, however, used public health, rather than economic health, as its organizing principle. The dissent therefore claimed that cigarettes fall under the FDA's ambit since the manufacturers' claims for a product are not the only—or even defining—characteristic of what makes it a drug. The dissenting opinion notes that "sometimes the very nature of the material makes it a drug," and even more radically, sometimes the "circumstances surrounding the distribution of an article" will affect how it is understood.[117] As we see here, whether economic or public health is the central goal has vast ramifications for how objects and behaviors are defined by judges: is the cigarette a drug or an ordinary product?[118]

I want to argue that a better understanding of this paradox between economic and public health is central to understanding how injury is managed and contained in American culture. In *Rule of Experts*, Timothy Mitchell paraphrases a key post-structural insight in his argument that the "principle of abstraction on which the order of law depends can be generated only as the difference between order and violence, the ideal and the actual, universal and the exceptional. But the violent, the actual, and the exceptional—all of which the law denounces and excludes, ruptures itself from and supercedes—are never gone. They make possible the rupture, the denunciation, and the order. They are the condition of its possibility."[119] In a similar vein, I want to argue that in American injury culture, understanding the economic-public health paradox is central to understanding how injury laws organize, frame, and ultimately lead us toward the "but for" assumptions with which I opened this chapter when ultimately, the kinds of calculations made by corporations about design and death rates, as we see in *Grimshaw*, are considered normal and acceptable behaviors. Regardless of one's position on the morality of such calculations, the fact that they exist articulates that moneymaking and human externalities in the United States are at odds and that the notion that progress improves the lives of all citizens will need some serious rhetorical shoring up.[120] Injury is designed in at the beginning and designed out at the end of the economic process of production.

The health care industry of the United States provides a ground-level view of the biopolitical paradox I raise here. The United States has a unique system of health care provision that fully enlivens the contradictions among public health, economic health, and health provision as a market good. How a nation understands basic medical care bears heavily on its notions of citizenship.

In the United States in 1998, private health insurance premiums ranged from $3,000 to $14,000 per year for a family of four,[121] and in 2002 health expenditures reached an average of $5,440 per insured person in addition to Medicare paycheck deductions.[122] Despite this, the United States has fewer physicians, hospital beds, and nurses per 1,000 people than the OECD average.[123] In 2002, 15.3 percent, or "43.6 million people were without health insurance coverage during the entire year."[124] These statistics can be compared easily to those of Canada, which has an equivalent—arguably higher—level of service, although in Canada care is offered to all legal residents with an average per capita spending of $2,791.[125] Slightly less than half of this is covered through insurance premiums, which range by province.[126]

The American health care system is uniquely costly compared to that of other advanced nations for three key reasons: the high cost of administration; physician and other personnel salaries; and "hardware," or pharmaceutical, service and hospital care costs. Studies have consistently shown that a for-profit system, such as that in the United States, will inevitably lead to higher administrative costs than government-run systems, and this is certainly borne out by comparison.[127] Health administration in the United States, on a per capita basis, is three times that of Canada.[128] On average, doctors in Canada and Germany earn significantly less than half as much as their U.S. counterparts; physicians in Austria, France, and Britain less than one-third as much; and physicians in Finland, Norway, and Sweden just one-fourth as much In addition, "the price of many U.S.-manufactured drugs under patent is 30% to 50% lower in Canada and other countries."[129]

The sheer economic power of this industry has created vast income disparity where the remunerations accorded to businesses related to health care create obvious stakes in maintaining an expensive health care industry. For one thing, 11.8 million Americans, or 9.1 percent of all workers, hold jobs in the field of health care.[130] The American Medical Association, which by the mid-century had become the "most powerful interest group in America," has lobbied consistently against government-run medical insurance. It branded insurance "un-American" in the 1920s; had a study of health care removed from the Social Security Bill in 1935; and launched its campaign against Truman's attempt to enact an insurance program by using vast financial resources, hardball tactics, and social prestige.[131]

These figures do not include the quite extraordinary, if invisible, personal and company time spent comparing, selecting, and administering care plans. They do not include the immeasurable psychic costs of job insecurity or having to stay with a job for medical insurance—particularly for people who have been seriously ill. Furthermore, they elide the extremity of the individuation of these high costs: the primary cause of personal bankruptcy in the United States is unpaid medical bills.[132] Studies report that between 300,000 and 500,000 families in 1999 filed for bankruptcy for reasons of illness or injury.[133]

Injury is good for the economy. The Bureau of Economic Analysis estimates that health services add $589.8 billion to the total GDP.[134] Car crashes alone constitute a multibillion-dollar industry. Motor vehicle collisions in 2000 had an economic cost, or "value," of $230.6 billion—2.3 percent of the U.S. GDP. This figure is based on 41,821 fatalities, 5.3 million non-fatal injuries, and 28 million damaged vehicles.[135] Similarly, the pharmaceutical industry pumps billions of dollars into the economy, albeit in ways that are not based in the good of public health.[136] The noted physician Marcia Angell has written, "The marketing budgets of the drug industry are enormous—much larger than the research and development costs. . . . According to its annual report, Pfizer spent 39.2 percent of its revenues on marketing and administration in 1999; Pharmacia & Upjohn is reported to have spent about the same. The industry depicts these huge expenditures as serving an educational function. . . . The conflict of interest is obvious.[137]

On this level of health and value, nothing has changed since Ralph Nader wrote in 1966 that "[i]t is in the post-accident response that lawyers and physicians and other specialists labor. This is where the remuneration lies and this is where the talent and energies go."[138] Another way to look at this, as Robert Proctor does in his book tracing the history of cancer research, is that research based in cure has not only trumped, but overwhelmed research in prevention in terms of budgets, prestige of work, and remuneration. As he points out, "No one's boat is rocked if our goal is to keep the carcinogen while searching for a cancer cure. . . . Basic research has produced . . . surprisingly little in the way of successful treatments and even less that is of relevance to prevention."[139] These debates about health care, insurance, cost, and marketing generally take highly moralistic tones in advocacy-based debates. However, I am not arguing that human health *should* particularly trump economic health. Rather, I am aiming to point out a series of unresolved paradoxes that result when these two primary rhetorical goals are placed in conversation and competition, and further noting the effects of the way in which these infrastructures tend to commodify injury, rather than value health.

Thus, another key irony in this contest lies in the way that the corporate side of the equation is able to absorb individuals into the project of consumerism precisely in such a way that it is difficult to do anything *but* work in the interests of American injury culture. Private sector jobs have become increasingly well remunerated in comparison to other jobs while the costs of "basic needs" such as housing, medical insurance, and education have increased dramatically. On the other hand, work for private health, rather than in the interests of public health, is vastly more prestigious. On the level of the individual middle- and upper-class worker, this means that the benefits package offered by the oil company lobbying against environmental protection measures that aim to protect human health tends to be better able to pay for an employee's chemotherapy than the package offered by the organization working to better understand the links between environmental degradation and human cancers. Finally, a crucial move in the last decade has been in the alliance of real and imagined social welfare on corporate well-being. The phasing out of pension plans and public education has meant the reliance for a larger portion of the citizenry directly on the stock market for retirement plans, college savings funds, and everyday well-being—things that a generation ago would be affordable through student loans, summer work, and pension plans. An anxious population is easy to tap into for the fears of corporate well-being.

The economy and its rewards have hardened, as it were, around these structures of value and reward. Every once in a while the apparent callousness of this version of economics emerges in the public eye. Philip Morris's 2001 report that calculated that the early death of smokers *saves* the Czech economy $24–30 million provides one recent illustration.[140] While this report spurred an international outrage when presented in defense of claims that the company should pay reparations to the Czech government, it made the point that health costs, injury costs, and life costs variously translate into economic terms. Allying the costs of ill health and premature death to economic remuneration will always be problematic and political, since life itself is expensive and the costs of injury are slippery.

The broader point is that for every level of the onion, injury in the United States is unreservedly saturated in money. The effects of inflated medical costs surge through the economy, only to fracture in quarrels over dividing up this increasingly large sector. As doctors and insurers charge higher rates, medical compensation awards will be higher and lawyers paid on contingency will receive more. As corporations grow, claims for punitive damages that will actually be deterrent will have to be higher. As punitive damages increase, they will likely continue to be lowered on appeal (and thus lose their punitive force) and be perceived either as unfair or as creating a lottery system of justice. In either case, punitive awards will be open to ridicule and in turn will be used to sell newspapers. Everybody wants a slice of the injury pie.[141]

Examples from Canada and Europe suggest that serious injury rates and their dire personal consequences can be both lowered overall and made less expensive by allowing everyone access to health care and increasing product and corporate regulation, thus undermining the two key rationales for the legal injury infrastructure.[142] So when we say that injury is good for or costly to the economy, we make judgments about how it forces individuals into a game of distributing resources.

In the United States, the redistribution of these resources requires that the physically injured body itself is the collateral of capitalist production—and in so doing, it implies that the safety and health of the citizen will ultimately act as the gold standard of economic production. With the material body as collateral, the contest between injured and injurer takes the semantic and performative form of *versus*. But unlike the consumer, whose injury "sticks" to her body, the corporation can never, in itself, suffer an equivalent corporal punishment since the product designers, marketers, engineers, and CEOs are consistently absorbed into the legal framing of the corporation, as are numerous others who work under the legal framing of the "corporate person." Thus the behaviors of an individual (smoker, overeater, bad driver) are ever pitted against a huge conglomerate of interests whose goal was ultimately, indeed, to have individuals buy more in order, in turn, to increase a company's stock value and, more generally, to increase the consumer spending index. While corporations do not want to injure per se, they *do* want people to smoke, overeat, and fantasize about driving fast. But the individuals that make up the conglomerate of the corporation have no accountability in the court; they cannot be "punished." Thus, a major contradiction exists between the legal mandate of the corporation, which is to maximize profit for its stockholders, and its supposed goal, which is to act in the consumers' interest of health and safety. In the legal semantic, this means not only that injury is built into the very structures of capitalism but that the injured person is literally separated out from the conditions of her injury.

Body as Culture's Repository

In thinking further about how culture resides in the materiality of human bodies, Elaine Scarry examines why it is that war requires the killing of enemy citizens. Could nations not agree that a chess game or a soccer match could settle the questions of a particular political disagreement? She asks, "What differentiates injury from any other activity on which a contest can be based in order to arrive at a winner and a loser?"[143] Her conclusion rests on the way that bodies and built environments both harbor and constitute culture: the promise of injury is that the victor can remake a destroyed culture. She writes, "The arms that had learned to gesture in a particular way are unmade; the hands that held within them not just blood and bone but the movements that made possible the play of the piano are unmade; the fingers and palms that knew in intricate detail the weight and feel of a particular tool are unmade; the legs that had within them by heart (that is, as a matter of deep bodily habit) the knowledge of how to peddle a bicycle are un-made. . . . All are deconstructed along with the tissue itself, the sentient source and sight of all learning."[144]

That the body is a repository for culture is in some sense intuitively true, reflected in aphorisms such as "you are what you eat." But to put consumer culture into terms of the physical making of Americans' bodies throws the assumptions of Scarry's analysis—that a nation will acculturate its citizens in terms of a set nationally determined values—into question; or, the United States provides an example of the handing over of the acculturation process in large part to private industrial interests. A super-sized portion of American capitalism is based precisely—and unapologetically—on convincing Americans to consume. Marion Nestle frames her recent book, *Food Politics*, on her conclusions that "many of the nutritional problems of Americans . . . can be traced to the food industry's imperative to encourage people to *eat more* in order to generate sales."[145] Billions of dollars are spent by the industry not on making hamburgers, fries, and salad dressing more healthy but on making them inexpensive and attractive through the use of cheap ingredients that have longer shelf lives; on lobbying governments to enact legislation in the industries' favor; and in finding ways such as advertising and packaging to make Americans consume more of it. Thus, American citizens are physically constituted through patterns of distribution and consumption.

Throughout the 1980s, the imperative of food consumption involved, as Greg Critser chronicles in his aptly titled book, *Fat Land*, the introduction of on the one hand vastly more unhealthy fats and sugars, such as palm oil and high-fructose corn syrup, in processed foods and without warnings or information and, on the other, "super-sizing" servings of all kinds. While many of the decisions to allow these new food products to be substituted without notice to consumers took place at the high echelons of government and corporate decision makers, the results of the decisions are clear in the bodies of Americans, 60 percent of whom are now overweight. In short, Americans are constantly barraged with a culture of "unhealth"—one in which regulatory agencies have conflicting roles. For example, the mandate of the Department of Agriculture (USDA) is to both advise the public on nutrition *and* to protect the interests of agriculture. As Nestle argues in detail, non-industry-supported studies consistently show that a large number of the conflicts of interest that arise from this contradictory mandate are resolved on the side of lobby dollars, from how budgets are allocated to how much meat is "recommended" in the food pyramid.

The targeting of kids that takes place through product placement, marketing, advertising, and vending machines in schools provides an excellent example of this process, as it is widely acknowledged and embraced by market researchers who can identify real and imagined vulnerabilities of kids, "tweens," and teenagers and use them to market their products.[146] For example, in his chapter titled "Kids" in *Why We Buy*, Paco Underhill advises the potential marketer of the importance of product placement for kids: candy at the checkout aisle, dog treats on the bottom shelf, and cookies with the baby food.[147] This way, kids will see and reach for the desirable product, and certain aisles will be unavoidable even for wary parents. What has become known to marketers as the "nag factor" has become important in corporations' ability to enter many Americans' most intimate relationships[148]— through estimated expenditures of $2,190 per American household.[149] Advertisers, for example, now work to train children in methods of nagging depending on what category their parents (nearly always the mother) fall into: "indulgers," "bare necessities," "conflicted," or, the smallest group, "kids' pals."[150]

Corporate spokespeople use vulnerabilities, such as children's and teens' dependence on acceptance into small social spheres, to create markets.[151] When criticized by parents' groups, they will claim either that they did not know that kids would be particularly attracted to their sales strategies (cartoons, high sugar content) or that obviously kids would be attracted to certain products and therefore parents need to take this into account in deciding what to expose their kids to. One clear example of this was the marketing of Camel cigarettes. While claiming that it does not want kids to smoke, the tobacco industry has typically allied tobacco in its ubiquitous advertising—even in their anti-smoking campaigns—with being independent, cool, and adult.[152] RJR Nabisco used Joe Camel as a James Bond/Don Johnson "cool" character to advertise its cigarette, and the campaign was effective in garnering the attention of young kids.[153] One study concluded that nearly one-third of three-year-olds could match Joe Camel with cigarettes and that six-year-old children were as familiar with Joe as they were with the Mickey Mouse logo on the Disney Channel.[154]

While cigarettes may be understood to provide an extreme example of marketing and injury (since most long-term smokers become addicted before the age of twenty-one and because of the high probability that smoke will wound a human host), their strategy of targeting kids is not dissimilar to the one used by McDonald's Corporation for its "happy meals" with Ronald McDonald and special toys (McDonald's is high on nag factor), Nabisco's for Oreo cookies, and Kellogg's for Pop-tarts. Indeed, as Marion Nestle has shown, food advertising makes up about half the marketing directed toward kids, and the Centers for Disease Control have found that poor diet and physical inactivity combined is only slightly behind tobacco as the leading cause of death in the United States.[155] Some studies have demonstrated that brand awareness can take place in children as young as six months and that brand loyalty can start as early as two years.[156] Advertising in this way is recursive: "kids" are now identified—and I identify them as a unique identity group—through their apparent affinity for their attraction to cartoon figures and to fried, high-fat, and sugary foods.[157]

But despite this sort of obviousness of marketing high-profit, low-health goods to vulnerable populations, the kinds of human wounding that results has been virtually untranslatable into proper "injuries." For example, in the 2003 *Pelman* case (in which two teenaged African Americans unsuccessfully sued McDonald's Restaurants for the injury of obesity), the complaint took on Rube Goldbergian extremes. Did McDonald's encourage "misuse" of its "product" (overconsumption of its foods)? Did McDonald's have a "duty to warn" since "their products have been so altered that their unhealthy attributes are now outside the ken of the ordinary consumer"? Have they "become completely different and more dangerous than the run-of-the-mill products they resemble"?[158] The wide coverage received by this case indicates precisely this ambivalence about the power of corporations to target consumers and bend their options and preferences, as well as widespread perceptions of the frivolous use of the law to compensate for individual frailties.

This disjuncture in what kinds of claims can be made in injury law, and the broad and seemingly inevitable production of unhealth in American capitalism, lies at the heart of what I am calling injury culture. That the body is at once the repository of culture and the main form of collateral against injury inevitably obfuscates the ways in which relations of inequality are encoded into commodities. Thus injuries and deaths may be unintended, but they can often be predictable in structural ways. The airbag example mentioned above further shows how both the creation of subject positions related to technology—such as "accident prone" drivers (or fat kids)—and the risk of physical injury is embedded in social inequity—an inequity that may find its roots in the misogyny that has interpreted drivers as tautologically male since the early days of automobiling. A woman seeking compensation for injuries caused by airbags may rightly be at a loss as to whether to blame the car manufacturer, NHTSA, or the masculinist education of designers. Furthermore, she may be at a loss as to who would be able to compensate her for such an injury—ultimately the injury of gender—and from which position to claim that injury. Thus the technology itself, with its promise to eradicate injury and its presentation of injury's new form, presents a key biopolitical issue through its distribution of risk and injury.

But the injury of the airbag can only be understood in the broader context of automobile culture. As Carol Sanger analyzes in her article "Girls and the Getaway," the car was one site through which gender was distinguished and naturalized, and then through which women were subordinated. She writes, "[T]he car has reinforced women's subordination and made it seem ordinary, even logical through two predictable, but subtle, mechanisms: by increasing women's domestic obligations and by sexualizing the relation between women and cars."[159] With the rise of the suburbs and the isolated stay-at-home mother, the car became the means by which women's time was taken through expectations that they would drive children to ever more far-flung lessons and sports events. It also provided a space in which rape consistently, in law, was invisible. This social construction of the car within women and men's work, and women and men's sexuality, was perhaps not an *inevitable* social use of the car, but it was a primary way that this commodity was taken up in American culture.[160]

If, as Sanger and other technology theorists such as Ruth Schwartz Cowan and Cynthia Cockburn argue, objects can materialize and naturalize certain identities, injury law demonstrates the recursive way in which design issues also materialize and naturalize sets of injuries as visible and compensable or invisible and non-compensable and how assumptions are made and articulated within discursive fields with arguments about choice, cost, and production. Thus, if American citizens are made through the practice of consumption as a nearly abstract ideal (as Lizabeth Cohen argues, and as I detail below), the actual items designed, advertised, and deployed as consumables can be understood as objects of governmentality, focusing differently distributed ideals and potential for action and possibility. Some of these possibilities depend on how products are taken up and used to shore up, supplement, and perform identities in familial and communal fields of power. Overwhelmingly, these opportunities for taking up objects are caught within dynamics of inequity that play out through unevenly distributed risk and injury. These dynamics become uniquely visible through critical readings of injury law; that is, legal contests provide a site at which such issues are struggled over. However, the form of the law overwhelmingly forecloses such discussion of risk and prior discrimination. Furthermore, the way in which injury law distinguishes persons and things makes it virtually impossible to understand how human wounding circulates as an economic and social fact.

What happens, then, when we see the law not as a neutral adjudicator but as constituting the terms of citizenship? How does injury culture instruct its subjects to understand wounding? Biopolitics is often talked about in terms of "normalizing," but it also differentiates, constituting difference within promises and fantasies of equality. Where the goals of the economy seem to oppose those of health, what kind of citizens are produced, enfranchised, and discarded?

Citizen Consumers

In her book *A Consumers' Republic*, Lizabeth Cohen has traced out in detail the ways in which American notions of citizenship became intertwined with consumerism during the twentieth century.[161] Particularly in the post—World War II period, the increasing consumption required for citizenship had to be performed in certain prescribed ways, and the common good was thought to emerge through the private and rational acts of consumption. However, as she notes, the state structuring of consumptive regimes also rendered certain forms of social engineering virtually invisible. She analyzes, for example, the GI bill and its consistent favoring of middle-class white men to the exclusion of women vets, widows of vets, and African American vets. "The fabled 'corporation man' of the 1950s . . . was as much a product of federal policy as corporate priorities, and was by no accident a man."[162] Furthermore, "The Consumers' Republic developed a structure of taxation that rewarded the traditional household of male breadwinner father and homemaker mother, thereby making women financially dependent on men at a time when the transformations of the depression and war might have encouraged alternatives."[163] The nuclear patriarchal family (re)emerged as the ideal consuming unit, and the commodities that were available for purchase served to entrench these roles and inequities.

This structuring of a consumers' republic and its private enterprise underpinnings came about not without struggle. A history of consumer movements charts against broader struggles of notions of patriotism in the twentieth century and the values of the consumer movements (who lobbied for fair trade, good design, and safety standards) pitted quite visibly against the private corporate interests in profit, obsolescence, and unregulated markets. Thus, the consumer movements of the 1930s were viciously uprooted after World War II when both private and governmental interests drove consumers to ally their personal interests with the good of the newly defined "economy" to such a degree that consumer groups of all stripes were targeted as communist. The alliance of consumption and freedom was most clearly presented in the infamous Nixon-Khrushchev kitchen debates, in which

Nixon defended obsolescence in the name of American choice, while Khrushchev held that a home should be a basic right. From here it was a short step to imagine that products could be used to distinguish and reflect on the value of the consumers themselves, and consumption became a primary way both to build communities (through Tupperware parties, for example) and to display and perform upward class mobility.[164] The rise of consumer interests in the 1960s and 1970s again receded with the gutting of most of these institutions (including OSHA, the FDA, and NHTSA) through the 1980s.[165]

Despite the viciousness with which they were attacked, consumers' movements never were a full critique of the consumers' republic.[166] They were merely attempts to gain fair prices, more voice in design issues, and more information on which to base decisions, and to have consumer interests voiced in regulatory arms of the government. They tended not to critique the broader fields of consumption and production to expose worker injury, pollution, or international trade inequities. They also did not critique such issues as nuclear families, gender, or, more generally, the centrality of consumption to American life. In other words, they did not concern themselves with the pivotal role that commodities play in governmentality.

To turn to the framing questions of this book, what kind of citizens are produced, enfranchised, and discarded in what I am describing as American injury culture? Obesity, the physiologist James O. Hill claims, "is a normal response to the American environment."[167] Yet it is perhaps the most feared and discriminatory body taboos and one of the fastest growing disabilities in the country. Plaintiffs in cases such as the McDonald's obesity case (*Pelman*) use law as a way to reassert a citizenship denied through the social and physical injuries of obesity. Along these lines, Adriana Petryna claims in her recent book on the Chernobyl nuclear disaster that "[a]cts of suffering can carry stakes beyond themselves, organize social behaviors, and inform policy actions regarding welfare and insurance, health care delivery, and courses of scientific investigation and its funding."[168] She calls the organization of these claims "biological citizenship." In the United States, I am arguing, biological citizenship is uniquely entwined with consumer citizenship, and as in the history of the use of consumer boycotts to instigate civil rights, consumption and its nemesis, litigation, entwine uniquely with health and with claims about suffering.

Claims about suffering are of course complicated. Pain is precisely that which cannot be fully communicated or fully known by another. The traces of this doubt infuse social understandings of injury law, from the repetitive strain injury sufferer who testified that "I never believed in RSI until I got it" to the need for plaintiffs' attorneys to have

good (read: bad) photographs for the jury. These slippages often con-
verge in moralistic claims on both sides—precisely because in American injury culture subjects understand injury as a compensatory site,
rather than integral to design, production, and consumption in a commodity culture.

In a short analysis of the way in which pain can become a moral
touchstone, a "universal true feeling" on which political appeals can
be made, Lauren Berlant outlines two ways of understanding citizenship. In the classic model, she argues, "each citizen's value is secured
by an equation between abstractness and emancipation: a cell of national identity provides juridically protected personhood for citizens
regardless of anything specific about them." This contrasts with a second version in which the "nation is peopled by suffering citizens and
noncitizens whose structural exclusion from the utopian-American
dreamscape exposes the state's claim of legitimacy and virtue to an
acid wash of truth telling that makes hegemonic disavowal virtually
impossible at certain moments of political intensity."[169] Citizenship,
then, might be taken as a two-way street. On the one hand, as in Berlant's first definition, certain rights, privileges, and responsibilities are
granted by virtue of the terms of belonging and, on the other, rights
are claimed and asserted, as she describes in the second definition. We
might term these "endowed" by the state and "asserted" by (potential)
citizens. Laws, in the first model of citizenship, work to distribute
goods and bads: rights can be either rules in themselves or reasons
for rules based in humanist assumptions.[170] The endowed rights might
instead base the distribution of goods on models of efficiency or an
interest in the overall social benefit.[171] The various theories of torts scat-
ter along a continuum of framing efficiency and various moral stand-
ings on how injury should matter and be made matter. Each judge in
such cases will also come with her own view.

The second version of citizenship correlates roughly with "asserted"
rights. This offers a more troubling prescription in rights claims as a
route to a healthy civic culture. To come back to Berlant's own words,
the use of pain as a measure of exclusion and legitimacy may "actually
sustain the utopian image of a homogeneous national metaculture
which can look like a healed or healthy body in contrast to the scarred
and exhausted one."[172] Similar to this second model of rights, injury
law suggests that consumptive regimes could take place either without
injury or within the bounds of acceptably spread and compensated injury. Through these models, citizens are encouraged to understand injury as a compensatory state, identifying as universal subjects.

But as Wendy Brown has argued, appealing to the state to adjudicate
injuries renders invisible the ways that the state is deeply invested in

injury production in the complex ways outlined above. The state makes injury visible only on its own terms, through its own mechanisms.[173] Asking the state to protect against injury deeply legitimizes the state as it disavows its role in injury production and distribution.[174] Suffering can carry a unique value—but only when it is registered in a meaningful way. So, bizarrely, suffering turns out to be uniquely meaningful even as it is easily dismissed in very narrow terms.[175] Furthermore, the ability to register suffering is highly contingent. Wealthier people have access to and use the tort system both more often and more successfully than less wealthy people.[176] Furthermore, wealthier people have more ability to override the usual limitations of law. The Air Transport Safety and System Stabilization Act of 2001 provides one potent example of this. This act, through the September 11th Victim Compensation Fund, offered the best of a workers' compensation system (guaranteed award) and the best of the tort system (very high awards) to a group of injured people who may not have had the evidence to bring a successful tort claim.[177] These cases illustrate Sheila Jasanoff's observation of a contemporary move toward the "transformation of the trial court's passionately personal gaze into the dispassionate processing routines of an administrative agency that puts efficiency and risk mitigation for all above the classic 'day in court' for each."[178] That these awards were paid from a taxpayer (rather than a corporate) purse also demonstrates the disparity in the ways that risks and injuries can be articulated: where some injuries are apparently issues of "national security," others lay buried as the side effects of business as usual.[179] Thus, sometimes injuries can link to a way to engage the structures that distributed those injuries, as they did with September 11, and sometimes not, as they do not with obesity.[180]

Conclusion

Design decisions ineluctably code danger and injury at the outset of the production process. Products anticipate the agents that will animate them temporally and statistically; products and humans simulate imagined relationships and worlds. In this sense, Pintos and cheeseburgers are not so dissimilar, as they both demonstrate how American injury culture injures as a matter of course.[181] Accidents and human wounding provide a boost to the economy that is astonishingly undertheorized in economic and social theory. Elucidating the issues in this way raises the question of how human wounding counts, who "owns" health, and how it is to count as a social good.

But within this ambivalence, an uneasy nostalgia for the human folds all too easily into rhetorics of social good and technological progress. This nostalgia makes legible sentiments such as: "Even if cars [substitute: pesticides, mercury amalgam fillings, nuclear power, ad infinitum] kill or sicken some of us, overall, they lead to a better quality of life for all of us Americans." The overlapping privileging of the human and the inclusive "us" presents the baseline for the imagined "utopian image of a homogeneous national metaculture" that Berlant writes about, and leads to the rhetorical power of injury law in its promise to right the wrongs of egregious corporate practices visited on specific persons (rather than statistical futures). The idealization of the ways that objects act in the world makes us into persons that can wield rights to ensure our place in that world.

The rights-bearing person who claims the right not to be hurt, however, is hurt with a wound that carries its own mode of circulation through the economy. As I pointed out, the existence of human wounding on the production and consumption side is integral to the economy for its infusion of billions of dollars. It has no "production" value in itself per se—only produced through compensation (otherwise calculated as a cost for its host). But as an economic force, as the wound circulates among lawyers, various kinds of doctors, accident investigators, insurance brokers and administrators, benefits officers, and wheelchair designers, it changes meaning as each practitioner turns it into a different sort of raw material for their services. If cancer were eradicated, a billion-dollar industry and millions of jobs would go with it. This point about the economic and social trade-offs of injury has been explicitly made by the Supreme Court in at least two opinions on cigarette litigation.

As it comes under rubrics of the discourses attached to each of these professions, the wound is reified as a distinct thing—always separate from the body it adheres to. Anthropologists Minnegal and Dwyer use an example of a pig to consider how value mutates in commodification:

> A pig is brought to an exchange not as a pig *per se*, but *as a particular* pig. Its particular constellation of attributes, and its history, make it not only appropriate but in a real sense, the only appropriate offering. Where pigs are sold, by contrast, attributes such as size, sex, and colour . . . no longer bear upon the appropriateness of the particular pig to the intended transaction. A pig is suitable for sale simply (i.e. universally) because it is a pig. *Thus, it seems that the idea of "pig" itself has become reified.*[182]

Marilyn Strathern draws attention, through this quote, to the way that the "'thing' created through commodification carries information about itself within it, and does not require contextualisation beyond its evaluation in relation to similar entities."[183] Similarly, wounding is put on the marketplace: a doctor will charge a certain rate to repair a similarly broken leg, no matter how it was broken; an oncologist will "hope" against all odds that a standardized round of chemotherapy will shrink a cancer tumor.

Wounds, then, ambiguously circulate as owned, embodied, materially distinct (such as cancers, broken arms, illnesses of all kinds), and diffuse (such as generalized unhealth). For this reason of definitional haze, wounds have tended to be counted as externalities to the economy. Externalities are the costs, such as pollution or noise, that remain unaccounted for in economic calculations. Michel Callon puts the question of externalities in terms of the framing or bracketing of which series of exchanges will be rendered legible and be counted as an "economy." Callon recognizes that in the creation of an economy, the "framing process is necessarily incomplete: first because a wholly hermetic frame is a contradiction in terms, and second because flows are always bidirectional, overflows simply being the inevitable corollary of the requisite links with the surrounding environment."[184] In other words, any economy will have externalities, good and bad.

Bringing injury (or any externality) into the economy requires rendering it measurable. A damage award, a bill for the treatment of a broken leg, and a calculation inferring that traffic injuries or cancer deaths pose an economic "cost" or "benefit" to a society all put a measurement on wounding—they each bring the wound into the economy. But they do so in different ways, as one sees in the documents presented by tobacco companies that discussed money saved by governments as a result of the early deaths of its smoking citizens. And as the outrage spurred by those calculations demonstrated, setting these equations is a moral project replete with the full ambivalence of the costs of everyday life. In economic terms, Americans would ideally die, and quickly, between the morrow of their last social security tax payment and the eve of their first check.

These ambiguities begin to show how wounds can carry economic meaning in multifaceted and complicated ways. Wounding is simply not quantifiable: "the frame or border of the economy is not a line on a map, but a horizon that at every point opens up other territories."[185] How wounding will count and for whom is a political decision that has everything to do with the meaning of citizenship in a given social and political sphere. Bodies carry different kinds of materiality and wounds adhere differently to different people. Where injury is understood as a rights project, the complicated questions that attend human wounding, such as how they are integral to the economy, are simply foreclosed. Health and its political, economic, and social value become rhetorical values rather than subjects of debate, and debate turns to terms of denunciation rather than analysis.

Law carries the full ambivalence of these promises. In its monetary valuation of the body, personal injury law merely echoes the broader logic of commodity culture. This logic renders invisible the inequities through which injuries are distributed. But institutions of injury law also strangely carry the potential to decommodify the wound—to make visible the "particular constellation of attributes, and . . . history" that belong to the wound that do, sometimes, matter. These trials present fascinating fields of play; someone's "day in court" is a powerful social moment. However, that day in court will ultimately disappoint. Unless better analytics are built for apprehending the meaning of human wounding as an economic and social force, with the full force of its ambivalent moralism and economics, a suit addressed to a personal injury will always tend to reiterate the same logic that led to the particular constellation of the injury.

Chapter 2

Sentience and Slavery

The Struggle over the Short-Handled Hoe

KNOWN AS *EL CORTITO* (the short one) or *el brazo del diablo* (the arm of the devil), the short-handled hoe, which measures 10–14 inches long and weighs 3–4 pounds, was regularly used by farm workers in California until it was outlawed in 1975.[186] In conjunction with hand weeding, it was useful in singling out lettuce, celery, and beet starts, which were planted in heavy rows to guarantee that sprouts would survive the ravages of birds, bugs, and the weather. Use of the hoe required the worker to fold over at the waist, constantly raising and lowering the hoe while walking sideways down the row of plants. The needs of agricultural mass production were such that workers were required to use the hoe for hours and days on end. Symptoms of short-handled hoe use included not only crippling injuries to the back but also nosebleeds, kidney malfunction, headaches, runny eyes from dirt, fever, acid urine, kidney pains, arthritis, exhaustion, wrist swelling, and poisoning from inhaling pesticides. One farm worker testified at a hearing in front of the Division of Industrial Safety that "I began using the short-handled hoe at the age of 11, [and] I have seen my body waste away."[187] A 1970 study found that the short-handled hoe caused health problems in 87 percent of respondents,[188] and of workers age thirty-one or older, 91 percent complained of back pain. Despite these figures, however, 50 percent of injured farm workers never saw a doctor due to intimidation, bureaucracy, inaccessibility of medical services, the language barrier, and possibly "macho" pride.[189]

To many workers, the short-handled hoe seemed to be a normal enough, self-evident tool. Indeed, one farm worker described how she initially thought the work would be easier with the short hoe. "I really thought it was cute," she said. "But then when I had started working about 2 or 3 hours I started feeling first of all the blood started coming to my eyes and my eyes started to hurt and then the next thing my legs started to hurt. After then it was my back and the pain was great."[190]

The short hoe is generally thought to have been introduced to California agriculture late in the nineteenth century as intensive crop farming took hold. When Japanese workers first came to California, they

FIGURE 4. A demonstration of racialized worker efficiency from the 1950 California Annual Farm Labor Report. Original photo caption reads: "Mexican workers are efficient at stoop labor tasks. Here Auburn Coe, Farm Placement Representative for Monterey County, notes worker's use of short handled hoe in thinning lettuce."

organized their own farms and thus had the freedom to use tools on a rotating basis and regularly change body position. A change in appellation from what was then known as "squat labor" to "stoop labor" reflects the change in farm work itself. If at one time workers could kneel or squat while intensely cultivating an area, a stooped position allowed a worker to make his or her way hurriedly down crop rows. This change in working postures was one indicator of the loss of control over working conditions more generally, as the economic and political persecution of the newly organized Chinese and Japanese immigrants was supervened by Mexican immigrants.

Unlike their predecessors, the new immigrants were typically not from farming backgrounds. However, "controllable labor was more attractive than skilled labor by this time, and so agricultural production underwent a reorganization."[191] The reorganization of labor established a labor contractor, or "crew pusher," who made sure that farm workers were working as productively as possible. An increasing division of labor established what the renowned journalist Carey McWilliams dubbed "factories in the field."[192] The short-handled hoe was an instrument of mass production in the sense that it was used for hours and days without recess and it allowed crew pushers to watch over large fields to see "malingerers" who stood up to rest their backs. A steady stream of labor was available to compensate for workers who left the job due to injury or fatigue (daily turnover in short-handled hoe gangs was as much as 85 percent).[193] The short hoe remained a standard tool of agriculture in California through most of the twentieth century. The legal struggle that resulted in the abolition of the short-handled hoe started with a petition by the California Rural Legal Assistance (CRLA) in 1972. The case went through three hearings before the Department of Industrial Labor and was appealed twice before being accepted for hearing before the California Supreme Court. The case was heard twice more in front of the Department of Industrial Labor, and the hoe was banned in 1975.

Contemporary safety laws structure "fair" relations of production and injury. They encode what may be demanded of the worker's body in the process of work—on an everyday level and in terms of risks undergone for production and service. In a market economy where cheap production is the essence of profit, the well-being of the worker and the necessity of production are always put in balance. These contests are considered in different ways; for example, a cost-benefit analysis may be performed to decide what is reasonable risk. But these "tests" always leave room for questions such as, "reasonable risk" for whom? In what circumstances? Given how many unknown factors?

Safety laws also open a way for us to better understand how injuries and objects come to carry meaning. As this case demonstrates, safety codes are always open to contestation, and these contests are crucial events through which social relations are built into and performed through objects. Furthermore, these contestations force parties to articulate positions and assumptions about objects and people. The short hoe provides a particularly interesting place for this type of interrogation for several reasons. First, the political economy and the semiotics of race allow us to see blatant articulations of racist assumptions that are these days rare in such public fora. Second, the 1960s and early 1970s provide a unique period in California history where the face-offs between the "right" and the "left" were particularly clear-cut in the Berkeley free speech, anti-Vietnam, civil rights, and feminist movements. Within these movements, race in America took on a broad-based visibility and racism became unacceptable to a wider group of Americans. Taking its place within this set of domestic and international struggles, the short-handled hoe became the pivot point around which repetitive strain back injuries emerged *as injuries* in the context of racialized bodies that were contradictorily considered to be both ideal for stoop labor *and* "naturally" prone to back injury, and of the activism of a growing number of Californians who believed that the racist underpinnings of agricultural production were wrong. Thus, *el cortito*—described by farm workers in the legal struggles variously as an instrument of torture, surveillance, indifference, and sheer pig-headedness, and described by the growers as simply a tool of the job—consolidated a unique showdown over political power, race and class, working conditions, and legal services for the poor. In so doing, it can illuminate how bodies and objects are co-constituted and made to "count" in different ways.

In pulling together the arguments that follow here, I have relied on the work of my historian colleagues who have created narratives about California's agricultural history. I have also worked from a series of interviews with community workers, doctors, attorneys who argued on both sides of the case and those who were more distantly involved in the case, and people who have been involved with farm working issues.[194] I have analyzed an archive of materials, most of which are on file at the CRLA's office in Salinas, that includes the legal briefs and petitions prepared by the attorneys, attorney correspondence, the transcripts of the hearings that took place before the Labor Relations Board, the studies used by the CRLA, press releases, newspaper reports, and other ephemera.[195] Without this archive, it would perhaps not be hyperbolic to say that there would be no short-handled hoe, no related back and other injuries, no poorly treated workers. Refracting the issue in this way, I pose that it is only through the archive created by this lawsuit that human bodies (that is, potentially injured bodies) were created and registered as something different than machinic cogs in the factory of the field.

"Archives assemble," says Michel-Rolph Trouillot. He argues that this assembly work is not the "passive act of collecting" but "an active act of production that prepares facts for historical intelligibility. Archives set up the substantive and formal elements of the narrative. They are the institutionalized sites of mediation between the sociohistorical process and the narrative about that process . . . they convey authority and set the rules for credibility and interdependence; they help select the stories that matter."[196] The short hoe, although barely mentioned in the literature on Californian agriculture, became a story that matters precisely for the ways that the suit both framed and forced articulations (articulations that are astonishingly frank in their racist underpinnings) about how sociohistoric events such as imported labor racialized bodies and how dangerous tools would be acted on and remembered. That the key CRLA lawyers pursued successful legal careers—one in the California court of appeals and the other in a large San Francisco law firm—while the doctor who testified on behalf of the growers and argued that Mexicans had congenitally disfigured backs wanted to forget the whole thing and refused an interview are reminders that these narratives inscribe how right and wrong will affect configurations of memory, success, and shame.

The suit in itself was not the entire story; it came to matter because of a number of threads that came together to enable its existence and its success: poverty law, a new "leftist" state governor, the United Farm Workers (UFW) movement, and its charismatic leader, Cesar Chavez. Additionally, the short hoe came to symbolize the degradation of farm laborers. *El cortito* was taken up in various representational regimes, from Dorothea Lange's famous photograph of three heroically portrayed workers hurtling up the rows of the field to posters for the farm movement. But the short hoe as an object and a symbol became an archive in Trouillot's sense through this legal case: a case through which Mexican and Mexican American workers asserted their bodies as "human." Thus, on the one hand this chapter is about figuring out how the hoe, the injuries, and race as a category are mutually constitutive and crystallize in different ways for pernicious and progressive reasons. On the other hand, it is about examining the ways that the law, the archive, and history, as mutually constitutive, write the story of culture and its struggles over who gets to be human—and as human, who gets to be injured. The hoe, which clearly does not *in itself* demand a certain posture, came to be injurious at a specific geopolitical moment of Californian agribusiness. Thus, it became in the late 1960s and early 1970s a crucial actor in the ways that race and citizenship were consolidated and played out.

Relying on the archive in this way, in all its details and countervailing contradictory stories, also allows for a fuller accounting of the way the hoe circulated in everyday narratives about contemporary life— quite literally, of the social work done by the hoe in maintaining relations of inequality. A close examination of the transcripts of the hearings illuminates the way that the growers' claims to economics and efficiency underpinned premises about the bodies of Mexicans and Mexican Americans. These assumptions about what Mexican bodies were did more than infect agricultural production; they structured it. In this sense, *el cortito* was as important an actor as any worker in the story of California agriculture.

The popular story that has emerged in California since the 1970s has consolidated an encounter between the evil growers and the liberal lawyers who harnessed the law of the land for just ends. This story is a tempting one—how else to account for the truly vicious racism, the murderously anti-labor stance, the unabashed intervention into affairs of the state, and the pitiable greed of California growers in the nineteenth and twentieth centuries? How else to account for the brilliant use to which the law was put by dedicated CRLA lawyers and staff in preventing the use of the short-handled hoe, or for the coalitions of activists, artists, and lawyers that arose during the struggle? This oppositional model, though, highlights the clumsy tools that law confers as a way of examining—let alone adjudicating—social struggles. After all, as Douglas Murray notes in the only published social analysis that focuses on the short-handled hoe, the structure of law insists that the arguments about the hoe were circumscribed within a narrow set of issues: "By identifying the problem as the hazardous use of a tool, the statutes deflected the attention away from the hazardous nature of production organized, directed and controlled by a corporation."[197] This model also tends to efface the workers themselves—they are deleted from both the account of *Growers v. the CRLA* and the continued conditions of their lives and labor.[198]

What follows here is divided into three sections. In the first I present an abbreviated history of California agriculture and its dependence on racial categories. The emergence of agribusiness in the state has been unique because of its concentrated ownership that was passed down from the Mexicans after 1848, the aridity and difficulty of irrigation, and the availability of waves of cheap alien workers who labored for barely subsistence wages. This will provide some context of the *bracero* labor policies, the establishment of the CRLA, and Governor Ronald Reagan's illegal attempts to cut social programming. In the second section I outline in some detail the testimony of the short hoe hearings, outlining the contours of the suit and the stories told about the short hoe. In the third section, I analyze the junctures of race, labor, injury, and the short hoe, examining how in the litigation, each party depended on racialized discourses through which to understand and articulate short hoe injuries and Mexican American bodies.

Race and Agribusiness: California

When Mexico surrendered California in 1848, the United States inherited large tracts of land from rancheros and passed these directly into the hands of corporate commercial agriculture.[199] The resulting concentration was further consolidated through railway land speculation.[200] Land remained uncultivated until toward the end of the century, when farmers sought to reap profits through bonanza wheat farming, which was popular because of the shortage of labor. Several successive droughts left this business in shambles, and with the development of the ice-making machine in 1851 and the refrigerated freight car in 1868, which made possible the transportation of fruit and vegetables, specialized crops were introduced[201]—oranges in 1873 and sugar beets in

1888.[202] This specialized farming and the highly technologized irrigation of the Imperial Valley further concentrated landholdings.

During this time of incipient landholding consolidation—between 1887 and 1893—Chinese immigrants formed the bulk of farm labor, and they virtually taught crop farming to the large farm owners.[203] With increasing Chinese immigration, exclusion became the foremost issue of California politics; white laborers saw the Chinese as stealing jobs and assisting large farm holders in monopolizing agriculture by helping them make the transition to crop farming. When the Chinese began to organize themselves by opening small businesses, employers' interests allied with labor and attempts to restrict immigration began.[204] Exclusion laws were passed in 1882, 1892, and 1902, in addition to the Nationality Act, which specified that only "free whites" and "African Aliens" could apply for naturalization in a country that was, by design, to be one of "Nordic fiber."[205] Thereafter, the Chinese—excluded from farm and public works labor, land ownership, access to business licenses, testifying in court for or against a white man, public education, citizenship, and naturalization—were confined to urban ghettos and faced vicious racism, violence, murder, and expulsion, as well as extra financial burdens in the form of taxation (shrimping and police taxes, among others) and specifically anti-Chinese laws and ordinances.[206]

I use the Chinese as an example here, but this cycle of using cheap labor and then maliciously dispossessing groups when they organized themselves was typical in California agriculture: South Asians, Japanese, Filipinos, and Armenians had similar experiences to those of the Chinese. Growers' strategies ensured ethnic factions and a chronic oversupply of labor in a market that was already only seasonal.[207] These tactics have been supported by the state government. One author notes that "confronted with an increasingly organized and militant agricultural work force, the state response typically has been to help promote the migration or immigration of a replacement supply."[208]

Unlike groups of Asians who came to work the fields, the Mexicans who arrived shortly after the turn of the century on the newly built railways had not been farmers.[209] Skill was no longer an important prerequisite for farm workers who labored increasingly in assembly-line agricultural production. Although the Mexicans were able to initiate some labor organization, the coming of white laborers who refused to organize with Mexicans stifled further organizing during the depression.[210] By 1935, three-quarters of all harvest labor was hired by one-tenth of growers who controlled over half of the production.[211] Growers began to further consolidate their power. In 1934 they organized the statewide Associated Farmers, whose explicit mandate was "to foster and encourage respect for and to maintain law and order, to promote

FIGURE 5. Filipinos cutting lettuce for Japanese owners, Salinas, California, Dorothea Lange, 1935. U.S. Farm Security Administration, Prints and Photographic Division, Library of Congress, LC-USF347–000826-D.

the prompt, orderly and efficient administration of justice."[212] Since agribusiness interests had been so successful in infiltrating government agencies, "justice" was also a term of art. Because they dealt in highly speculative markets with perishable commodities,[213] and because seasonal farm labor was almost the only cost that growers had control over, they argued that they were not responsible for working conditions and they protected this privilege savagely.[214] In 1947 one Professor Cleland wrote that "California's industrial agriculture can exhibit all the customary weapons . . . gas, goon squads, propaganda, bribery."[215]

Between 1942 and 1964, a bracero program recruited Mexicans to work in U.S. fields as a cheap labor supply. Public funds were used to initiate and maintain the program, and the terms of employment (most of which were never enforced) were negotiated by the United States and Mexico in 1942.[216] The goals of the program were succinctly encapsulated by the governor of California in 1947: "Mexican workers . . . should constitute a flexible group which can be readily moved from operation to operation and from place to place where local help falls short of the numbers needed to save the crops. These workers should be in a sense 'shock troops' used only in real emergency as insurance against loss of valuable production."[217] A labor force that could be sent home was ideal for underpaid, difficult, and migratory farm labor, and labor shortages were always the reason given for importing labor (braceros and, later, illegal immigrants). However, braceros were used as strikebreakers and to maintain low wages—indeed, during the bracero era, agricultural wages declined drastically in comparison to those in manufacturing: from 65 percent in 1948 to 47 percent in 1959.[218] One employee of the U.S. Department dubbed the bracero program "legalized slavery."[219]

The attitude toward Mexican laborers during that period is reflected in this quote, taken from a book published in 1971: "To toil endless hours in stifling heat and under generally adverse conditions demanded more than mere physical attributes. [It] required a somewhat unique personality type: one accustomed to living, indeed thriving, in a virtual state of physical and mental peonage. The Mexican peasant was ideally suited for the task. . . . [T]he sociopsychological milieu in which the average Mexican peasant was reared, prepared him ideally for his role as the servile, hard-working, seldom complaining, perpetually polite, bracero."[220] By the 1950s, braceros constituted well over half the laborers in many crops,[221] and although growers again cried labor shortage, braceros were clearly used as cheap subsidized labor.[222] This point is corroborated by the fact that when the bracero program ended, the predicted disaster failed to materialize: crop production did not lessen and consumer prices did not increase.[223]

After a series of extensions to the program, the importation of bracero labor was officially halted in 1964. In 1965 United Farm Worker strikes began, and farm workers gained citizen support during the civil rights era.[224] The CRLA was one other result of this support. Initiated in 1966 as an element of President Lyndon Johnson's War on Poverty program, the CRLA included a core group of public service lawyers who cast about for broad-based issues with long-range consequences.[225] Among these, the short-handled hoe—much to the lawyers' surprise—staked a claim as a farm worker issue of major proportions.

The ten offices of the CRLA began with money ($1 million annually) from the Office of Economic Opportunity (OEO) and the dedication of young civil rights lawyers. The introduction of legal services to the poor of California was to fulfill Johnson's mandate of "equal justice under the law." A large percentage of the rural poor in California consisted of farm workers, who had no right to form unions, were in chronic oversupply, and earned less than minimum wage (one of the first CRLA suits was to enforce a newly instituted minimum wage of $1.65/hour).[226] Considering the odds—40 lawyers and 25 community workers served 16 counties and a population in excess of 550,000 (at a time when the national average was one lawyer for 640 persons)—the CRLA was tremendously effective.[227] They won 90 percent of the class action suits brought between December 1966 and January 1970.[228] Two CRLA attorneys describe the paradoxical role of the CRLA as "a genuinely *conservative* force regarding the written laws and administration regulations of the State and Federal Governments. But it was a genuinely *revolutionary* force in relation to agribusiness's law and order."[229]

In order to not get bogged down with individual cases such as family or landlord disputes, the CRLA took on broader-based issues that would have a structural effect on poor people.[230] Its first major-impact cases in the late 1960s included three key suits. The first illegalized bracero labor;[231] the second contested Governor Ronald Reagan's 1967 $240 million cut to Medi-Cal as unconstitutional;[232] and in the third they halted the practice of having Mexican American children placed into "special classes" for the mentally handicapped by ensuring that the intelligence tests were administered in Spanish.[233] In addition, the CRLA brought a number of suits similar to the one brought against the Madera Unified School Board. The school board annually closed schools so that students could pick grapes in nearby fields, which were in violation of state health and sanitation laws—no toilets, drinking water, or hand-washing facilities. In addition, suit was brought against the state welfare department, which had terminated welfare to families who had refused to allow their children over ten years old to work in the fields.[234]

By 1970 Governor Reagan had had enough of equal justice under the law. At the height of the farm workers' activism, as the Delano grape strike boycott was gaining momentum, and the month after he was elected governor for the second time, he vetoed CRLA funding. In order to justify the removal of funding for a group that was renowned for its excellent track record, he had a report written with charges that "range[d] from the libelous ('CRLA attorneys tried to arrange a meeting between Angela Davis and the Soledad Brothers') to the ridiculous ('CRLA attorneys appear in court barefoot')."[235]

After a long battle, during which the author of the report, Lewis K. Uhler, refused to provide evidence to an OEO panel for any of the claims he had made, Reagan's veto was overridden.[236] The events of this proceeding have been well documented elsewhere. Suffice it to say here that by all accounts, including an independent report of the commission enlisted to examine Uhler's claims, the Reagan-Uhler report offered an account full of unfounded accusations. In the words of one former deputy attorney general of the state of California who had represented the state against the CRLA, "I am convinced . . . that this is a

report that the State officials issued containing charges that they know
are not true. . . . I think this report is a very bad example of what happens when the philosophy against certain groups overcomes people's
rationality."[237]

The Hearings

In 1969 Maurice Jourdane was a young graduate of Hastings College
of Law and a newly appointed CRLA attorney. When farm workers
approached him with the short-handled hoe, they tested him: if you
really want to do something for us, you will get rid of this instrument.
Like many of the farm workers had, he shook his head in disbelief—
that is, until he went out and tried it himself. He spent the next six
years on the case.[238] His first step was to spend a week at Stanford's
law school library searching for a legal hook that might sidestep the
powerful agribusiness interests that permeated most state institutions.[239] On September 20, 1972,[240] he and the CRLA posed the issue to
the Industrial Safety Board (ISB) of the Division of Industrial Safety.
This document mandates that workers in California have the right to
"such freedom from danger to the life, safety, or health of employees
as the nature of the employment reasonably permits."[241] Jourdane argued that the short-handled hoe contravened one of the health and
safety standards in the California Administrative Code that prohibited
the use of unsafe hand tools.[242]

While Jourdane had hoped that the issue would generate publicity
and then legislation, the board took up the petition by setting up three
hearings, one in San Francisco, another in Imperial (El Centro), and the
final in Salinas, to hear testimony from farm workers, doctors, lawyers,
and growers. The ISB, appointed by the governor, is legally bound to
include representatives of labor, management, and the general public.[243] Reagan had named a "former FBI agent, a corporate director of
an oil equipment manufacturing firm, the supervisor of employee relations for a major gas company, and the owner of a construction company," leaving the vice president of Operating Engineers Local 3 as the
only labor representative.[244]

By all reports, the hearings were packed and raucous affairs, with
growers' comments mixed in with those of farm workers and doctors
in no clear order. Nevertheless, it is possible to gather the arguments
generally under the categories of growers, the CRLA, and the farm
workers.

The growers' statements are familiar in their resonance with contemporary U.S. tort reform laments. These complaints tend to express a

fairly typical array of concerns, mourning the costs of injuries to both businesses and the state; blaming the workers for the injuries; and casting injuries as an inevitable, if not regrettable, side effect of agricultural production (and as such, one they could not be held responsible for). The testimony included claims that there were no reasonable alternatives,[245] that workers chose to use the hoe,[246] that companies would go bankrupt if the hoe was banned,[247] that the state would suffer economic losses,[248] and that it would cost too much to replace the hoes.[249] Richard Hubbard, an owner and operator of Hubbard farms in El Centro, discussed the decisions made about farm technology in simple market terms. He talked about the technical difficulty of having to "dribble out 500,000 seeds to the acre, and then try[ing] to thin it down to 24,000 to 25,000 [seedlings] per acre."[250] Hubbard was clear on the question of technology, arguing that "[m]ost farmers are not altruistic, and if it is cheaper for them to go to a mechanical thinner, if they can obtain a better product by going to a long-handled hoe, we would have done so long ago."[251]

The growers also dismissed complaints of injury as misattributed, since the hoe is simply comparable to other tools such as wrenches and carpet layers' tools.[252] They further expressed fear that all stoop labor would be eliminated, thus, rendering much of farm labor problematic.[253] One grower raised the issue of fault: "We're not in the business to hurt someone's back. It's a necessity."[254] Finally, they resorted to barely veiled threats: "if you can't do the job we have braceros that can do it,"[255] or "if you take away the control that we have with the short-handled hoe, we ... will have to mechanize."[256]

The real legal crux of the argument, which is to say the only argument that sufficiently narrowed the issue to the legal nugget of "unsafe" and whether or not the short hoe was, in fact, unsafe regardless of the many reasons that it may be desirable to keep it in the fields, was the suggestion that the problem was not the hoe but that people did not use it properly.[257] The other main argument along these lines was a simple denial that the short-handled hoe use caused back injury.[258]

Some farm workers testified that the hoe was fine, and their testimony fell into three categories.[259] They claimed that they would rather use a short-handled hoe than a long-handled hoe and that people who were injured were not using it properly, and they expressed fear about being replaced by technology in claims such as "if they take the short-handled hoe away. ... [t]hey're going to put [in] machines."[260]

Legally, it was incumbent upon the CRLA to demonstrate two key points: first, that serious and irreversible back injuries were caused by the short-handled hoe, and second, that the long-handled hoe was as efficient as, if not more so, the short-handled hoe. To demonstrate these points, they had the results of two studies. The first was a survey compiled from a questionnaire that the CRLA sent out nationally, finding that other states with similar crops (Washington, Idaho, Minnesota, Texas) did not use the short-handled hoe but the long-handled hoe.[261] The second study was a comparative one illustrating that agricultural workers who used the short-handled hoe had a drastically higher rate of back pain than those who did not. The rest of the testimony fell into roughly two categories—expert and experiential. Doctors and a workers' compensation attorney testified to the medical severity of the injury, the loss of productivity that resulted, the cost of compensation, and the reasons why injuries from the short-handled hoe did not appear in workers' compensation records.[262] Farm workers testified to the severity of the injury and the labor conditions of farm work.

Eleven doctors testified as to the severity of injury resulting from short-handled hoe use, explaining to the board in layman's terms yet in great detail the mechanisms of the spine, disks, muscles, and tendons; the mechanics of spinal injury resulting from short-handled hoe use; and the effects of lifting weight while bent over.[263] The doctors agreed that use of *el cortito* causes major degeneration and weakening such that the equivalent of a seventy-year-old back will be found on a person of thirty-five; that it causes arthritis, herniated or slipped disks, fracture, or spondilolosis that would not be caused by use of long-handled hoe; and that the injury is irreversible.

Even after surgery, 50 percent of patients with back injuries are never able to return to work. Dr. Robert Murphy testified that "[t]he worker loses a tremendous amount. He loses his livelihood. He never gets compensation that's equal to what he can make by working. He loses his family status. He loses his re-employability because these people do not get rehired. And from our studies at the University of California, I can tell you that the incidence of psychiatric disease in patients who have had chronic low back pains following injuries is tremendous."[264] While the growers tried to limit the scope of the injury, the doctors showed that the expense of injured workers is paid not only by the individuals but also by the state. When interrogated about the importance of the "productivity" of California agriculture, Dr. Murphy balanced productivity against the expense of back injuries. He said, "I'm sure you can buy a lot of beets for $100,000,000. I don't know what you mean by productivity, but it wouldn't even approach the cost of workmen's compensation for back injuries."[265]

A main obstacle to the CRLA's case was that very few workers' compensation cases had been filed that would demonstrate the direct link between hoe use and back injury.[266] There are two main reasons for this. First, agriculture was not covered under workers' compensation until the late 1950s, so legal firms did not handle farm workers, and they did not know farm workers' needs or language.[267] Perhaps as a result of not having been covered, farm workers did not complain about their pain. Dr. Robert Thomson mentioned that "I have the feeling that they sort of expect [back pain,] that this is their way of life to have backaches, so they don't really come to the doctor complaining about it."[268] Second, because of the cumulative nature of the injury, a farm worker may be injured as a result of the hoe but while he or she was doing different work.[269] Another doctor stated that "the pattern of these injuries is not a sudden traumatic impact where the back goes out, but rather, because of this long period of weakening, finding then in the clinic later case after case after case of back problems in farm workers."[270] More crucially, even if the doctor could link the injury to the cumulative use of the hoe, workers' compensation claims require the doctor to report a specific incident that caused the injury.[271] As Dr. David Flanagan argued, injury using the short hoe is not "a reportable injury because there is no incident."[272] Thus, compensation records did not show the full story because other injuries happened only as a result of the already weakened back.[273] Furthermore, one doctor testified that he regularly sent injured workers to the welfare office rather than to workers' compensation because workers were so rarely compensated through this institution and when they were, the checks took months to go through the bureaucracy. Attorney Michael Rucka spoke for others when he argued that since they understood the injury as a result of the position, not the tool, they filed claims as "repetitive bending, stooping, and lifting."[274] Rucka also gave detailed testimony as to the difficulty and expense of representing repetitive trauma injuries, which were not generally worth it given the low wages (and thus predicted low settlements from which attorneys take payment as a percentage) of farm workers.[275] The added invisibility of these injuries relates to the fact that these tools are generally understood as ordinary products (like wrenches or carpet layers' tools), not as inherently dangerous.

Part of the CRLA's strategy to account for the low rates of reportage, the lack of workers' compensation records, and the difficulty of diagnosing the injury was the sheer number of doctors who testified, each from a different perspective. This attempt to stack the archive did not go unnoticed. Just prior to the statement of one of the doctors, the head of the commission, Edward White, deliberated on the necessity of yet another medical opinion, one that would likely repeat what had already been said, suggesting that they had heard enough medical evidence. CRLA attorney Martin Glick responded, "I think his testimony is quite different from some of the other doctors." White responded,

"We've already got nine doctors and we feel that perhaps we're adding icing to the cake."[276]

Farm worker testimony generally fell into four categories: the severity of the injury; the symbolic value of *el cortito*; the humiliation of the injury and of the stooped position; and the primitive state of technology. Many workers spoke eloquently of the sheer pain of using the hoe. Unlike other work that allowed the worker to switch tasks,[277] "after working with the short-handled hoe, one comes home without the desire to eat, to bathe, to communicate, to socialize. . . . I began using the short-handled hoe at the age of 11, [and] I have seen my body waste away."[278] Perhaps some of the most effective testimony was from a sixty-five-year-old man who had been an amateur and professional boxer in the 1920s before doing farm work. Mr. Hernandez said, "At the end of a week my body was pretty sore, especially the lower back. In the second week it was harder on me. I could hardly stand my lower back and my legs. On the third week it was just plain torture. . . . And I quit. . . . It was three weeks after that before I could . . . really straighten up without feeling pain in my back.[279] This man switched from stoop labor to lifting one-hundred-pound sacks over his head into boxcars. He did this for seventeen years and lifted as many as eight hundred bags a day. He said, "I have waited thirty-nine years for a hearing on this short hoe."[280]

Several reasons for the growers' preference for the short-handled hoe were suggested. Growers may have used the hoe to purposely degrade workers, to easily survey them across the fields, or to use them as a rite of passage. One worker testified that "the foreman will usually keep track in [his] own sort of tentative way of the number of times the person stands up to give his back a so-called rest. If a person stands up ten times or more, they'll keep an eye on this guy and he won't be there the next day. The sort of inherent relaxing mechanisms in harvesting other crops is built into it, but not the *cortito*. . . . It's very excruciating on the back."[281] This also explained, to the workers, the reasons why a few farm workers testified *for* the hoe at these hearings. "We know that the fieldworkers who are speaking up for the short-handled hoe are the ones who will be given the job of foreman because they are the ones who are always kissing up to the grower."[282]

It was not only the pain of the labor that the farm workers were protesting. According to one worker, "[There] is the terrific pain that the farm worker suffered while actually using the hoe during the end of the day. . . . And the second kind of pain they testified to is the pain that the farm workers had when they became thirty-five or forty and found themselves disabled, and having the problem of trying to get to sleep, trying to get up, having trouble walking and having to lie down again, and that kind of problem, I think as we all know, goes with back problems."[283] A few times, a farm worker would try to give a more general idea of the terms of labor and point out that the growers were giving an inaccurate account of labor conditions. Fred Reyes said, "The foreman brings some soda pop into the field and if the workers don't buy them, then [they're] fired. . . . They come in here and explain to you that everything is alright, and there's nothing wrong with the short hoe because they have tried to kill us with that hoe. They never paid the price rightfully for this kind of a job; now [in the hearings] they claim they pay $2.50 to $3.00 an hour." The board had no interest in the link between the short hoe and labor conditions. After this testimony the following dialogue ensued:

WHITE: Mr. Glick, would you keep this on target now. We're not getting into working conditions.
GLICK: I have nothing to do with this.
WHITE: Oh, you don't. Well, would you tell him we are interested in the injury and the effect of the short hoe on the working, but not when it gets into other areas, working conditions, soda pop, this sort of thing.[284]

Larger claims about technology were also made. One worker argued, "I say that if they have the technology to [replace lettuce crews], if they have the technology to put a man on the moon, if they have the technology to create weapons that can cause unlimited destruction, then certainly they can find the technology to replace the short-handled hoe."[285] The farm worker testimony made clear that they realized that the short hoe issue was one of both labor conditions under agribusiness and the technological stagnation that comes with a cheap labor pool.

In their rebuttals to the farm workers and the CRLA, the growers introduced virtually no evidence for their sweeping economic claims or for their dismissal of health issues. They claimed that California has more intensive agriculture than other areas and therefore cannot be compared with the other regions.[286] They also resorted to other, extralegal methods of persuasion. For example, during the time of the hearings, they arranged a tour of a couple of the farms for the Division of Industrial Safety (the CRLA did not know about this until after the fact).[287] Unlike Jourdane, who took the case on after using the hoe himself, the committee claimed that none of the workers at these farms had seemed discontented or had had any complaints. The director wrote, "We were all watching carefully for any evidence of discomfiture or even low morale, such as expressions or actions or whatever. I observed literally none. Note that I had visited two fields and the same situation existed in both."[288] In future litigation Jourdane did not let this event go unnoticed, wondering aloud in briefs and petitions how long the board members expected that a farm worker would keep her job after registering a complaint about working conditions.

On July 13, 1973, the board unanimously concluded that the CRLA "failed to prove the tool unsafe." Relying on statistics compiled by the Industrial Relations Board of work injuries in 1970 and on a few farm workers' testimonies in which they claimed that they did not suffer from back injury, the board ruled that not enough medical evidence had been presented by the CRLA. They wrote that "there are, in fact, many work operations that hasten aging of various body parts at varying rates according to individual resistance . . . [and] very few of these conditions are logically controllable by safety orders, because such orders have few ways of adjusting to the fact that some people are quite resistant to the related aging processes."[289] Thus, the board concluded that "the unsafe tool" clause was not intended to encompass tools that caused injury as a matter of everyday use, arguing that the prohibition on unsafe hand tools applies only to tools that are inherently dangerous and not to tools that cause danger from the manner of their use.[290]

Martin Glick expressed his disappointment in the commissioners, who, in the face of overwhelming testimony, were "surrounded by peer pressure, and engaged in secret processes."[291] The CRLA then appealed the case to the California Supreme Court, which only accepted *Carmona* after it was refused by the court of appeals. As chief justice of a notoriously pro-plaintiff court, Justice Tobriner wrote that "a defectively designed tool which causes injury as a result of the manner in which it must regularly be used can be just as harmful to employees as a defectively manufactured tool or a tool in poor condition." As he pointed out, "almost all tools are only unsafe when used and would not constitute an inherent danger if not in use."[292] The Supreme Court directed the division to reconsider its opinion in accordance with a wider standard of defective design.

By the time the second set of hearings (San Diego [March 24, 1975] and Salinas [March 27, 1975]) began, Jerry Brown had replaced Ronald Reagan as governor and had in turn replaced some of the key political figures in the state; California politics had swung to the left.[293] The short-handled hoe had received wide newspaper and television coverage and popular support.[294] Finally, in 1975, the short-handled hoe was legally banned, although enforcement of the ban has been lax.[295] The CRLA victory was sweetened several months later when Bud Antle, a corporation that had staunchly defended the short-handled hoe, publicly acknowledged that workers wielding the long-handled hoe were more productive than they had been with the short hoe.[296]

Embodied Technology: Race

In the context of production, when injuries suffered by workers are recognized as injuries (that is, they are not blamed on the worker's incompetence or preconditions and they are not entirely overlooked), they are often perceived as a side effect of production, and/or as a necessary by-product of production, and/or as an unintentional consequence of production. Put another way, the power of the growers was not only in the power to injure but in the ability to erase the traces of that injury *as injury* (traces that would otherwise be apparent in workers' compensation records, for example) as well as to describe farm worker claims as banal, unviable, or out of hand and thus to cede the conditions for continued injury. While the short-handled hoe might be understood as an instrument of surveillance such that a foreman looking across the fields would be able to spot a worker resting her back, it was also an instrument whereby the power of agribusiness was inscribed into that very body.

Thus, the success of the farm workers and the CRLA depended on their convincing the court and the Industrial Relations Board of two key points. First, they had to show that farm workers' bodies were worth something—that they could not and should not be merely discarded as by-products to the labor process and that as owners of worthy bodies, they should not be systematically injured in the course of work. Second, they had to prove that the short hoe has a systematic relationship to injury, even though it was clear from the testimony of the growers that all agricultural work hurts. What came to be at stake, then, was what the relationship between the racialized body and the short hoe would be. Whereas for growers, racial stereotypes were used to assert their entitlement over workers' bodies and "naturalize" the workers' relationship to the short hoe, strategic reconstructions of technologies and bodies were used by the CRLA to decouple this relationship.

It is not surprising that the physical characteristics of race took on a key importance in these hearings, given the way in which race has structured agricultural production in California.[297] In the set of hearings that took place after the California Supreme Court ruling, the growers reiterated their anecdotal evidence and introduced the new testimony of Dr. Oakley Hewitt, an orthopedic surgeon from the Palo Alto Medical Clinic. Dr. Hewitt reported in an affidavit that "certain groups of people, . . . because of racial characteristics, diet or lifestyle are more prone to symptomatic low back disease. . . . The Stewart study of the Eskimo . . . reported that approximately 60 percent of the

Eskimo tribe studied have a [back] condition called Spondylosis."[298] He then argued that "Mexicans" have a similar congenital weakness that can account for the high rates of injury. (I use scare quotes because Hewitt does not describe what he means by the term Mexican.)

But we have also seen how the growers argued that Mexican laborers were ideally *suited* for stoop labor. For example, Farmer Mervyn Baily testified, "I cannot remember one single case . . . where we had a back injury attributed to the short-handled hoe. My father ran a crew of Hindus in 1911. . . . Then Japanese. Then we followed with the Filipinos. And then the Mexicans. The stoop laborers, most of them are smaller or more agile than the ordinary Anglo due to their build and the fact that they seem to have a stronger body for the job."[299] If the racial marker of flexibility (echoed in the contemporary rhetoric of Asian women factory workers' "nimble fingers") christens racialized groups as consummate workers through the idealization of their bodies, in the claim that Mexicans have a congenital predisposition (similar to that of the colonially inscribed "Eskimo") to back injury the doctor inscribes Mexican laborers as radically embodied in a markedly different way. These people who neither had nor deserve toilet facilities, who were housed in old prisoner-of-war camps, who did not have access to fresh water or bathing facilities—the people who are always already physically inscribed with the stigmatic and semiotic mark of the "wetback"—are reinscribed as additionally always already injured by virtue of their genetic traits.

If having control over pain was one element of the power of the growers, the ability to bestow civilization and then eschew human rights on the basis of the lack of civilization was another crucial factor that describes the way in which growers maintained power.[300] The story told by Dr. Hewitt locates the fault of the short-handled hoe wounds with the body of the Mexican worker but then uses the observation to argue in defense of the continued use of the hoe. The trope of the radically embodied worker devalues the farm worker in a specific way by racializing him *as devalued*. The very marker of what it is to be Mexican is to have an injured back.

The fact that certain societies and cultures have constructed racialized Others for the purpose of doing semiotic or material work for themselves through that very construction is by now well accepted in cultural and anthropological theory. It is with this in mind that we recognize the plausibility of how representations deeply affect the ways in which groups of people enter political and economic life. Thus, Camille Guerin-Gonzales's conclusion to her carefully argued study rings true: "representations of the work force as temporary and male [both before, during, and after bracero labor] influenced both government policies and growers' practices, which severely limited the economic participation of Mexican immigrants."[301] I am arguing here that as well as being temporary and male, the representation was of a workforce that was uncivilized and preinjured—and consequently not susceptible to tangible or compensable injury. To put this another way, if the fundamental claim that Elaine Scarry makes in her book *The Body in Pain* about pain and injury is that the unmaking of the human being—the injury of tissue—is precisely the "unmaking of the civilization as it resides in each body," then it would be reasonable to assume that the uncivilized body cannot be unmade. The uncivilized body is the precisely the *pre*injured body discursively incapable of feeling pain.[302]

Trauma theorist Robert Jay Lifton makes a pivotal point about the particular enabling capacity of the racist epithet. He argues that the dehumanization of the Vietnamese people in the 1960s, embodied in the term "gook," provided the key means for the ruination of their way of life and ultimately for their torture and murder. Lifton discusses the way in which peasants became "psychologically functional victims," explaining that the "process is self-perpetuating: once seen as symbolically death-tainted, the victims can be more easily killed, which makes them still more death-tainted. They are cast out of history, denied the status of a people with cultural continuity. Since they are historically and psychologically already dead, one may kill them arbitrarily, without the feeling one is taking a life."[303] Once victimized, the imagined and real "gooks" entered the scapegoating cycle of victimization: "because he is an inferior outcast, he must do the polluted and defiled work of society; because he does that work he is death-tainted and contemptible; because he is contemptible, he must be forced to accept his degraded condition and may be brutalized and murdered at will."[304] The role of the physical body figures centrally in this cycle; the Mexican American body can be simultaneously all that is detestable: brown, good at stoop labor, *and* pre-injured and congenitally deformed. Though not a question of death and survival in the same way as was Vietnam during the war, race and the strategic positioning of victimization were certainly about economic superiority—in Californian terms, inferior lives were blatantly used and injured to create the wealth of agribusiness and the luxury of culture enjoying lettuce and strawberries.

In addition to this mode of racialization, a clear strategy of the defenders of *el cortito* was the despecification of the injuries rendered by the short hoe. Contrary to the testimony of many doctors who described in detail the effects of lifting the weight of the hoe while bent at the waist, Dr. Hewitt argued that "it may well be that all forms of stooped labor, which could include planting, harvesting, picking or cultivating in specific crops, would predispose a worker to an increased incidence of degenerative conditions of the lower back . . . and whether the short hoe, per se, is any worse than handpicking and harvesting lettuce is very difficult to say."[305] The defense attorney corroborated this point, saying that workers do not actually hoe very much, and "other work, such as cutting lettuce, is as bad."[306] Grower Paul W. Englund noted that the short-handled hoe accounted only for 20 to 25 percent of all stoop labor in agricultural work, and he asked the pivotal question: "Is the short-handled hoe worse than cutting lettuce, or packing lettuce, or picking strawberries, or picking onions, or all the crops that are grown on the ground? That's a question I don't know, but I can see what the result [of banning stoop labor] would be."[307] By broadening the issue to encompass all farm work, Hewitt and Englund dissipate concern for the specific work and injury while holding the question at the level of the ridiculous (who would outlaw *all* farm work?), thus aborting the question of how farm work might be more varied or technologically enhanced to limit injury.

In another example of this tactic, growers divulged and appealed to their own health problems. Grower Lloyd Heger said that when he injured his back, his "doctor told him to lose fifteen pounds and get more sleep." He said, "I know of several other growers that have back injuries . . . [that are] not caused by the short-handled hoe."[308] Another grower said, "[I]f I didn't have to work, I'd live longer. I have an implanted pacemaker."[309] These comments can be taken as a stab at attorneys who may not understand the everyday injuries of agricultural work and a testimony to all kinds of injuries that become ephemeral in industrial culture. On the other hand, the claims dilute the seriousness and systemic nature of short hoe injuries. Thus, growers made their case based in a combination of blatant social devaluation based on racial categories, the generalized injuries attributable to all kinds of work, and the threat of an end to agricultural production.

The very wording of the safe hand tool law compelled the CRLA and farm workers to prove the direct linkage between hoe use and injury. Yet their victory clearly depended on building a larger social movement publicizing the role of *el cortito* in farm workers' lives. The enforced use of the hoe was understood by the farm workers to be a blatant use of power for the purpose of reiterating the message of farm worker subordination.

Q. If you had a preference for using the long-handled hoe, would you use it?
A. I would rather use the long hoe.

Q. Why don't you use the long-handled hoe right now?

A. The company will not permit us to use the long-handled hoe because they want to take all the juice that they can out of us.[310]

Thus, the symbolic power of the hoe, which appeared in UFW posters of the period, was harnessed by the farm workers to change the meaning of the tool and invest it with the resonance of the power dynamics of agribusiness more generally. But this symbolic power, even as it was appropriated by farm workers, was a key aspect of worker degradation.[311]

In the introduction to *The Body in Pain*, Scarry discusses the ways in which pain entails the feeling of being acted upon. Even in cases where pain is purely internal, it is described with the metaphors of other instruments such as "hammering" pain or "knife-like" pain.[312] It is through this "expressive potential of the sign of the weapon" that she explains the communicative success of Amnesty International publications that prominently display the symbols of torture.[313] At the same time the expressive potential of the short hoe might be a reflection of the overt and abused power of the growers. This is reflected both in the UFW posters that featured the hoe as symbolic of the farm workers' struggles and in farm worker testimony such as "it was torture, it was torture."[314] The significance of the hoe itself lies in part in the work that was required by the CRLA, UFW, and farm workers in creating it as a tool of torture or a weapon in some sense. In this light, the particular choice of appellation for the hoe by the workers, *el brazo del diablo*, cannot be overlooked.[315] Conversely, the use of images such as Dorothea Lange's photographs of farm workers in the 1930s hinge on a slightly different strategy: humanizing and even heroizing the workers.

Mexican American arms had already played a pivotal role in Californian agriculture, as reflected in the bracero program—literally the "one who uses his arm" program. But the "arm of the devil" is additive—it connotes the appendage that, while *used* by the farm worker, is *of* the (perceived) devil-grower and situates the farm worker's body as an intermediary. The devil's arm was a tool but also the direct arm of the capitalist, the arm of the government, the arm that controlled the conditions of labor, as well as the arm that entered the workers' bodies through its ability to injure, maim, and disable. The devil's arm was indeed not the prosthesis of the worker but of the corporation. Just as in product liability suits in which the plaintiff's claim relies on her ability to denaturalize the taken-for-granted relations between bodies and technologies, the farm workers' claim to ban the hoe depended on their insistence on the material difference between the hoes and their bodies. After all, the worker's body, for the grower, is part of his own prosthetic assemblage—the technology of agricultural production of which the worker was one part and the hoe was another and the boundaries between the two were insignificant. On the other hand, for the farm worker the very appellation of the "devil's arm" connotes a sequence of moveable parts, in which the worker's body is distinct from the rest of the aggregate—the hoe is the distinct object with which he produces for the grower. Given the circulation of bodies within the system of agricultural production, the farm workers' bodies physically depended on their ability to convince the growers that their bodies were materially distinct from the rest of the productive prosthetic.

Conclusion

Before the short hoe's implication in injurious relations, workers were simply required as mechanical parts of the production process. These relations of production between workers and machines have been noted by authors as diverse as Karl Marx and Henry Ford. Ford wrote quite literally about how his workers were mere appendages to his machines, and thus how he could employ disabled men and even women in accordance with the exact requirements for production. Ultimately, one way to differentiate bodies and machines is in the designation of injury and the ways in which injury both becomes thinkable and carries meaning when it does. Ownership of a human body allows certain actors in the production process (that is, the human actors) to come to the table as legal actors and claim their bodies as basic, nondisposable collateral in capitalist production. This process was precisely at stake in defining the short hoe as "inherently" dangerous. Thus, the archive of the short hoe presents two key insights into the ways that difference, race, and subordination, as regimes of social injury, circulate and become naturalized within and between humans and tools and the physical injuries they produce.

First, the short hoe provides a place to examine how farm worker injuries gradually became legible as injuries. The law itself could not do the work of enabling this shift, but it offered access to institutional networks that became instrumental because of wider political shifts. If anything, this makes clear the extent to which justice is a political rather than legal issue. For the inequalities that stemmed from short hoe use, claims were made in terms of advocacy: inequality was intertwined with a concept of "injury." Thus, the CRLA attorneys argued that "my client is human—and has been harmed, as any other human would have been, by this product." Pain was used as the universal human touchstone. One of the first things one CRLA lawyer did was go to the field and use the short hoe himself. Furthermore, the ultimate victory for the farm workers was influenced by the way the case was picked up by white liberals of the era who joined the struggle to have the hoe banned and by a political era in which both consumer rights—and, not unrelated, civil rights—were being fought for and, in an incipient way, taken seriously. Universal civil rights was a necessary argument for plaintiffs in arguing to outlaw the short-handled hoe; since Mexican American "humanness" was at stake, lawyers argued that the work tool dehumanizes in the process of injuring. All of the CRLA attorneys to whom I spoke agreed that without Jerry Brown's election and his replacement of key political figures, the short hoe would still be in use. Additionally, by the time of the short hoe victory, Cesar Chavez and the UFW had developed a broad-based, continent-wide social movement for farm workers' rights, and this victory was one of a number of victories that reflected the growing visibility of and social support for farm workers' rights. Thus, as the short hoe became *the* symbol of farm workers' struggles, it gained additional power in the minds of radical and liberal activists.

Furthermore, the ways in which the hoe brought the injury into the story of agricultural labor after it had been ignored for so long entailed a collaboration between medical and legal discourses.[316] Although the concept of cumulative trauma was not a new concept at the turn of the decade—the California Labor Code had long contained the statutory bases for the concept of micro-trauma or cumulative injury[317]—the application of these laws to farm workers, who were not perceived as entitled to benefits, was radical. In the years just prior to the CRLA case, the labor code law had been incipiently used as a basis for finding liability for spinal disability. Thus, the physicians who were willing to testify in the short hoe case were the more "liberal and risk taking and for the most part not from academic medicine."[318] Michael Rucka explains that "the logical extension and application of what was known in medicine to what was known in the law was what brought about success."[319] Furthermore, once it became clear that the hoe was going to go, doctors were much more willing to diagnose the hoe-related injuries; repetitive strain injuries in general had more success in workers' compensation claims in the late 1970s and 1980s.

Second, the hoe made racial subordination seem natural, and the narratives that circulated in the hearings illuminate how this was so. In some key sense, Mexican American farm workers were produced as racialized beings through their relation to the hoe and through their bad backs. Thus, registers of physical and social injury (back pain, racial subordination) are produced, labeled, and crystallized for their utility on the one hand in dehumanizing and reifying labor, and, on the other, in recuperating the humanity of the workers.

In part we can see this through the different arguments that were made by the growers. One strategy disengaged injury from power relations (we, too, get injured). Another approach simply claimed the necessity of the work tool (like a wrench, it is simply a requirement to get the job done—we cannot halt all agricultural production). These two implicitly play out competing notions of economic and social goods (such as safety and production) and which costs are acceptable and by whom. In so doing, they ignored the problem of stuctural injuries and shifted them to unimportant side-effect status.

Another tactic attributed fault to the workers themselves. Unlike (and like) the flexible Filipinos and Hindus, but like the congenitally injured Eskimos, the Mexican American laborer was the one who was injured by his racial designation as always already injured. Furthermore, the Mexican American expected to be injured—he or she did not go to the doctor because of a bad back but lived with it, either because a bad back is a normal occurrence or because she did not expect that physicians could help her. Registers of injury circulate here; as the constitutive feature the social injury of racial designation is the physical injury suffered from farm labor. Social and physical injury are inextricable.

On the other side, the law was used to allow a disenfranchised group to literally have their stories entered into the historical archive. If the short hoe could be shown to be *inherently* injurious, issues such as fault, race, or economic consequence had nothing to do with its legality in the fields. Trouillot reminds us that the "constitution [of] subjects goes hand in hand with the continuous creation of the past. As such, they do not succeed such a past, they are its contemporaries."[320] In this sense, the constitution of farm worker subjects was contingent on the recognition of the injurious experiences of the short hoe; even the worker who switched work after three weeks had "waited thirty-nine years for this hearing" precisely because it brought recognition and a means to rejoin the racial category, albeit in its own problematic terms. Law, the historiographic archive, and citizenship are mutually constitutive. Simultaneously, the short hoe, injuries, and race were mutually constitutive.

The object of the hoe brought the disability into legal discourse—and then that discourse brought Mexican laborers into history, even as the hoe had not yet been acknowledged in workers' compensation or other medical records. The very form of safety laws is based on negotiating just how much injury an employer might ask of its employees—after all, as the growers testify, all work can result in injury. Ultimately then it was through the object and through the unsafe tool clause that the farm workers and the CRLA were able to argue—for the first time—that this injury *did* exist. But even as the clause allowed Tobriner radically to blame the tool rather than the user and thus to redefine the hoe as injurious and the bodies as meaningful, the short hoe and its legal hook of the unsafe hand tool clause necessarily circumscribed workers' ills within a narrow set of legal issues and away from the conditions of agricultural labor more generally. Thus, variations of the short hoe struggle continue with hand weeding, strawberry picking, and the use of curved knives, practices that continue to define racialized immigrant labor in California.

Chapter 3

Keyboard Design

The Litigation Wave of the 1990s

FOR MANY TYPEWRITER and computer keyboard users, these tools are a far cry from the "curiosity-breeding little joker" Mark Twain complained of.[321] Keyboard-instigated injuries attained the status of an "epidemic" in the 1980s and proliferated as a highly publicized—and politicized—litigation wave of the 1990s. Newspapers and computer journals mainstreamed a variety of soft tissue injuries (including nerve damage and tendonitis) as an epidemic that first afflicted keyboard operators in Australia before "migrating" to the UK and North America.[322] In Australia repetitive strain injury (RSI) was at first considered a compensable work injury but later dismissed as a symptom of malingering. In the United States, reports claimed that computer-induced cumulative trauma disorders (CTDs) reached nearly a million cases per year by 1995, a tenfold increase since the preceding decade,[323] and that workers' compensation and health insurance providers were paying an average of $29,000 in health care costs and lost wages.[324] Since OSHA stopped logging CTDs and removed them from the list of conditions that employers are required to report, it is very difficult to determine what current rates are.

In this context, computer keyboards became the focal point of several hundred lawsuits in which plaintiffs claimed that keyboards were the cause of severely disabling hand and wrist injuries. Many of the cases were settled, which means that the records are sealed. Of the suits, only a few went to trial, and of these, all were won, ultimately, by the defendants—although a notable case won a large jury award before it was overturned on appeal.[325] Though the suits used a different set of laws to try to materialize injuries than the litigation of the short hoe did, they reflect similar issues. Was the keyboard defective in itself—or defective only in use? What would such a distinction mean? How is cause to be located in a repetitive injury? Furthermore, the keyboard is only one aspect of a workstation: a computer user will have to sit in a chair, have the keyboard and monitor at a certain height, and decide how long he will engage in data entry. Given the right circumstances, any prolonged activity will certainly result in injury; why should typing and keyboards be considered unique?

This is what the court in *Howard v. Digital Equipment Corporation* decided when it said, "plaintiff has failed to establish that harm associated with using the LK401 keyboard is not from the repetitive use of the product itself. . . . In this respect, the LK401 keyboard is no different than the bells used by members of the Salvation Army to attract donors at Christmas. . . . The proper way to alleviate this discomfort is open and obvious—the individual should either pause or place the bell in his other hand."[326] Similarly, Michael Cerussi, a New York attorney who successfully defended IBM against many of these liability suits, stressed the role of common sense in the courtroom.[327] He argued that the computer industry won the cases because "every case we've tried, we've tried in front of intelligent jurors who understand the law and more important, apply their common sense to these claims."[328] But what could a common sense be in the case of such a historically loaded object as the interface for standardized type? In what possible world could the object that has been credited with virtually enabling the rise of the corporation be akin to a Salvation Army bell?

But I am getting ahead of myself here, for I want to examine the trajectory and language of these cases in the context of the history of upper-extremity cumulative trauma disorders, and then of the development of typewriters and office politics. That the use of standardized type since the late nineteenth century has had a crucial influence on the ways that business and personal communications have taken place is a standard story. Within this normative history of the instruments of mass corporate industrialization (typewriters, adding machines, filing cabinets, and cash registers) exists also an archive of how these objects were built into and constitutive of gender in the twentieth century. Some of this is standard heteronormative stuff. Inevitably male bosses courted secretaries; inevitably female office assistants made coffee. Sexual innuendo pervaded the office hierarchy and to a certain extent women had to play along to, quite simply, keep their jobs. Office decor and secretarial manuals have made these relations manifest as they have offered instruction on the proper habitation and performance of these roles, particularly for women. But the instrument that provided the initial entrée for women to join the formerly masculine space of the office—the machine that heterosexualized the office—was the typewriter. This history poses a critical dimension to understanding both the keyboard and its role in injury, and the lawsuits as a broader cultural phenomenon.

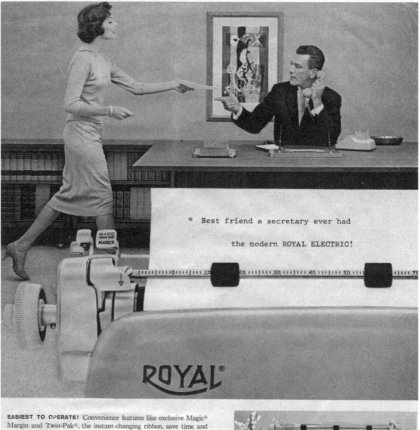

FIGURE 6. *Life Magazine*, 1965.

Thus, I offer a history of the present to think about the co-constitution of gender, injury, and keyboards, and the categories that hold each of these in place. The categories came to hold a particular configuration at the moment of the litigation wave. Not only has gender played a role in how the medical establishment recognizes and treats RSI,[329] but the history of clerical labor in the nineteenth and twentieth centuries, the development of the typewriter, and the recognition of RSI, taken together, establish that gender is also pivotal to the design of the keyboard in its incarnations as typewriter and computer-input device.

Litigation Wave

In many ways RSI litigation followed a classic curve of contemporary product liability litigation. RSI began as a working-class injury afflicting secretaries, data input workers, and users of digital scanners whose work demanded repetitive motions on cheap equipment, whose output demands were high and strictly surveilled, who may have had little access to the kinds of medical treatments required by soft tissue injuries, and who had very little choice over their work conditions. Thus, RSI litigation can serve as an example of one way litigation has been used as a strategy in a broader social movement. Litigation took place after the failure of OSHA to set ergonomics standards and the failure of a vast number of companies to educate employees about RSI.

As the litigation gathered publicity, journalists from the *New York Times* and *Newsday* entered complaints, creating the "critical mass and push" to move a working-class injury into a middle-class tort.[330] This also gave rise to the high profile of the cases. At the height of the wave there were thousands of cases; New York attorney Steven Phillips had an estimated 2,000 clients.[331] In 1992, when he had 37 out of the 44 RSI cases, Phillips won a motion to consolidate, a move he had used in his earlier asbestos cases. This strategy, which Phillips refers to as introducing an "economy of scale," had several ramifications. It meant that they could proceed together and use the same motions and discovery, thus saving resources. It meant that they would have one judge, whom they could "educate" about the issues, and the attorneys did not have to travel around the country. And it also led to more publicity and new plaintiffs.

Two key early victories further set the cases in motion. One case extended the statute of limitations; in another, a jury awarded a secretary $5.3 million, leading to a flurry of news coverage.[332] Ultimately this case, along with two others, was dismissed on appeal and a series of defendant victories followed.

Five key issues hampered the plaintiffs' cases. First, the injuries could always be made to seem multifactorial both in terms of office equipment and in terms of the individual and her activities. In the legal forum, this had major implications. As physiologist Dr. Laura Punnett (who testified as an expert in several cases) says, even when scientists were able to present multivariate analyses that factored out other issues, these studies were "not easy for people to grasp," and the defense was able to make it seem as if plaintiffs were "trying to have their cake and eat it too."[333] Second, by the mid- to late 1990s when the cases were coming before juries, keyboards were common domestic devices—many people used them without being injured and perceived them as benign devices. This misunderstanding of the keyboard also meant that even those who suffered from RSI did not realize it until much later, thus posing a statute of limitations problem in many states.[334]

A third difficulty was classifying the symptoms of upper extremity musculo-skeletal disorders, in which many of the symptoms carried no clear diagnosis. In one of the early cases, *Urbanski v. IBM*, a high school secretary was severely affected by pain and disability that did not correlate with any clinical labels and thus was not perceived to have clinical credibility. This was one reason that carpal tunnel syndrome (CTS), even though it accounted for just a small percentage of CTDs, gained such high visibility. The quantitative test for CTS was a nerve conduction velocity test, and even though it has been criticized for its imprecision, it is considered the gold standard of quantifying injury. CTS is the only CTD with an objective, quantifiable method of diagnosis. In addition, the treatment for CTS was a surgical procedure, which for lawyers meant that costs were easy to demonstrate and work time missed was easier to justify. The treatment of carpal tunnel however, also revealed the paradox of doctors—who are generally poorly trained in soft tissue injuries and in occupational health—offering surgery as a treatment even before information had been gathered about workplace activities and ergonomics. Fourth, since the injuries were not spectacularly visible, juries could be difficult to convince. Fifth, the stakes were high because of the number of pending cases; one plaintiff victory could cause a landslide of claims because of the sheer number of RSI sufferers.

After a series of settlements and dismissed cases, the litigation dwindled by the late 1990s. By this time, new working conditions also led to a decrease in the number of injuries: keyboard designs improved vastly, and there was a diminution of data input jobs as a result of new scanning technologies that rendered the task of data input obsolete. In part because of the lawsuits but also because of the vast coverage of the issue in magazines and newspapers, a new awareness of the injury may have caused people to change work habits. Ultimately, though, as I mentioned above, OSHA stopped collecting data on CTDs, and thus, as Dr. Laura Punnett says, it is virtually impossible to track the number of these injuries.

The plaintiffs' arguments hinged on several key design issues and two main legal theories. The legal theories were, first, failure to warn, since computer manufacturers' files showed that they had known about these injuries for decades. The "smoking gun" of these cases was a video produced by Apple Computer in 1990 to inform its employees about possible injuries and how to avoid them. This video was destroyed in 1991 because of the legal department's concern over RSI-related litigation.[335] It was the key to one early case that led to a settlement when the plaintiff's lawyers were able to show a pretrial discovery violation and the defense lawyers faced jail time for denying the video's existence.[336] But even without such a smoking gun, plaintiffs could argue that it would have been reasonable to expect manufacturers to have known about potential injuries resulting from keyboard use, given the history of research on the topic.

The second legal issue was that of defective design, which applied to individual keyboards. Varying slightly by keyboard, there were four main components of the defective design argument. The first was that for many of the keyboards in question, the force required to depress keys was significantly higher than what was required by the American National Standards Institute (ANSI). This meant that some typists were being required to carry literally tons of extra work on their fingers per day.[337] Second, keys were designed with no tactile feedback loop. This meant that the typist would not know how hard to strike the key until the key had bottomed out and exposed the fingers to sharp blows on each keystroke. Tactile feedback involves some sort of an indication that the key has been struck hard enough to register the letter, such that the typist will release pressure before the key hits the hard surface underneath. In an analysis comparing a Digital Equipment Corporation (DEC) keyboard to the ANSI standards for key design, engineer and ergonomics expert David Thompson found that the poor design of the keys translated into "31,658 to 37,989 pounds of *added* force per day, transmitted through the fingertips, fingers, hands, and arms (emphasis original)."[338]

Force factors and tactile feedback were both design features that typists, even experienced ones, would not normally be aware of; nor would they be aware of the severity of the injury that could be induced by the repetitive use of such keyboards. Tactile feedback, Thompson stated, is something that "trained typists learn unconsciously."[339]

The third and fourth main design flaws relate to key layout, particularly the placement of function keys and numeric pads which, by increasing pronation and finger stretch, increase the force profile on the fingers. When workers are required to type constantly for several days in a row, the body is unable to heal from these exertions, and injury can result. The design issues, then, were fairly straightforward and relatively easy to understand: force, repetition, hand positioning. However, they were not uncontroversial. Attempts to create an American national standard for computer use had been underway for six years when it was not adopted in 1992. Furthermore, the National Institute for Occupational Safety and Health (NIOSH) had focused on breaks and work periods but not keyboard design in its considerations of RSI. At this time OSHA was suffering from major cutbacks (during the Reagan and Bush administrations) and there was tremendous pressure not to criticize business. As David Thompson claimed, there were "no decent RSI guidelines for ten years," and these were the first ten years of the introduction of computer keyboarding.[340]

In the lawsuits, the computer manufacturers consistently resorted to the argument that the keyboard was not in itself at fault, and thus it was not defective and did not need a warning. In product liability law, a warning is required when the "foreseeable risks of harm posed by the product could have been reduced or avoided by the provision of reasonable instructions or warnings by the seller or other distributor."[341] A manufacturer does not have a duty to warn the user of a danger obvious to the user. Thus, the manufacturers rebutted the failure to warn claims by arguing that people were not using keyboards properly, or that any dangers were obvious and could have been rectified by taking breaks or adjusting other office equipment. Michael Cerussi has claimed to the press that "[t]hese are keyboards we're talking about, not asbestos, not lead. Just keyboards."[342] Any tool is dangerous if used excessively, and the keyboard no more so than hammers or screwdrivers. Based on the published opinions, this was by far the more successful argument, though plaintiff's attorney Phillips claims that he settled all his cases and believes he would have "won some and lost some in front of juries." Manufacturers used a similar argument in defending against defective design, claiming that injuries were caused by activities other than typing, or that once they realized they were being hurt, plaintiffs could and should have ceased the activity.

The other key successful defense in the early litigation related to statutes of limitations. In New York, for example, legal action must be commenced within three years of injury. Since RSI poses no distinct date of injury and can last for months or years before becoming disabling, the statute of limitations initially posed problems for plaintiffs.

In 1996, plaintiffs' attorneys attempted to have RSI considered as a "toxic tort" as a way to extend the statute of limitations.[343] In so doing, they attempted to redefine commonsense notions of contact with the keyboard as a creative way to circumvent statute of limitations barriers. To do this, they needed to explain "contact" in terms of "exposure," where the "toxic substance" statute defines exposure as "direct or indirect exposure by absorption, contact, ingestion, inhalation, implantation or injection."[344]

The first court found that the keyboard was not a "substance in any form." The judge found that, "simply put, the keyboard is not a substance, toxic or otherwise. Plaintiff's injuries were allegedly incurred by direct contact with a tangible object, not a substance, and the term 'substance' was no more meant to encompass a piece of office equipment than it was meant to include any other ordinary product."[345] The Supreme Court of New York, however, accepted the toxic tort argument in part, ruling that accrual date for action against a manufacturer is at the onset of symptoms or at the last use of the manufacturer's keyboard, whichever is earlier.[346] This decision was widely reported in the lay and legal press as opening the way for the litigation wave. Nevertheless, by the late 1990s, the wave had nearly died out: of over twenty jury trials, all but two were in ruled in favor of the defendants, and those two were either vacated or reversed on appeal.

I will introduce one representative case, *Shirl Jeanne Howard v. Digital Equipment Corporation and Honeywell, Inc.*, decided in 1998 in favor of DEC and Honeywell in Pennsylvania.[347] After an analysis of the social history of the typewriter and the keyboard in the next section, I will return to these issues at the end of the chapter.

In *Howard*, a data entry clerk brought a complaint for failure to warn. The court dismissed the claim on the basis that "the law was well-settled that keyboard manufacturers had no duty to warn" and that the "user failed to proffer sufficient evidence to establish that the alleged danger involved in using the keyboard was anything other than the repetitive motion required to operate the keyboard."[348] The court thus defined Howard's injury as precisely antithetical to the conditions of its production, since Howard was, indeed, claiming that repetitive use of the keyboard caused her injuries.

The court cited from a number of other RSI decisions as precedent for this case. In *Creamer v. IBM*, the plaintiff claimed that she sustained injury by using an optical scanner at a grocery store. The court stated, "If she may establish a case against IBM here, by analogy one could argue that similar warnings should be attached to screwdrivers, tennis racquets, typewriters, musical instruments, bread dough, garden gloves, pencils, pens, floor mats, brooms, golf clubs, footballs, base-

balls, baseball mitts, and indeed, milk cows. By analogy, warnings
should be made that physical manipulation inherent in their use can in
some persons and under some circumstances be associated with varied
ailments."[349] In going through several other cases where carpal tunnel
was alleged to be caused by computer keyboards, the court concluded
that products "whose use requires physical activity often entail a risk
that such use will cause harm—harm not from the product itself but
harm from the manner of a product's use."[350] This was precisely the
distinction that, in the short hoe case, California Supreme Court Justice
Tobriner would not accept.

Evidence submitted by plaintiffs that DEC knew of the dangers and
warned their employees of them without putting warnings on its consumer products was also raised by the court. In dismissing this evidence, the court quoted from an article written by an occupational
health nurse hired by DEC in 1988: "Repeated exertions in combination
with static loads have also been shown to have a detrimental effect on
the tendons." The article continues by comparing workers who completed tasks that required high repetition and high force, who were
"five times more likely to have hand and wrist disorders than were men
in the low-force, low repetition activity group. For jobs that are repetitive, rapid-paced and require forceful and awkward postured [sic], the
optimal solution is one geared toward job redesign. . . . [U]se of *better
designed tools and equipment* . . . will minimize, if not eliminate, the risk
to the worker."[351] The article continues by emphasizing that the worker
must be educated about early signs and symptoms of soft tissue disorders so that the worker may alter work habits and seek care "when
problems are in an early stage, eliminating the change [sic] for irreversible tissue damage or impaired function."[352] Clearly, the article states
that injury can be mitigated through education (read: some sort of
warning about the possibilities of injury) and well-designed work tools.

Nevertheless, regarding this evidence, the court claimed that "[i]ron-
ically, the excerpts quoted by plaintiff . . . actually favor the *defendants*
on the issue of failure to warn."[353] It is hard not to read the court's statement as anything other than a willful misreading when it states that
"there is no duty to warn where the only danger results from repetitive
use of keyboards. The writings . . . demonstrate that the best way to
alleviate the problem is not by placing warnings on keyboards but by
educating the worker so that the worker may alter work practices."[354]
Other plaintiff evidence about force, repetition, contact stresses, and
awkward posture was similarly reduced by the court to an attenuation
of the design issues of the keyboard to the fact that keyboards need to
be used in a repetitive way and therefore it is the repetitive movements,
not the keyboards themselves, that are the cause of RSI.

The court concluded by stating that the

> plaintiff has failed to establish that any harm associated with using the LK401 keyboard is not from the repetitive use of the product itself. Moreover, the discomfort and pain associated with repetitive use of keyboards in general is open and obvious. In this respect the LK401 is no different than the bells used by members of the Salvation Army to attract donors at Christmas. Ringing the bell requires the individual to constantly flex the tendons in his wrist. Obviously, this motion can . . . result in great discomfort. The proper way to alleviate this discomfort is open and obvious—the individual should either pause or place the bell in his other hand. No one would rationally argue that the bells contained a design defect. . . . It is the same with keyboards. . . . [T]here is simply no duty to warn about the physical manipulation inherent in the use of certain objects which can in some persons and under some circumstances cause carpal tunnel syndrome.

The court distinguished between the product and the practices required to use the product, and then it presented what it understood to be an analogous case of physical manipulation and discomfort. I will return to this after presenting a social history of the typewriter and its associated injuries.

Social Nexus

A twelfth-century manuscript epilogue reads, "I can't feel my hand, my head's awhirl, I'd swap my pen for a beautiful girl."[355] RSI was recorded in 1713 by the surgeon Ramazzini as a disease of scribes and notaries.[356] With rising industrialization, repetitive strain injuries erupted in major proportions at the end of the nineteenth century with writers' cramp. Symptoms of writers' cramp, also known as scriveners' palsy, reported from 1820 and increasingly through the 1880s, included symptoms similar to those of computer-related RSIs—intense pain, prickling, stiffness, eventually anesthesia and paralysis. The condition overwhelmingly affected males of prime working age. Reasons given for this outbreak were the prevalence of poor penmanship, the introduction of the steel nib, and the rise of a clerical class.[357] One contemporary commentator blamed "the increased speed and recklessness with which [the pen] is driven in our modern struggle for existence."[358] One of the recommended treatments, ironically, was switching from handwriting to typewriting.

Thus, injuries of the hand and wrist resulting from repetitive activities—particularly those based in written communication—were well-known by the time of the introduction of the typewriter, and more so with the introduction of the computer keyboard. In fact, judging by the history and severity of hand injuries and the corresponding importance of the hand to human functioning, the factors of causation of the RSI epidemic of the 1990s would have been mind-bogglingly predictable for anyone who cared to look at the historical record. It is precisely this record that I will offer here.

In this genealogy of the lawsuits, I juxtapose histories of the typewriter, women's entry into the workforce, and twentieth-century injuries of the hand and wrist to offer a social ergonomics through which women as bodies with particular social positions and typing as a practice uneasily circulated in fields of social relations. These relations were constitutive of women, keyboards, and ultimately, I suggest, the injuries themselves—even as the lawsuits led to vast improvements in keyboard designs and the end of the epidemic.

Between 1829 and 1873, some twenty inventors in the United States, England, France, and Germany worked to develop an operational typewriter. Shortly thereafter, literally hundreds of writing machines, chirographs, typographs, keyframes, parlographs, writing balls, and printing devices with a vast array of type mechanisms, inking systems, shapes, and key layout designs littered the market.[359]

The breakthrough for the typewriter as we know it came in 1865. After the Civil War, the U.S. government canceled the Remington Company's arms contract and the company cast about for mass-producible items. When approached by the inventor Christopher Latham Sholes in 1873, the Remington brothers signed a contract to be the first to produce his typewriter, and after a rickety start Remington became the foremost typewriter manufacturer.[360] Between July and December 1874, 400 Remington typewriters were sold; by 1886, 50,000 machines were sold; and by 1888, the Remington Standard Typewriter Company (under new management) was producing 1,500 machines a month.[361] In 1917 Remington declared a profit of $2.3 million.[362]

Although typing was almost immediately identified as a woman's vocation, the machine was far from easy to use. Jack London had perhaps the most famous bouts with the typewriter:

And then there was the matter of typewriting. That machine was a wonder. . . . I'll swear that machine never did the same thing the same way twice. . . . The keys of the machine have to be hit so hard that to one outside the house it sounded like a distant thunder or someone breaking up furniture. I had to hit the keys so hard that I strained my first fingers to the elbows, while the ends of my fingers were blisters burst and blistered again. Had it been my machine I'd have operated it with a carpenter's hammer.[363]

Not only did the stiff early mechanisms render typewriter use tremendously taxing, but the key layout required awkward finger gymnastics. The initial impetus for the QWERTY key layout remains contested, although the usual explanation is that Sholes developed the layout to overcome type-bar clash in early machines by placing the most frequently used type bars as far away from each other as possible.[364] Others claim that the letters for the word "typewriter" all appear on the top row to facilitate the demonstrator's work in marketing.[365] Regardless of the reason for the QWERTY design, its mass production by Remington guaranteed its formal acceptance as the standard in 1905 despite the literally hundreds of patented layouts, shapes, and sizes.

Despite these controversies, historians agree on the major debacle of the design. Typewriter historian Wilfred Beeching wrote that the sale of the QWERTY keyboard

> was probably one of the biggest confidence tricks of all time—namely the idea that this arrangement of the keyboard was scientific and added speed and efficiency. This, of course, was true of his particular machine, but the idea that so-called "scientific arrangement" of the keys was designed to give the minimum movement of the hands was, in fact, completely false! To write almost any word in the English language, a maximum distance has to be covered by the fingers.[366]

The QWERTY keyboard was designed for use with two fingers, and ten-finger typing was not commonly recognized until 1889, when the term "touch typing" was introduced.[367] The keyboard layout did not change with the new ten-finger method and the design was severely criticized at the turn of the century for being worse than an arbitrary arrangement of keys, severely overloading the left hand and certain fingers, causing excessive row hopping and requiring exorbitant finger travel.[368]

While at the time typewriters were not used enough to cause an outbreak of injury, by the early twentieth century there were at least forty other documented varieties of occupational hand disorders, all named after the jobs in which they occurred: milkers' cramp, pianists' cramp, sewing spasm, and silk-winders' dermatosis, to name just a few. Although differently named, the medical establishment recognized that the ailments shared common symptoms and gradually etiological studies became more anatomically based.[369] Telegraphists' cramp was perhaps the most intelligible of these disorders, both because of its magnitude and because of the group that suffered from it.

The first medical case study of telegraphers' cramp was reported in 1875.[370] In 1908 Great Britain recognized telegraphers' cramp as a com-

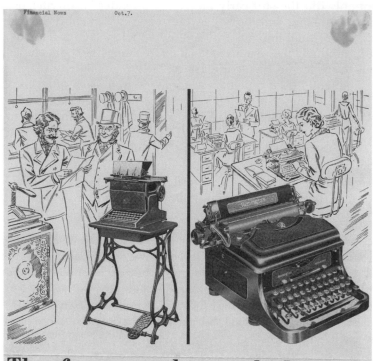

FIGURE 7. Financial News, ca. 1930, NW Ayer Advertising Agency Records, Archives Center, National Museum of American History, Behring Center, Smithsonian Institution.

FIGURE 8. Hand position for telegraphing, 1895. J. H. Lloyd, *The Diseases of Occupations*, London, 1895.

pensable disorder under workers' compensation laws. By 1911 telegraphists' cramp had become such a serious issue in the UK that a substantial departmental committee report was published on the subject.[371] The study found that some 64 percent of 8,153 telegraphers were affected and 9 percent were medically diagnosed with telegraphers' cramp—statistics stunningly similar to contemporary computer users' incidence of RSI.[372] In his well-researched history of the social recognition of cumulative trauma disorders, Allard Dembe compares the compensation of telegraphers' cramp to the lack of compensation for a very similar injury known as "twisters' cramp." Twisters' cramp affected a relatively small group of older women lace makers while telegraphers' cramp afflicted a well-organized group of white-collar men who were able to garner media attention and initiate public discussion about compensation. Despite the obvious correlations to the typewriter, these histories have been told separately.

When mainstream typewriter histories discuss gender, it has most often been to credit the invention of the typewriter with giving women the ability to earn a living. An early version of this notion appears in a 1875 Remington typewriter advertisement, which paraded:

> And the benevolent can, by the gift of a "Type-Writer" to a poor, deserving young woman, put her at once in the way of earning a good living as a copyist or corresponding clerk. No invention has opened for women so broad and easy an avenue to profitable and suitable employment.[373]

Sholes echoed this view when, toward the end of his life, he said, "I do feel I have done something for the women who have always had to work so hard. It will enable them to earn a living."[374] Obviously the advertising copy hews to a specific marketing agenda, but the typewriter's introduction into the hitherto all-male office space served as

FIGURE 9. Typewriter advertisement, 1921. Warshaw Collection of Business Americana—Typewriters, Archives Center, National Museum of American History, Behring Center, Smithsonian Institution.

the symbolic pivot around which the feminization of secretarial labor took place. In the space of thirty years, women came to make up 95 percent of the clerical and secretarial labor force.[375]

But it is worth looking at these correlations and assumptions more carefully to provide a broader cultural analysis of how the typewriter and women's bodies came to be so easily coupled, and what was at stake in these couplings. The historian Margery Davies notes that it was not the typewriter per se that allowed women into the work-place—women have always worked for a lower wage than men, and there is nothing about the typewriter that makes it easier or more effi-cient for a woman rather than a man to operate. Rather, the structural changes in capitalism at the time of the typewriter's invention "under-lay [its] successful manufacture . . . [and the] usefulness of a writing machine became self-evident."[376] The rise of the industrial complex and consequent increase in statistics and census gathering, accounting, and record keeping marked a structural shift in the scale of the U.S. econ-omy, and an increased demand for clerical labor was met by a ready pool of women workers.[377] One historian goes further, insisting that the popularity of typewriters was due to the fact that women operated them. He cites a 1904 secretarial employment agency manager who noted that 90 percent of callers asked specifically for a female typist, usually in terms such as, "[h]ave you got a pretty blond?"[378]

Until the last quarter of the nineteenth century, male clerks had en-joyed a high status in terms of respectability, and their work was skilled and varied although they rarely earned enough to move up to the middle class. As women entered the workforce, both wages and status decreased for male and female clerical workers, and with in-creased office sizes, even the distinction between superior and inferior

FIGURE 10. Dictating machine of 1890.

clerks eroded.[379] It was widely claimed that women do "more and better work for $900 per annum than many male clerks who were paid double that amount."[380] Whether women were willing to work harder for less or whether they had no choice but to accept less, it happened that as women joined the clerical workforce, clerical wages dwindled and factory wages increased.[381] Gendered skill levels were thus mutually defined, where the material of "skilled" work traveled with men.[382]

Furthermore, the introduction of the time clock and the application of scientific management techniques subjected each clerk's work to surveillance and control such that lower-paid clerical labor came to resemble factory work.[383] The development of the dictation machine in the 1910s further deskilled clerical laborers by rendering redundant one of their two skills, shorthand, and thus shifted even more of the physical labor of clerical work to typing. Adrian Forty describes the truly amazing results promised with scientific management: correspondents who had previously managed with difficulty to handle 20

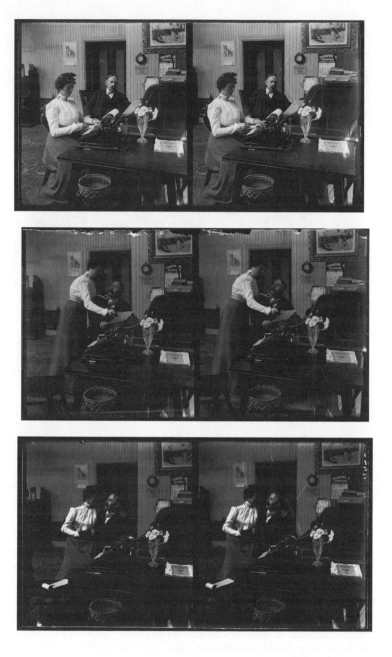

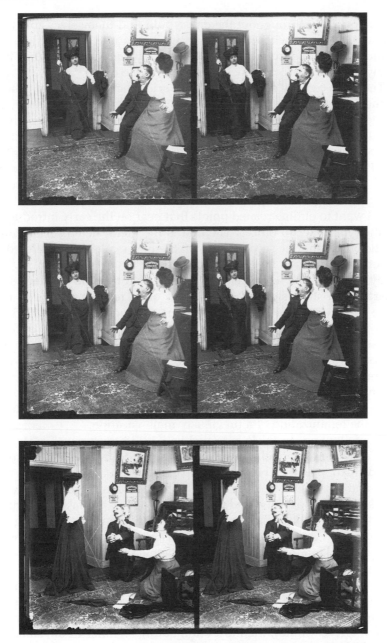

FIGURE 11. Underwood and Underwood Glass Stereograph Collection, ca. 1906. Archives Center, National Museum of American History, Behring Center, Smithsonian Institution.

letters per hour throughout the day would find themselves able without strain to deal with 60 per hour, while the rate of opening letters
could be increased from 100 to 300 per hour when the process had been
analyzed and the correct method taught to the clerk.[384]

The early century's infatuation with scientific management ushered
in the first office "ergonomic" systems.[385] Designs for desks, chairs, and
moveable walls made workers conform to fixed systems of management, giving the impression, if not the results, of increased efficiency.
These early managers similarly paid close attention to typewriters.
Stroke character recorders counted each character typed and standardized dictating times were established.[386] I want to return to these notions of thought and work that correlated to ideas about "flow." But
first I want to outline related points that bear on the early introduction
of the typewriter to offices. The first is the literal heterosexualization
of the office, and the second bears on the new explanations offered for
repetitive injuries in the 1910s and 1920s.

By the 1920s the female clerical worker had become an identifiable
character in short stories.[387] Employers quite regularly married their
type writers, and vaudeville jokes, films, and novels characteristically
played on these liaisons and the "mingling of the sexes and different
classes."[388] Before that, however, the woman in the office was a character of significant cultural ambivalence. While clerical labor held the
promise of limited freedom for young women, these women were not
easily absorbed into the office as neutral workers—rather the expectations of patriarchal heterosexuality mingled oddly with trepidation
over the feminization of a previously male vocation.

The following chronicle is recited in a 1913 screenplay, *The Lyre and
the Typewriter*.[389] A freelance typist sits down to take dictation from a
young man, who then blurts out: "Miss, I love you." She types his message and bills him. There are many facets to this humorous tale, which
turns on the automation and commodification of the labor of writing.
The woman cannot hear the content of the young man's message—it
is not within the purview of her role as a worker. She is there not to
comprehend but to transcribe—she is the medium of the change of medium, voice to text, content to inscription. The joke, ironically, rests on
her fulfilling precisely the requirements of her job. In his analysis of
this story, Friedrich Kittler argues that through typewriting and the
commodification of the word, "messages containing meaning or love
do not arrive. Money, the most annihilating signifier of all, standard-
izes them."[390] For Kittler, the exchange value of words evacuates meaning and reifies words into units of economic exchange.

This message can be squeezed for still more meaning. The tale is
funny insofar as it plays on male *anxiety* about women as commodifi-
ers and that their new role makes them legitimately unavailable to

FIGURE 12. "Elbowing Him Out," 1900, shorthand writer.

their messages. As solely the vessel for his words, the woman ensures that his standardized words will meet only an audience beyond—and only one that can meet it in economic terms. In joining that marketplace through her labor, this woman demonstrates through her literal transcription of his message that her body is no longer on the heterosexual marketplace in quite the same way.

Homi Bhabha argues that anxiety can take on the characteristic of a social identity with its own agency of affect.[391] Bhabha argues that anxiety emerges in a subject when the ego harnesses the potential to change an uncomfortable situation. Anxiety in the context of the woman-machine coupling has several nuances, as the above joke illustrates. The joke hinges on the ambiguity of the woman's role—as "woman" and as worker—and the woman's obvious preference of roles in the face of the man's confusion between the two. This anxiety over the indeterminate place of heterosexual relationships in the drenched office politics and popular culture at the turn of the century, and apprehension concerning women's new roles and the heterosexualization of office work was certainly a significant impetus behind such joking strategies. As Wendy Brown notes, consent is a response to power; consent adds or withdraws legitimacy "but it is not a mode of enacting or sharing power."[392] The proposal—"Miss, I love you"—is one akin to a marriage suit, that is, an admission of desire that implicitly necessitates a capitulation. Consent withheld is pivotal to the humor of the situation; the woman is able to sanction her own withdrawal from the fellow's request for legitimation through another channel of male authority—her absorption into a communications network of the capitalist exchange on which her labor, as labor (and not the unpaid housework that would have resulted from her consent), depends.

FIGURE 13. Advertisement for Royal Typewriter, 1935.

But while sexualized jokes, cartoons, postcards, and editorials relentlessly triangulated the boss-secretary relationship with the typewriter,
the marketing of the typewriter conflated the secretary's body and
labor into the office equipment itself. A 1935 advertisement for the
"New Easy-Writing Royal" shows how the synecdoche of the typewriter stands in for the woman/labor/tool. It promised that "[t]he

shortest distance between the thought and the perfectly typewritten letter is the New Easy-Writing Royal Typewriter," illustrating a woman's hands operating the machine horizontally sandwiched between an illustration of a man having a thought and another of him signing a typed letter.[393] The illustration suggests that when one owns the Royal Typewriter the document magically appears, derived solely by the thinking of it.

To be sure, typewriter advertising carries a particular valance in that it was one of the few machines of which women were allowed to become expert users (albeit with the diminished prestige of expertise). In her article subtitled "The Visual Economy of Feminine Display," Abigail Solomon-Godeau analyzes the visual collapse of femininity, display, and spectacle, arguing that femininity became, in the twentieth century, a "supplementary emblem of the commodity itself."[394] The "coupling of eros and commodity," or the use of the feminine-as-spectacle in order to sell products from cars to cigars, is so ubiquitous as to have become cliché.[395] Examining this issue in relation to office technology turns up some of the ways that objects distribute differences and hierarchies.

Certainly in the office women were literally on display, and typewriter advertising evidences an ambivalence between what Solomon-Godeau argues is the feminine supplement to the commodity form ("the feminine image operates as a conduit and mirror of desire, reciprocally intensifying and reflecting the commodity's allure")[396] and the representations of women as conduits of masculine power. (It is no wonder that the preparation of coffee became, in the 1980s, the locus of resistance among some secretaries.)

The images of typewriters and other office technology of the early to mid-century portray women's work in several ways. Often images show only disembodied hands at the typewriter. Ellen Lupton, who has studied the ways in which women are gendered through everyday products, puts it this way: "the woman and her machine act as a technological conduit for male thought." Other ads foregrounded women's natural propensity toward "agility and musicality,"[397] or conflate the secretary and the typewriter in other ways, such as in the Royal ad that pictures both a woman and a typewriter and says, "Certainly, you choose the finest." Rosemary Pringle has written about the relationships among men, women, and technology in the office in this way: "Both secretaries and technology appear as men's possessions, a measure of their worth, the objects as well as the basis of men's power and control. The secretaries are there to operate men's machines and to service men—in ways that are, by implication, rather intimate."[398] The point is simply that the semiotic work of these advertisements and the lived experiences that they tap into is not incidental, but structures and naturalizes the meanings of women, work, and office technology.

At the same time these fantasies were playing out, a gradual shift occurred away from physiological and toward psychological explanations of repetitive strain injuries. The 1911 British Departmental Report on Telegraphists' Cramp, for example, gave equal weight to two causal explanations of telegraphers' cramp: a nervous instability on the part of the operator and fatigue caused by repeated hand movements when operating the Morse key.[399] Pre-Freud, occupational neuroses had indicated nervous disorders of unknown etiology. Freud was one of the first to introduce the notion that mental disorders might by caused solely by psychological factors, and he distinguished between diseases that had psychological origins and those that originated in organic disorders.[400] This Freudian distinction between physiological and psychological neuroses was lost on the public. Dembe observes that "[d]espite the fact that the original descriptions of chronic hand and wrist disorders as occupational neuroses did not imply any psychoneurosis in the Freudian sense, they were nevertheless typically conceived as possessing an underlying psychological component."[401]

The misunderstanding of this key difference resulted in the relegation of cumulative trauma disorders to psychological rather than physiological origin and the particular attribution of such "nervous disorders" to women, Jews, and immigrants. In his history of cumulative trauma disorders of the hands and wrists, Dembe writes,

> Between 1900 and 1930 white-collar employment in the United States rose by almost 800 percent, . . . more than two-thirds of whom were women. After 1900, occupational neuroses of the hands and wrists increasingly came to be interpreted by physicians as forms of neurasthenia, psychoneurosis, and other psychological abnormalities. At the same time, physicians continued to allege that women, Jews, and immigrants were especially susceptible to these types of psychological disorders. Physicians' linkage of such groups with psychological abnormality was part of a broader social reaction to the unprecedented entry of large numbers of these individuals into the modern workplace.[402]

Thus, physicians adopted discourses of hysteria that had been used to dismiss women's complaints and began applying them to occupational disorders. The lack of compensation and treatment left women with little choice but to leave jobs, and evidence suggests "that many women during the 1920s either decided to leave their employment or were forced to leave because of sickness, exhaustion or injury."[403] Due to saturation of the job market and the depression, employers cut wages in the 1920s and 1930s by as much as half and employment was extremely low among clerical workers.[404] RSI sufferers' lack of credibility is likely a significant factor in low reportage rates of RSI in the early century.

This is not to say, however, that injuries were not being researched and better designs to the QWERTY keyboard imagined. For example, in the early 1930s, August Dvorak, a professor of education and psychology at the University of Washington, and a team of industrial engineers tested 250 keyboards. From these tests they developed the Dvorak Simplified Keyboard (DSK) that reduced the number of miles traveled by the fingers in an eight-hour typing day from sixteen to one, while maintaining other essential design features of the keyboard. The DSK design was specifically created to be inexpensive, altering the manufacturing process as little as possible. The DSK design simplified the stroking of common letter sequences, alternated strokes as much as possible between hands, and factored in the structure of the hand to increase speed while reducing errors and fatigue. The DSK design was intensely investigated by the U.S. Navy in 1944 and the Australian Post Office in 1953. Both investigations found that the DSK decreased fatigue and improved accuracy and speed and would probably result in a "very substantial increase in efficiency of typists."[405] "Efficiency" here is an ergonomic term describing wasted energy and useless gestures.

The development, testing, and patenting, throughout the twentieth century, of alternative typewriter designs also indicates a concern regarding the physical harm caused by the design of the typewriter.[406] A split and laterally angled keyboard,[407] for example, was found to significantly reduce "aches and pains" even with the QWERTY key layout.[408] Eberhard Kroemer, who later testified as an expert in the RSI litigation, summarized the German literature on alternative keyboard designs and key layouts of the 1950s, 1960s and 1970s that specifically addressed documented syndromes of the hand-wrist, spine, and shoulder, thus illustrating their existence even before the vast increase in the use of the QWERTY keyboard in the 1980s and 1990s.[409]

Part of the reason for RSI's prolonged invisibility despite this research was the fact that between 1950 and 1980 carpal tunnel syndrome remained unrecognized under workers' compensation in the United States; it was—astonishingly—understood to be a disease of middle-aged women attributable to hormonal changes. Despite some doctors' careful scrutiny of the problem, the opinion of one Chicago surgeon, Dr. George Phalen, remained enormously influential.[410] Although he recognized that cumulative trauma disorders were aggravated by use of the hands, his premise before, during, and after his studies was that women do not, by definition, do "manual" work and therefore their hand and wrist problems cannot be occupationally caused. This assumption spared him from the more intensive research in which his lesser known colleagues were engaged: documenting the specificities of hand and wrist motions in rigorous attempts to link the disease to specific causes.[411] Despite Phalen's surgical interventions into the wrists of 40 percent of his female patients, he maintained, even in retirement, that "it's in their minds, not their wrists."[412] It is worth noting, as a contrast to the American systems, that in 1958 so many Japanese punch card perforators, typists, and keyboard operators had crevicobrachial disorders that the Japanese government introduced a work maximum of five hours per day with no more than 40,000 keystrokes.[413]

There is more to the story of the ongoing mass production of inscription injuries, such as RSI, than is supposed by past and present models of efficiency and ergonomics.[414] After all, once the ergonomic research and alternative designs existed and the injuries were documented, why did the keyboard remain unchanged even with the introduction of computer input devices? Studies demonstrate that typing injuries are related to inefficiency, to the poor ergonomic design of the keyboard, and to other office equipment that result in awkward physiological positioning and asymmetrical use—as well as plain and simple overuse. The only real explanation for the recalcitrance in adopting new designs is that the effort or expense of retraining typists was simply too great, and the costs of injuries and inefficiency did not warrant this expense to those who were in the position of making these changes.[415]

But injury also results from definitions of efficiency that factor out ergonomics and human wounding, and also factor human injury out of ergonomics. "Wasted energy" and "useless gestures" are terms used by efficiency experts and scientific managers who are not concerned about the health of office workers if they are easily replaced. As evidenced by the ongoing use of the demonstratedly hazardous QWERTY keyboard, office managers were hesitant to "jam up a system" that already worked *well enough* by introducing equipment that in the short run would require practice time, retraining, and financial outlay for unskilled and easily replaced workers.[416] In part they worked "well enough" because they were not being paid for by the people who were making these decisions. Thus, it is worth looking further at the cultural stakes in how the heterosexualization of the office played into fantasies about writing, thinking, and writing implements—fantasies that underwrote the ways that injuries were received by the courts.

The material practice of writing in the Renaissance turned on a fascinating genealogy of the hand, the "relationships between the hand writing and handwriting."[417] Whether with pen, typewriter, or word processor, one *writes* a letter by virtue of having signed a letter. Jonathan Goldberg explains in his history of Renaissance writing that the secretary—etymologically the "guardian of the lord's secrets"—is the necessary absence (or absorption onto the writing medium) through which the master has a presence. The secretary functions as the attached-detached hand of the master and his very body is regulated by the signing hand. "The signature is not imagined as the same hand as that which writes the letter, because it will be written by a secretary and in secretary's hand. Not part of the letter, the signature's authenticity derives from elsewhere—from the system of the re-marking of the writer within the privileges of the italic hand."[418] Goldberg traces this history through the use of writing instruments and the proper training of the hand until finally the hand is considered to be the sole instrument of script, detached from a body that can only be an impediment to a writer. I suggest here that in the early twentieth century, as a part of this genealogy of writing, the instrument of script—the woman and typewriter—was similarly detached from the thinking, or active, masculinized body. This point has crucial repercussions for the marketing of computers and consequently for the cultural recognition of RSI.

In a regime of print culture, especially since the advent of the typewriter, the meaning of "hand" has itself changed. The handwritten note or letter gestures toward the personal and the informal—the positive sense of eccentricity. Both handwriting and the symbolic investment of the signature signal personal speech rather than mechanical repetition and production. Conversely, the type writer's inscriptions dent a standardized gridded page in which the very design and mechanics of the machine mandate the bodily posture and discipline of the user as it erases the signifiers of the body from the resulting text. The gap in the production of writing (or the juncture between the body typing and the type writing) is thus materially widened as it is metaphorically erased. If the typewriter formed the catalyst for women's hands' entrance to scriptive domains, typewriters coded the instrumentalization and expunging of any trace of those bodies.

The authority and personalization of inscription carried a correlate worry: the problem of flow. The course of thought from brain to technology to paper has been a continuing theme in the poetics of writing technology. Consider the moment at which the continuous flow pen was introduced:

> Quill pen or steel pen, there could be no doubt that one of the great disadvantages of either was the need to constantly replenish the nib with a fresh supply of ink. This inevitably broke the flow of writing which the writing masters recommended to their pupils as being a desirable acquirement. Equally inconvenient was the break in thought which might occur as the pen made its way from paper to ink pot and back again.[419]

Flow concerns were similarly tapped into with the advertising attempts to gain a market for the dictation machine. It was advertised—with limited success—to allow for closer concentration and guaranteed privacy: "Men who formerly dictated stilted letters . . . have been taught by the dictating machine to express themselves lucidly."[420] This concern with the necessary continuity of thought can be seen in typewriter ads through the first decades of the twentieth century, which poetically represented women's white, graceful fingers completing the act of translation into the typewriter. These ads represent female hands, with the typewriter, as literally the medium of the message.

These semiotics of the QWERTY keypad in its typewriter form underwent significant conversion in its iteration as a computer input device. There were, first, the different physical requirements: while touch typing carried over, there were no built-in pauses in typing, such as for adjusting paper or awaiting a carriage return. In his ethnography of CAD/CAM, Gary Downey compares "the joy of getting something to work inside the computer and the frustration of being chained for hours to a seat and keyboard." Sitting at the computer, he writes, poses a reduction of all "significant bodily movements to linear terms. In sharp contrast with, say, riding a bicycle, driving a car, wielding a hammer, or fixing the plumbing, all of which required variable movement and involvement of my body, transforming myself into a CAD/CAM user reduced my body to an analogue of the computer."[421] Thus the actual disciplines of the body for computer use contrast starkly with the way in which it ushered in a new set of engagements, or a involvement with the "inside" of the machine. This was the case with handwriting to some extent, as I argued above, but the potential was all the wider with computer games, programming, writing, and even to a certain extent with data entry, where the new engagements encouraged one to literally lose oneself in the interaction between mind and computer—to forget the work that was being performed by one's own hands and wrists.

The presence of women's bodies as models and typists in typewriter ads contrasts rather markedly with the lack of bodies, particularly typing bodies, of the computer ads of the 1990s. Typing was reformulated to be less about writing and flow and more explicitly about power and access; in short, typing itself was backgrounded.[422] Not only was it typical for typewriter advertisements to show women in the act of typing, but even the early room-size computing devices were advertised with female bodies—not typing at them but posed in front of them as part of the display.[423] These changing representations indicate a changing fantasy about machinic production. If earlier, the type writers worked in albeit sexualized and invisibilized ways, computers, on the other

FIGURE 14. Advertisement for IBM VoiceType software, 1995.

hand, are, in the economy of the signifier, not about typing, repetition, or work but about personality, signature, and agency. The male body is not a part of the work act, but still the thought—his thought—is magically inscribed. Earlier it was the sexualized female body that did the work. Now, it is the fetishized computer. Thus, the history of body-machine interface is erased in a fantasy that slips among thought, paper, and power—the middle point, be it the woman-machine or the (assumed male consumer) body at the machine, is consistently under erasure.

One place to see a sort of apotheosis of this point is in IBM's advertisement for its voice dictation software:

> Gavin just finished his epic poem, "The Iceberg, the Walrus and the Fisherman's Elbow." It took nineteen years to complete. His publisher said, "You are brilliant. You are profound. But you've got to get faster on the keyboard." [And then in smaller type,] "You'd rather be a poet than a typist."[424]

The software—the mode of communication, it is supposed—is what would allow Gavin—illustrated in a close-up double-spread black and white photograph as a weatherbeaten old fisherman full of tales and adventures—to blossom fully as a poet; never mind the act of typing, which stultifies his mind and trips his fingers.[425] If typing is an act of labor, speaking is apparently a natural expression of one's inner, true, and poetic self.

FIGURE 15. Advertisement for IBM ThinkPad, 1996.

Speaking is just the flow from thought, and in the cybernetic computer fantasies of marketing even that step can be eradicated. IBM peddles their ThinkPad thus:

> The evolution of thought. Crying equals food. Four plus seventeen, carry the one, twenty-one. Conjunctive adverbs. Deductive reasoning. You are already in possession of the most amazing computer on the planet. Now you need its companion: a machine capable of capturing and communicating your thoughts with unparalleled precision. When a spark jumps from one neuron to the next and a message goes from your brain down to your fingertips and into a keyboard, you should have in front of you the most thoughtfully designed, intelligently built machine possible. A computer that reflects all of the thinking and ardor and insight of the human mind. ThinkPad. A better place to think.[426]

The isolation of body parts in the configuration of thinking's relationship to the machinic computer assumes that the substance of thinking itself—the traversal of the spark from neuron to fingertip to keyboard—is contained in that very loop. This "thinking" is a curious sort of spirit—an immaterial activity wholly caught up in mind-body severance. The ad implies a relationship of machine-human/thought-communication whereby both computer and human are transformed.

If it is just a fingertip that operates the computer and really the interface is between two highly sophisticated brains, then of course keyboard design hardly matters. The 1935 Royal Typewriter advertisement ("The shortest distance between the thought and the perfectly typed letter") presages the idea of a causal relationship between thought and production. Whereas 1930s-era typewriter advertising concretized thought with long, slender, royal-looking fingers and the overtones of sexy legs and bodies, the bodies of ThinkPad advertisements are placed within the imaginative space of three computer screens illustrated along the margins of the page. These bodies relax in the green hues of nature (two children), or peruse the golds of the art gallery (a young, wealthy woman of color). Bodies are being sold in each of these images. If in 1935 the typewriter symbolically included the woman operator, in 1996 the bodies are offered as synecdoches of leisure, wealth, youth, and beauty.

Perhaps the clearest example of this refiguration can be seen in an advertisement for the Microsoft Natural (ergonomic) Keyboard, which shows a man's casually crossed arms with an overlaid graphic line stylishly joining one hand to a miniaturized image of the keyboard in the bottom corner—"made for each other."[427] The new Microsoft Natural Keyboard, designed precisely as a reaction to and to guard against RSI, merges the man and the machine with the sexual overtones of its slogan as it spatially and cognitively divorces the man from the feminized act of typing. Whereas in typewriter advertisements the woman's hands *at the typewriter* are symbolically for sale with the machine, in the Microsoft Natural Keyboard ads the product simply *is* both the woman and the typewriter. Thus, a combination of fear of "women's work" and a symbolic condensation of the woman and machine combine to erase, even as they foreground, the ergonomics of the machine.

Thus the multiple relationships between the possession of women's work and bodies through eroticism, anxiety, and fantasies about creativity and flow gain concrete specificity through analyses of these popular representations. The shift toward personal computing marked by the demise of the personal secretary and the marketing of the machine to men for their own use rested on similar tropes as the secretary-typewriter duo. The signifying of the computer as an eroticized commodity, as equally possessable as the woman and the typewriter, has shifted the relays among possession, femininity, and commodity. Whereas women had been displayed using and adorning typewriters to sell (materially and semiotically) the product to male employers, the actual feminized work practice has been disavowed with the introduction of the computer. This disavowal has resulted in the erasure of the hands and bodies at work, and the reconfiguration of the computer commodity. With the rise of the personal computer, this invisibility of

FIGURE 16. Advertisement for Microsoft Natural Keyboard, 1996.

work took on a new valance for several reasons. As Downey's ethnography demonstrates, and as the advertisements corroborate, computer work (as opposed to data entry work) encouraged users to see through the physical requirements of the machine; to link the computer with the brain as the hands did the invisible work of data entry. Second, with the rise of computerization, a vast new need for data entry came about.[428] A significant part of this labor has now been rendered obsolete by computerized scanners, but in the 1980s and early 1990s, the very companies that claimed that computer keyboards were obvious tools rather like "hammers" and "pencils"[429] were developing software that counted data entry personnel's keystrokes as systems of surveillance to allow management to ensure maximum input rates. These companies were also lobbying against OSHA's proposed office ergonomic regulations.

Furthermore, the computer keyboard was simply a different kind of tool than the typewriter. Despite its purposefully mimetic appearance, it required different force factors to operate it and it did not have built-in break periods to load and adjust paper. Early computer keyboard designs took away these built-in breaks but added poorly designed function keys that required use of the weakest fingers and awkward finger positioning, required excessive force for key depression, and lacked tactile feedback to allow the user to "aid the nervous system's control of the motor responses involved in keystrokes."[430]

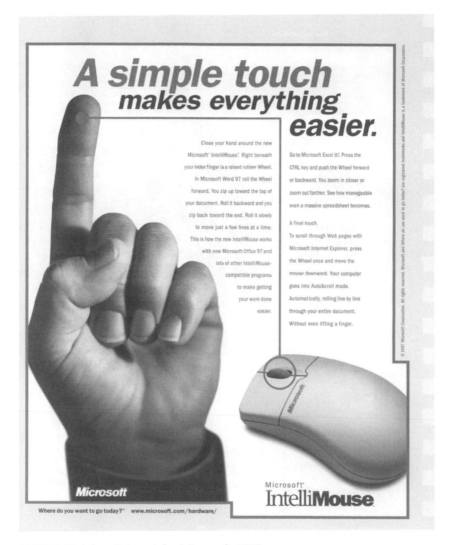

FIGURE 17. Advertisement for Microsoft, 1997.

Industrial Design

The sweeping consequence of RSI litigation lies in the correlation among the necessity of the hand for human functioning, its extraordinary physiology, and the severity of the injury in impeding everyday life. Scientists from Stephen Jay Gould to Sherwood Washburn and

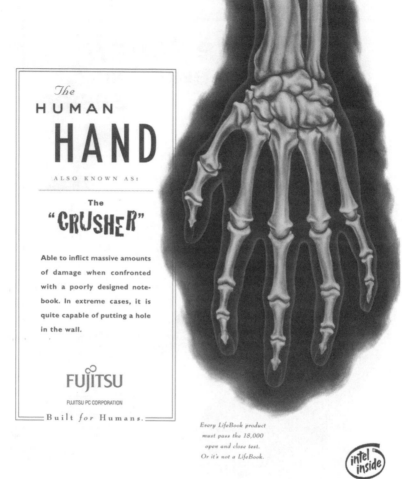

FIGURE 18. Advertisement for Fujitsu Notebook computer, 1997.

Mary Marzke have linked the development of the human hand and intricate tool use to the development of the brain.[431] One worker laid off after a bout with RSI wrote, " 'Rest' meant avoiding every object that caused pain: my car, my bicycle, my violin; the key in the lock, the quarter in the vending machine, the cap on the Calistoga bottle;

We've changed the

dreaded, backbreaking,

mind-numbing, painful

task of communicating

through your computer.

(All right, slight exaggeration.)

FIGURE 19. Advertisement for FocalPoint Communications Software, 1996.

clapping hands, shaking hands, holding hands. It stripped me of my independence and self-esteem."[432] That so many people were suffering with such serious consequences and that neither the courts nor the regulatory systems seemed to be able to enforce changes in product design or office ergonomics, or effect warnings or education, raises crucial questions about American citizenship.

As *Howard* demonstrates and the other cases corroborate, the law offers a promise of making injuries visible while in practice it offers limited ability to do so. In understanding Shirl Howard not as a consumer or a worker but as someone who is at once dependent on her employer for education on typing injuries and a freely choosing subject analogous to a volunteer collecting donations on a Saturday, the court is unable to understand her as a subject that has been coded in a particular way—as gendered, virtually through her relationship to a set of work practices that includes the history of typing and women's work. Thus, the law was unable and unwilling to understand the conditions of inequity that virtually enabled the injurious design of the keyboard to begin with.

To be sure, the *Howard* court pointed out weaknesses in the plaintiff's case. It drew attention, for example, to the fact that the plaintiff had no expert witness testifying specifically about the details of the keyboard. There are several points to be made about this. First, it demonstrates that expert witnesses are expensive and need to be paid by the plaintiff's attorney whether or not the case wins (and thus, regardless of whether the attorney is paid). Thus, plaintiffs' attorneys may hesitate in bringing the strongest possible case on every front and instead make a series of compromises based in educated decisions about the machinations of the court. Second, in other RSI cases where experts were called, they made no difference to the rulings, as the *Howard* court noted. Third, the court makes clear on several occasions in the written decision that expert testimony of this sort would not in fact have made a difference to the opinion. This latter point dovetails with the actions of the plaintiff's lead attorney, Lee Balefsky, who says that he did have expert witnesses who analyzed the keyboard but that their testimony was ignored.[433] The court makes it clear that no amount of evidence would persuade it that the keyboard is any more injurious than a chair, or that the keyboard is similar to a chair, or that the relation of secretary to keyboard is any different than Salvation Army volunteer to bell.

It is true that RSI is multifactorial. Injury depends not only on individual physical traits but also on personal practices; someone who jogs to work and practices yoga will be less likely to suffer from it. Furthermore, as virtually all ergonomics manuals and physical therapists agree, there are ways to organize workstations such that some of the awkward postures required for typing can be alleviated. These manuals lay out precise guidelines for how high to set a screen and keyboard, where to place wrists and feet, what stretches to do in well-defined breaks. This is an ergonomics that sets out the parameters that will enable the body to engage in one activity: data entry into a computer through a typewriter-like keyboard.

The typewriter was an object that built in breaks for its user. No doubt typewriters and their operators were badly positioned. Yet they required the use of a full hand and needed users to change paper and wait for carriage returns. Also, the keys required enough pressure so that fingers could fully rest on them without striking the key and thus alleviate static loading of the fingers. These factors may have been just enough to allow operators to escape injury. Or, perhaps RSI remained invisible because low-paid, easily replaceable women, whose injuries were dismissed by the medical field as psychological, had few ways of making their injuries matter. Computer keyboards changed typing qualitatively and quantitatively. Unlike the Salvation Army bell, the computer keyboard demanded a total body analogue: it allowed for faster typing but no breaks, it was impossible to rest one hand without halting work entirely, and typing was the sole activity for many jobs. In addition, because keyboards were attached to digital memory systems and not to paper, this work correlated with a broad economic expansion in the need for data input. Office ergonomics provided one route around that difference between typewriters and keyboards in its new disciplining of the entire body for computer keying.

In claiming that the problem was the repetition necessary to use the keyboard rather than the keyboard itself, the *Howard* court made a distinction between the object and the practices required to use it. Since any foreseeable use of the keyboard would require repetitious acts, the court's distinction was far from self-evident. Rather, it embodied assumptions about what adequate design should entail and far-reaching assumptions about where the costs of predictable injuries should fall: on the statistical victim or on the manufacturer with control over design enhancement. Dr. Laura Punnett, who testified for plaintiffs in several cases, said, "[T]he principal of a school may have no idea about CTDs, and yet IBM had all the information at its fingertips and was training its own workers."[434] So while it seems clear that we could terminate the account of fault in either the keyboard or the person who used it repeatedly, how one traces these explanations will have high costs for how the politics of injury create both injured bodies and material worlds.

The RSI cases demonstrate that the terms of law required an intense attenuated understanding of the worker, the keyboard, the work, and the injury. In addition, these injuries come to court only after a series of failures: of employers to set up ergonomics workstations; of federal regulatory agencies to set out adequate ergonomics standards; of venues to educate those engaged in data entry at all levels; of the legislation of minimum design standards for computers and keyboards. The fact, however, that the epidemic was not avoided should not be taken as evidence that it could have been. The conclusion here is not that OSHA needs to be better funded or that we need more research on ergonomics. The conclusion is not that the courts made mistakes with regard to these cases and they fell through the cracks. Rather, these cases demonstrate the difficulties courts had in determining how objects and humans act in relation to each other.

The keyboard was defective not only in each individual keyboard's specificity (how much force required to press keys and so on) but in the very requirements for its use. The repetitive act of typing on an instrument requires fine finger work with force at a fast pace, while the body is still and the arms are pronated. The activity of typing on an instrument designed with these requirements simply will be injurious for a certain percentage of people who engage in it. This has been true in hand-centered vocations that vary from telegraphers to musicians to chicken pluckers. The body can heal itself if allowed to take breaks and certain positions will allow bodies to maintain higher outputs, but the fact remains that office ergonomics exist for one purpose: to enable the worker to partake in the repetitive act of data input. Regardless of cultural fantasies about flow, ideas, power, and brains, data input is what occurs at the physical juncture of the keyboard and the hands. For this reason, where chairs and desks are purchased through separate orders for many purposes, office managers may not be interested in ergonomics training for many reasons, and consumers do not all belong to these institutions, the keyboard is really the only place where a product warning makes sense—a warning precisely about the consequences of the physical requirements for using the product.[435] The cornerstone of product liability law in the United States has been that a "manufacturer is strictly liable in tort when an article he places on the market, knowing that it is to be used without inspection for defects, proves to have a defect that causes injury for a human being."[436] Tort law posits that placing an item on the market meant representing "that it would safely do the job for which it was built."[437] While other legal scholars pose different theories of how and when liability should be attributed, this statement still stands in for the rhetorical value of injury law in capitalism. The laws are meant to protect individuals who cannot possibly know about the products they purchase and, in the larger sense, to protect the citizenry from the temptations of capitalism.

But as the RSI litigation demonstrates, the law is fraught with problems. Even this statement, taken by legal theorists to be the foremost articulation of strict liability, does not distinguish between the product itself and the practices required to use it. Furthermore, the law requires each plaintiff to come to the law separately; then the court can openly dismiss a case precisely because it is individuated, precisely because only some individuals suffer from this injury. The defense in *Howard* similarly insisted that each keyboard had to be studied in the context of users with the exact same symptoms, and claimed that it was impossible to draw conclusions from the wider occupational literature. This legal approach was quite different from that of science, which moves from the general to the specific—examining physical repetitive manual work and then honing in on its details.[438] The legal framework, requiring an attenuation of person and thing that are then set against each other, reflects, rather, a consumer logic. The logic is of a piece with ideologies of consumption in which sovereign consumers are set against selectable objects. While the failure of OSHA to set adequate ergonomic standards might be traced back to corporate lobbying, the lack of medical treatment for soft tissue injuries might be framed against the training and class experiences of physicians, and the lack of adequate keyboard design can be traced to cost-saving measures, the larger issue is the inability of these institutions to comprehend the co-constitution of objects and persons. I have suggested here that the typewriter, in the fullness of its office politics, marketing, and injury histories, can be seen to embody a critical hinge for the production of twentieth-century heterosexuality—and more particularly, how these politics simultaneously apotheosized women's bodies as supplements to the typewriter as a commodity and downplayed the injuries that resulted from their work. In its analogies of milk cows and tennis rackets, the court showed that the law was unable to understand the very semiotics that give meaning to the everydayness of the QWERTY keyboard and the invisibility of typing. In its failure to understand RSI, courts demonstrated that they were merely symptoms of the continuing dynamics of social and material subordination.[439]

Chapter 4

"Come Up to the 'Kool' Taste"

African American Upward Mobility and
the Semiotics of Smoking Menthols

ALTHOUGH MOST OFTEN considered with alcohol in policy debates, tobacco more readily compares to sugar or coffee in its ubiquitous availability (and, until recently, acceptability) to all classes. The intimate pleasures of the cigarette—from the flip-top box to the smoker's perfected flick of an ash to the excuse to ask a stranger for a light—should not be underestimated. The cigarette's social rituals have made it truly iconic of popular culture through the twentieth century. Consider its adaptability: readily slipped into a pocket or behind an ear, it is a means to a private or social moment. Useful as a lift or a sedative, the cigarette stands in as a snack, prop, drug, or coping mechanism. The commodity achieves its most refined, profitable, and complete incarnation in the cigarette, with its inexpensive, efficient, short-lived gratification. Consumed nearly completely, literally disappearing into a puff of smoke (the butt easily disposed of under a shoe), the cigarette's solitary fault lies in the fact that, over time, the cumulative effects of its debris slowly and irrevocably sicken and kill its consuming host.

In the legal framing of capitalism in the United States, this one flaw—that cigarettes injure when used as intended—could be enough not only to regulate but also to ban the cigarette outright. In the United States, product liability law is the imperfect but established infrastructure by which Americans can claim that they were unjustly injured by an object purchased and used in a predictable manner. But despite three decades of litigation, people have been able to consider themselves injured by cigarettes in the legal sense only since the late 1990s. This change is due to the work of a recent wave of litigants who have successfully shown that tobacco corporations falsely advertised, defectively designed, and knowingly sold an addictive product. Although dismissed by the U.S. Court of Appeals for the Third Circuit in 2001, one of the most interesting of the recent spate of lawsuits was brought in Pennsylvania on behalf of black smokers. In this suit, the Reverend Jesse Brown attempted to highlight the economic racism of cigarette marketing through a civil rights claim. Brown's complaint stated "that

Defendants have for many years targeted African Americans and their communities with specific advertising to lure them into using mentholated tobacco products."[440] Brown raised the issues of niche marketing, discrimination, and the "staggering loss of life, premature disability, disease, illness, and economic loss," which has resulted from "the Tobacco Companies' intentional and racially discriminating fraudulent course of misconduct."[441]

The *Brown* complaint contended that mentholated cigarettes (also known as menthols) contained enhanced dangers. First, the complaint explained that the ingredient menthol itself contains compounds such as benzopyrene, which are carcinogenic when smoked. Second, it argued that mentholated cigarettes contain higher nicotine and tar levels than nonmentholated versions. Third, *Brown* claimed that menthol encourages deeper and longer inhalation of tobacco smoke, increasing the addictive properties of the cigarette and decreasing the lungs' ability to rid itself of carcinogenic components of smoke. According to evidence submitted in *Brown*, mentholated cigarettes account for between 60 and 75 percent of the cigarettes smoked by African Americans—and 90 percent of African American youth who smoke, smoke menthols.[442] Thus, *Brown* claimed, as a result of the increased danger of mentholated cigarettes and "a conspiracy of deception and misrepresentation against the African American public," African Americans have disproportionately suffered the injury, disability, and death that invariably follow from smoking mentholated cigarettes.

Reverend Brown brought this injury claim as a civil rights suit, providing a radical departure from product liability approaches to legal retribution for dangerously defective products. By claiming transgression of the Civil Rights Act of 1866, originally written to protect recently freed slaves from a variety of discriminatory practices, the complainants of the *Brown* suit sought to show the unconstitutionality of targeting African Americans with defective products. This strategy sidestepped the problematic way in which product liability law seeks to reestablish the status quo through compensation and its corollary effect, which is its tendency to undercompensate women and minorities—meaning they are both less likely to be compensated (as a group) and tend to receive less compensation. Furthermore, it sought structural redress by attempting to have advertising directed toward African Americans banned, a remedy that would not be available through product liability law.

There is no doubt that cigarettes have had a devastating impact on the African American community: tobacco smoking is the number-one killer and disabler of African Americans. It results in more deaths among black Americans than homicide, car accidents, drug abuse, and

AIDS combined. It intensifies serious health problems that disproportionately affect black Americans: hypertension, diabetes, low birth weight, infant mortality, and hazardous occupational exposures.[443] Blacks have a higher incidence than whites of tobacco-related illnesses such as cancers of the lung, esophagus, oral cavity, and larynx, heart disease, and cerebrovascular disease. In 1992 lung cancer became the leading cause of cancer mortality among African American women aged fifty-five to seventy-four.[444] Compared with whites, blacks also tend to be diagnosed when diseases are at a later stage and have a significantly lower survival rate after diagnosis.[445] It is thus precisely the aggressiveness of the cigarette in the making of smokers that makes it a fascinating way to engage questions of its mediation through designers, sellers, and users.

Although the complainants submitted substantial evidence on target marketing and design defects—including evidence of industry research on the health effects of menthols dating possibly to the 1930s[446]—the structure of civil rights law placed these key issues beyond what the majority in the court understood to be their field of judgment. For example, plaintiffs needed to show intentional discrimination on the part of the defendants that would impair the plaintiffs' ability to "make contractual arrangements for the sale and purchase of tobacco products." In dismissing *Brown*, the court set aside the issue of targeting because plaintiffs were unable to show that they were offered less favorable contractual terms than whites were. Essentially, the court determined that plaintiffs had in fact been free to buy any type of cigarette, and the mentholated products that many did smoke were "just as defective and dangerous as the mentholated products" that were sold to whites with equal terms of sale.[447] In other words, the court was unable to calculate the ways in which different educational, medical, and other factors played into the constitution of choice in an implied market contract. Thus a federal district court dismissed *Brown* in 1999 on narrow but important legal grounds, and the plaintiffs' charge of targeting a dangerous product at racially defined markets was not considered.

Nevertheless, the *Brown* case is one in an important series of attempts by culturally and economically defined groups to mobilize against extreme target marketing. But it is also much more than that. I contend here that the structural issues raised by *Brown* cast into relief the difficulties of demonstrating how social and physical injuries are imbricated—a central problem in understanding how injury and inequality are distributed through consumption in the United States. It reveals the structural complexity—indeed the impossibility—of articulating in legal, compensatory language the process through which individuals and communities are socially and physically constituted by the products they own and consume. Thus the complaint both points to, as it is a symptom of, the complexities of the ever-circulating contingent relations among injured communities, niche marketing, and dangerous products. Analysis of it in context poses radical challenges to articulations of American injury law.

This case is about a vernacular right not to be injured through the products one consumes; in this sense it directly parallels a product liability claim. Not surprisingly, the significant media attention *Brown* garnered tended to fissure along the same lines as a product liability case would. One side, seemingly allied with tobacco corporations, claimed that African Americans are as capable as anyone of making choices, and everyone makes choices they regret. The other side consolidated around the position that tobacco corporations have behaved reprehensibly and are unquestionably responsible for injuries resulting from smoking. Neither side necessarily portrays African Americans as naive dupes or hapless victims—indeed, both sides went out of their way to claim the contrary. But each carries assumptions about human, nonhuman, and institutional accountability, as well as about choice, injury, inequality, agency, and regret.

Product liability law's key assumption is that given adequate product design, human users will be able to make responsible choices. This perspective assumes that consumers and corporations enter contracts (through consumption) as two equal and sovereign subjects. *Brown* deeply questions this premise by showing that, in fact, products are powerfully produced by factors such as advertising and, furthermore, that choice is a highly social practice. Profoundly implicating the corporation in structural racism on multiple levels, *Brown* claims that tobacco companies targeted a much more dangerously designed product, through deceptive advertising, to a group of people who are statistically more likely to be influenced by advertising claims. The transparent veracity of *Brown*'s claims to racism and the ease with which it was dismissed demands critical attention. The suit's framing the issue of defective products as one of civil rights rather than product liability interrogates the very core of rationalist injury frameworks and sheds light on the broader structure of capitalism and the always already unequal social terms of consumption.

To place *Brown* in a more textured context, this chapter focuses primarily on the growth of black consumerism in the 1950s and 1960s for several reasons. First, the number of black smokers increased dramatically during this twenty-year period, and smoking by everyone was at its twentieth-century peak: 52.5 percent of Americans were smokers by 1966.[448] Second, during these decades African Americans were "discovered" as a viable market and targeted in innovative (but not necessarily progressive) ways for a slew of new products, including mentholated cigarettes. According to evidence submitted in *Brown*, the tobacco company Brown and Williamson (B&W), which produced the Kool brand, advertised proportionately more to blacks than whites throughout the 1960s (while 10 percent of the population is black, B&W spent 17 percent of Kool's advertising budget on "black advertising").[449] But although much was made of this statistic by complainants, I argue here that this greater spending was not the main factor in the sway of this campaign, nor is it constitutive of race targeting. Indeed, that cigarette companies led target market campaigns was nothing new. Despite awareness of their product's dangers, Philip Morris and others have been marketing cigarettes to particular ethnic or economic groups with abandon since the earliest years of the century. While *Brown* correctly contends that race targeting, in the absence of information about the hazards of smoking, might have influenced many more African Americans to smoke than might have otherwise, a deeper investigation of the politics and culture of the 1950s and 1960s reveals a more complex and insidious culprit.[450]

The semiotics of marketing menthols and other leisure products toward African Americans emerged in the context of the civil rights movement's boycotts against discrimination. Breaking down barriers to consumption, these boycotts aligned blacks' dignity with their right to consume quality products and services as freely as whites. In short, in a nation that defined citizenship largely in terms of consumption, civil rights claims tended to emulate these terms of citizenship. In this context, tobacco companies also aligned consumption of their product with equality and upward mobility, creating intersecting agendas. During this period, as Michael Omi and Howard Winant argue, the "black movement redefined the meaning of racial identity, and consequently of race itself, in American society."[451] These decades are key in understanding the circulating figurations of race in a semiotics of smoking. Moreover, the links among consumption, race-based marketing, and smoking menthols, claimed in the *Brown* case, crystallized during this period.

Making the Menthol Smoker

Tobacco and mint leaves have doubtless been mixed together and smoked since antiquity, and menthol crystals have been added to snuff for hundreds of years. In the age of the contemporary cigarette, however, mentholation, acting as a mild anesthetic, numbs the throat to the

FIGURE 20. Award-winning advertisement for Kool cigarettes, 1946, *tobaccodocuments.org*, "Pollay Collection."

harsh elements of tobacco smoke and thus allows a deeper and longer inhalation. In 1926 Axton-Fisher introduced a mentholated cigarette called "Spud," named after its original patent holder.[452] B&W, formed in 1894, launched the mentholated Kool in 1933 and priced it at 15 cents, 25 percent cheaper than Spud, which it outsold swiftly.[453] The first Kool ads featured a penguin and inaugurated the seventy-year marketing bid to associate menthol cigarettes with refreshment and health. "Like a week by the sea, this smoke . . . is a tonic to hot, tired throats."[454] The award-winning ad of 1946 focuses on the pharmaceutical value of Kools: "Head stopped up? Got the Sneezes? Switch to Kools . . . The flavor pleases!"[455]

Notwithstanding recent sales taxes, cigarettes have traditionally provided a cheap and accessible indulgence to all classes, and, gaining momentum throughout the century, cigarette companies have ensured that smoking has been introduced to literally hundreds of cross-referenced niche markets. According to contemporary industry documents, sometime in the 1950s or 1960s mentholated cigarettes came to be identified—at least by black people—as a black product. Sociologists, marketers, and smokers have offered various reasons for this notable association. Industry attorney Jeffrey G. Weil claimed, "The targeting is not because they're African-American—it's because they like menthol cigarettes."[456] Conversely, Charyn Sutton, a plaintiff in the *Brown* class action suit, testified that B&W "put extra effort into promoting menthol cigarettes to blacks." She said, further, that "when I was in high school [B&W] made the penguin into a person, and we really thought he was a stand-in for African Americans because at that time African Americans really couldn't be portrayed in ads in the general market. . . . The class took that penguin and made him the class mascot—that's how intense the identification was by that kind of advertising."[457]

It has been suggested that African Americans' preference for menthols may be explained culturally as an identification with the vernacular origins of the word "cool" and its manifest attitudes and gestures. Another possibility for the preference lies in the resonance of mentholed cigarettes with menthol's roots in folk medicine and over-the-counter drugs. Menthol is steam distilled from oil of peppermint, which has been used as an ingredient of medicinal mixtures for thousands of years. Peppermint oil's popularity as a home remedy stemmed from its effectiveness, when combined with sodium bicarbonate or powdered rhubarb, as an antacid, an appetite stimulant, and a purgative. Mentholated commercial products, such as lozenges, inhalers, and chest rubs, were common in Britain and North America by the mid-nineteenth century and have remained so, although contemporary evidence suggests that they have no beneficial medical effects.[458] Reports that African Americans have spent two to four times as much as white Americans on over-the-counter medications more generally, likely as a result of restricted access to health care, suggests a reliance on mentholated products.[459] These hypotheses aside, B&W capitalized on many African Americans' positive view of mentholation's purported medicinal properties in its advertisement of Kools.[460]

Market studies attest to a strong preference for mentholated cigarettes among African Americans, both for the qualities of the cigarette as well as for its image. For example, in 1980 Philip Morris, planning its own niche advertising strategy for the cigarette Merit, had a 166-page document prepared on ethnic marketing.[461] Several pages are dedicated to analyzing the success of Kool cigarettes, and the document quotes African American smokers who focus on taste, style, and loyalty. Black participants in the study considered Kools to be "so smooth and mild you can smoke them all the time," and they work "like an anesthetic." Many of these smokers said they experienced Kools as "relaxing," a means of "escape," and a way to meditate. Kool style was considered the crucial element to Kool's success and the brand was "heavily" associated with a very positive, often glamorous self-image: "To be cool you smoke Kool"; "Smoking a Kool? Like riding a Rolls Royce." The study concludes, "Kool smokers see themselves as very stylish and apart from other smokers who haven't made it to Kools"; they were separate from the crowd. These reactions to the Kool advertisements recurred in one black smoker's reminiscences in 2000: "I don't know if I smoked because I saw the ads. I do know that they made me feel a certain way, like I was part of that whole glamour thing."[462]

The smokers' testimony collected by Philip Morris suggests an uncritical assimilation of advertising rhetoric and makes clear the extent to which the identity of the Kools smoker was wrapped up in the expression of taste as a measure of class and good breeding. Like Coca-Cola, which is consumed for pleasure, or like other personal embellishments such as Gucci, Victorinox, or Mustangs, which are meant to be seen, cigarette brands are used to express, through their consumption and display, an identity, a style, and a self. Thus, for a large percentage of African American smokers, the Kool cigarette was interpellated as an object with evolving meanings and multiple uses. It is this multiplicity of meanings that the *Brown* complaint poignantly suggests as it defers to the necessity of focusing on the attenuated and quantitative issues of targeting and cigarette design.

One telling place to open this exploration further is through an investigation of a 1967 ad for Kools that appeared in *Ebony*'s August special issue on youth. The ad not only appeared at the height of the civil rights movement but itself offers an instance of what might be read as an anti-racist pro-corporate movement on the part of African American marketers, including *Ebony*'s publisher and founding editor, John H. Johnson. In his editorial for the youth issue, Johnson explores "the challenging and bewilderingly complex world of the more than eleven million Negroes who are below the age of twenty-five."[463] Although Johnson stresses his concern with youth, the issue is also about civil rights. It features articles on activist movements; the dearth of educational opportunities; Jesse Jackson's views on economics, unemployment, and Vietnam; as well as a protofeminist piece on the successes of a female pool player in Iowa. This content generally fits into the human interest, celebrity, bootstrap rubric under which Johnson had founded *Ebony* twenty-two years prior. As befits the predominant readership of the magazine, the preponderance of its advertisements are geared to women. Through the 1960s *Ebony* covered civil rights issues, but as the movement became increasingly radical, the magazine reverted to an orientation of self-help rather than protest.[464] In the early to mid-1960s *Ebony* readers were better educated, held more white-collar jobs, had a much higher mean income, and were ten years older than the average of the ages of the general black population. In addi-

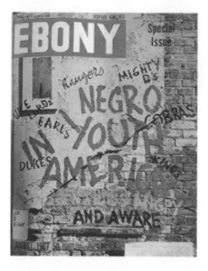

FIGURE 21. Cover and inside cover from *Ebony*, August 1967.

tion, 31 percent of readers earned an annual income of less than $5,000 and 41 percent had not completed high school.[465]

The youth issue's editorial content and advertising offer a conflicting pastiche of preoccupations and priorities. Advertisements portray that summer as one of leisure and luxury. The *Ebony* women of the advertising pages appear to be ecstatic over visiting the manicurist, straightening hair, quaffing Pepsi, lathering down in the shower, and ironing clothes. Meanwhile, articles address a female readership occupied with meetings, day jobs, and childcare. The cover pictures conflict, illustrating a broken-down brick wall, painted with the graffiti sign that provides a title for the issue: "Negro Youth in America Anxious, Angry, and Aware." In the midst of this confusion and crisis of identity, the reader turns from the front cover to find an invitation to "Come up to the Kool Taste." The moment of calm on the cover's flip side transports the reader to a stream babbling through a forest as the blurred background to a couple relaxing on a quixotic wooden bridge. Although the couple seems to be about the same age as the "youth" featured in the magazine, they are certainly of a different generation.

In this leisurely pose in the woods, the woman in her turquoise-green dress with matching shoes and bracelet seems to emerge, genie-like, from the box of cigarettes. Even the twist of her body, highlighted by the folds of her frock, echoes the curling smoke of the fairy-tale genie as it emerges from Aladdin's lamp. But if this is so, it is the only suggestion of smoke, for these white-toothed models do not even have their cigarettes lit. The couple is confidently heterosexual, overlapping if not touching; a wedding ring is conspicuously absent. He, dark and handsome, and she, light-skinned with straightened hair, promise a romantic afternoon. Perhaps they are courting; they are certainly upwardly mobile. These charming people wait curiously, invitingly, genuinely, for some sign from the observer, and the cigarette box below reflects this offer. The invitation of this scene, untarnished by the now familiar product warnings, is unabashed in its class and assimilationist aspirations. If the appellation "kool" plays on a real or imagined black vernacular, the enticement is to a middle class. The Kool brand was hailed by *Advertising Age* as a success for its call to upward mobility, and well-dressed couples in outdoor scenes were depicted in the advertisements for Newport and Salem menthols throughout the mid- to late 1960s.[466]

Although this duplicitously slick ad promises a prosaic menu of success, achievement, and pleasure—the standard fare of advertisers everywhere—it can more radically be read as the culmination of the struggles of John Johnson and other black conservatives. These trials are central to the ethos that leads to the kinds of claims made by *Brown*, for they bring together the stakes in nonracist advertising for both desegregation and community building through the cultural production of magazines in the context of civil rights struggles. These were underpinned in no small way by the local and institutional power of tobacco companies. Only by tracing each of these can we analyze the travels of race and its consolidation in what are sometimes conflicting ways. This inquiry provides crucial insight into the civil rights claim underpinning *Brown*.

The rise of the lifestyle magazine as a form of popular culture after World War I helped strengthen the ideal of an American middle class— one that was largely racialized as white.[467] The uneasy position of all people identified as and with black Americans in the middle class was clear, however, as the *Ebony* reader in August 1967 turned from the cover image of the graffitied wall to the Kool advertisement on its backside. The cover hints at the violence of the era, in which Martin Luther King and Malcolm X were both shot. Moreover, while he was alive Malcolm X surely frightened black conservatives, many of whom were also readers of *Ebony*, as much as he did whites. The FBI infiltrated the Black Panthers and other political groups as young black men were being drafted for Vietnam. Perhaps readers of *Ebony*, having grown up in the era of Jim Crow when "talking back" could be a capital crime, were terrified for their more radical grown children.[468] The Kool advertisement, in contrast, offered other fantasies based in the history of a civil rights movement that had used the law to open new possibilities in education and employment even as it evacuated the energy and potential dangers of black identifications in the more radical wing of the civil rights and other contemporary revolutionary movements of the era.[469] Thus, if the contrast between the cover and the inside page of the 1967 issue illustrates the broader ambivalence of the magazine's content and perhaps its readership, then the ad itself exemplifies the values of a long tradition of black conservatism, whose roots in Booker T. Washington's reliance on hard work and self-improvement found voice through twentieth-century women's clubs, black churches, and appeals to the U.S. Supreme Court.[470]

The ad's design and placement in the magazine reflect this social history, but its actual existence in 1967 is emblazoned with Johnson's struggles as an African American editor. His 1989 autobiography, *Succeeding against the Odds*, is one diffracted through the lens of a foundational belief in equal opportunity capitalism. Born in 1918, Johnson completed the eighth grade twice because it was the last grade available to blacks in Arkansas. Meanwhile, his mother earned enough money to move with her son and daughter to Chicago so that he could attend high school in the growing metropolis. Johnson epitomizes the American Dream, and his autobiography is largely a story of overcoming difficulties, though perhaps not as many as he would have liked. He writes, "If I hadn't operated with the handicap of racial barriers, I could have made billions, instead of millions."[471] To be sure, compelling evidence buoys this observation.

Johnson's initial success with *Negro Digest* (1942), which he initiated with a $500 loan that used his mother's furniture as collateral, led him to found *Ebony* (1945), *Tan* (1950), and *Jet* (1951). *Ebony*'s first issue, launched with nary a subscriber as an oversized monthly of "Negro news and pictures," had by 1966 reached a circulation of close to a million.[472] One of Johnson's main obstacles, after having overcome so many to have *Ebony* published at all, was finding advertisers for the magazine. Even after *Ebony* reached a staggering circulation of 400,000, Johnson still struggled to attract advertisers; the ambitious editor wanted the big four-color ads "that were the staple of white magazines" rather than the inferior black and white small-scale ads typical of black publications.[473] Johnson shares several anecdotes in his autobiography—in a paternal "you can too" guise—of how he was able to reach the offices of a significant number of CEOs and finally convince them to advertise.

As editor of *Ebony*, black middle-class America's premier magazine, Johnson played an instrumental role in shaping his readership into a lucrative marketing demographic. One of his broader-range strategies involved a two-pronged operation to convince white corporations of the size and profitability of the Negro market and, ultimately, to teach them how to cater to this market. Publishing in the early 1950s, Johnson spearheaded a burgeoning industry of market consultants involved in a similar venture. Johnson's goal was clear: "To increase the profits of corporate America and, incidentally, the profits of Johnson Publishing Company, we have to change the perceptions of corporate America."[474] By 1967 *Ebony* had the lion's share of the annual $8 million spent on black-oriented magazine advertising.[475]

The strength of the African American market and the community's positive response to respectful advertising had been demonstrated as early as the mid-1930s. The Kellogg Company was among the first U.S. food corporations to pursue this market by broadly advertising Cornflakes in a nonderogatory manner in the black press.[476] This invitation to consume must have been powerfully compelling to a group of people that had been so violently disregarded. As historian Grace Elizabeth Hale shows, in the early century Southern segregation enforced systems of consumption that involved brutally suppressing the "uppity" Negro who emulated the white middle class in part by selling only poor quality goods to blacks.[477] Thus, even wealthy blacks could not access goods and other signifiers of their class, and when they could they found that the symbols of oppression went far beyond second-class service and goods. They were met at the country store with not only staggeringly racist advertising and product labels but also sales counters stocked with souvenirs of the latest lynching, including postcards of the event and victims' severed fingers and toes.

Northern and Southern blacks relied on brand-name products, as they became available, to avoid discriminations such as short weights and poor quality goods. Similarly, the growth of supermarkets and standardized services such as self-serve and mechanized checkouts saved the black shopper from continually being bumped to the back of the line.[478] Nevertheless, the elementary tutorials offered by Johnson and others indicate the egregious baseline of advertisers' racism. He began with such rudiments as: "Don't exaggerate Negro characters, with flat noses, thick lips, kinky hair, and owl eyes. . . . Always avoid the word 'Pickaninny,' or lampooning illustrations of Negro children. They are as dear to their parents as are other children, irrespective of race."[479] The secondary effects of racism also needed to be spelled out: "Don't set up contest prizes that a Negro winner could not enjoy, such as a free trip to Miami Beach, or a new suburban house in an area where the Negro might not want to live."[480] Changing the perceptions of corporate America meant nothing less than refiguring popular representations of race in the media, and the latter required a drastic change of race perception.

For example, in trying to off-load their racist practices, many corporations claimed that integration in advertising would offend a large portion of the white market, which was ten times larger than the African American market. African American market advisors took several tactics in addressing this concern. One response was to emphasize the sheer size of the market. By the mid-1960s, market researchers were tracking the income levels and spending habits of this demographic, claiming that "Negroes, as a group, represent a purchasing power of around $20 billion, approximately as large as the markets of Belgium, Sweden, Denmark, and Norway combined."[481] Size by population was not in itself the crucial factor, so attempts were also made to diminish the notion that African Americans were poor. Johnson, for example, commissioned a survey on the brand preferences of black families to discredit the "general assumption that this is simply a market for low cost goods."[482]

Other advisors tried to put a positive spin on the particular experiences of African Americans. One claimed that hired domestics "exert a direct influence on the purchase of several commodities in the home."[483] Johnson focused on the fact that some African Americans had "become acquainted with expensive merchandise through working with wealthy white people—as butlers, valets, maids, housekeepers."[484] Inequities were recast as marketing opportunities: since African Americans had far less access to recreation and housing, it was argued that they tended to spend their money on commodities, thus matching and exceeding white disposable income in several categories. The categories most often mentioned concerned "looks" and "prestige items," such as scotch. This questionable analysis is typical of the marketing literature of this period, with claims such as, "The Negro . . . will spend much more money on food, clothing, appliances, automobiles, and other items in order to help overcome his insecurity neurosis. The result has been that Negro standards of living in many categories of goods are a match to white standards."[485] The "insecurity neurosis" and "inferiority complexes"[486] that African Americans purportedly suffered provided an opportunity for advertisers to offer what Jackson Lears has since called the "therapeutic ethos" of consumption.[487]

Other consultants studied the ways that race exceeded the problems of class and the accessibility of products. For example, African American sociologist Henry Allen Bullock's 1961 two-part study in the *Harvard Business Review* was based on a survey of nearly two thousand people and in-depth interviews with a further three hundred. Bullock's most interesting data have to do with blacks' and whites' approaches to consumer choices, which detail varying moral codes of consumption. Consider the example of credit: to justify its use, black people "felt obliged to display an elaborate system of rationalization." For whites, credit tended to be used more liberally for products that they wanted rather than "needed."[488] Overall, whites tended to be more accepting and even envious of higher consumption levels, whereas blacks held a more traditionally Protestant view of consumption above and beyond financial liberty. In considering air conditioners, for example, a white person said, "They [owners] are spoiled, but I think it's wonderful. I wish I could afford to do it."[489] African Americans tended to feel that air conditioning was an unnecessary luxury. These examples suggest a different approach to class privilege and consumerism that goes beyond a simple ability to buy more; they indicate the ways in which class transformation also required a resocialization about consumption and entitlement.[490] In his 1963 study of advertising in *Ebony* and *Life*, Dave Berkman noted this ambivalence between race and class in consumer decisions in a slightly different way. He concluded that what the black man "does want is to be a middle-class Negro; but for right now, and for as long as the two are, to a large degree, essentially contradictions in terms, he will find most appealing those items whose consumption most clearly say 'white'—but only because they also say 'middle-class.' "[491]

Class, race, desegregation, and entitlement tied in with consumptive behaviors and aspirations in complicated ways. Likewise, motives for altering corporate racism surely ranged from racial integration to career trajectories and personal gain, though certainly many white and African American market consultants genuinely believed in the integrity of their work. One 1961 article claims, "Children, for example, do hear and learn the advertising message. They, too, are destinators [*sic*]. What kind of people they become is determined, at least in part, by the tonal quality of the advertisers' message. When sellers turn communicators, they inevitably become educators."[492] Another African American consultant wrote, "As the Negro becomes freer, he becomes more race conscious. There would be no Negro market in the United States if it weren't for the racial tension."[493] This evidence suggests that consultants believed that the eradication of racism in marketing and advertising would redress the vicious racism of the early century.

The work, however, was not universally celebrated as progressive. Sociologist E. Franklin Frazier cited statistics in his 1957 study of the "black bourgeoisie" indicating that by 1938 blacks already spent about 90 percent of their incomes in white-owned businesses.[494] Frazier wrote that "the myth that Negroes were spending $15 billion in 1951 [nearly three times what could be demonstrated using available statistics] was widely circulated by Whites as well as Negroes in the U.S. and whet the appetites of the black bourgeoisie, both Negro businessmen and

Negroes employed by American corporations in their efforts to reap benefits from the increased earnings of Negroes."[495] Indeed, the broadcast advertising trade journal *Sponsor* reported that "[t]he growing awareness that understanding is the key to effective advertising has created a boom for 15 or 20 Negro public relations firms. Billings for D. Parke Gibson, for example, are up 40 percent over a year ago."[496] It is not at all clear that target marketing brought more money overall to white companies, though it seems to have provided (limited) job opportunities for black consultants and magazine editors. Frazier argues that this misrepresentation of the size of the market served a tripartite purpose. First, it gave an exaggerated sense of worth to bourgeois blacks; second, it strengthened the false notion that the accumulation of wealth could solve African Americans' problems; and third, it presented integration as a possibility for African Americans (an idea he disagreed with).

The differing stakes in corporate capitalism and desegregation in employment, advertising, and selling can be seen in Johnson's outspoken opposition to a Christmas boycott that had been suggested by James Baldwin, Louis Lomax, and Ossie Davis in the wake of the 1963 Birmingham church bombing.[497] Yet despite Johnson's unwillingness to risk antagonizing wealthy corporate sponsors, once companies accepted the importance of black consumers they recognized that civil rights concerns affected consumption patterns. One article, describing black women's purchasing habits, reports, "Further, she is militant in her pursuit of economic and civil rights, and will cross off her shopping list the name of any company she believes or suspects practices discrimination."[498] By 1964 when this article appeared, companies had had ample opportunity to experience the effects of boycotts; the previous year *Advertising Age* had puzzled over the fine lines among placating, fearing, and bribing angry black boycotters.[499]

Some corporations were willing to capitulate, at least rhetorically, to some civil rights demands. After the lunch counter boycotts in 1963, for example, Woolworth's decided to "really get a very strong, positive program—one which includes employment opportunities and perhaps scholarships—to overcome the bad reputation it acquired."[500] Other corporations, such as Greyhound, acted on African American marketing advice and installed a "total marketing" approach that included hiring black executives and drivers and picturing whites and blacks seated together in commercials.[501] On the other hand, companies were also quick to co-opt black culture by, for example, making short films depicting "the Negro in education, entertainment, agriculture, national affairs, and medicine," and illustrating ads with cultural icons such as jazz bands, sports idols, and civil rights activists. One remarkable

Advertising Age article, "L&M Cigarettes Pitched to Blacks as 'Superbad,'" served as a glossary of advertising's black-targeted lexicon. It describes a Liggett and Myers campaign for its overwhelmingly white readership: "'Super bad' actually means especially good or super excellent in the current black lexicon."

The stakes in systematic racism for cigarette companies were few. Thus, cigarette companies (unlike housing developers, for example)[502] were free to interpellate people of any race, class, or gender without fearing the loss of their other customers, and this liberty enabled them to ally themselves with any cause—from Billie Jean King's demand for an equal tennis purse for women to desegregation. Cigarette companies were on the leading edge of post–World War II segmented marketing; one of the first four advertisements that graced the pages of *Ebony* promoted Chesterfield cigarettes. This brand had already been advertising in target presses to Jews and Germans earlier in the century, and starting in the early 1950s Chesterfield's ads featured black models in black magazines and white models in white magazines, often with the same copy. Despite the seemingly progressive race thinking of tobacco companies, the advertising did not come without costs on several levels. First, quantitative evidence has suggested that targeted cigarette advertising can be linked to increased smoking in the targeted group[503] and tobacco documents have linked the high sales of Kools in the 1960s to the high nicotine and sugar content of the cigarette. The number of African American smokers increased significantly between 1955 and the mid-1960s, with the result that lung cancer, which accounts for 25 percent of all cancer cases in black males, increased 220 percent between 1950 and 1985.[504] Studies have shown that advertising works best for uneducated and underprivileged groups, and *Brown* cites studies showing that African Americans have been more inclined to accept advertisers' claims.

It is no secret that tobacco companies have been tireless in their tentacular struggle to hide tobacco's effect on the public health. This now well-documented united front included scientific obfuscation on a mass scale, tireless political campaigning, and the suppression of information. For example, in 1952 the advertisement-free *Reader's Digest*, the nation's then largest circulating magazine, had published the first widely read popular article on the health effects of smoking, bringing information on the health risks long known in medical communities to the general public. But the independent magazine underestimated the tobacco industry's power. During this period, American Tobacco and *Reader's Digest* shared the same ad agency, Batten, Barton, Durstine and Osborn. In 1957 American Tobacco's public relations employee J. T. Ross pressured Batten, Barton, Durstine and Osborn to drop the magazine's advertising account. Since American Tobacco billed about $30 million annually, compared to *Reader's Digest*'s $2 million, the agency dropped *Reader's Digest*.[505] This action is just one example of hundreds where tobacco corporations have stultified the press by any means necessary. *Ebony* has received a steady 10 percent of its ad revenue from cigarettes since 1947 and as many as one in three color advertisements in some issues is for cigarettes. Quantitative sociological studies find that "in its more than 40-year history, [*Ebony*] has never published a major article on the leading cause of death among Black Americans: tobacco,"[506] even as it has marked the deaths of celebrities, such as Nat King Cole, who died from smoking-related illness.

Magazine content studies also demonstrate a shift in the focus of marketing demographics as the health effects of smoking emerged in the popular consciousness. Richard Pollay's studies of *Ebony* and *Life* magazines show a steady increase in the percentage of cigarette advertising in *Ebony*. In 1950, there were sixteen ads for cigarettes in *Ebony* compared to thirty-one in *Life*, whereas in 1962, these figures were respectively fifty-seven and twenty-eight. During this period the dangers of smoking were becoming more widely recognized. Filter tips were now available, though they were marketed primarily to white consumers and were not advertised in black magazines.[507] As whites were quitting, companies were becoming more conscious about attracting niche groups and young smokers.

It may be true, as Thomas Laqueur argues, that "addiction is not only an attachment to a substance, it is also an attachment to a passion of great spiritual and cultural thickness."[508] But the terms of that cultural thickness are complicated and neither homogenous nor simple. Clearly, discrimination pervaded the rise of U.S. consumerism in the 1950s and 1960s. Key tensions arose in this period of intensifying popular and corporate activity that influenced the most prominent images in American culture—advertisements—to finally include groups of minority people in seemingly respectful ways. These embodied promises of the contemporary civil rights struggles—for education, jobs, and housing—not only through the fantasies that they portrayed but also through the economic channels of supporting African American market consultants, publishers, magazines, models, and writers.

Tracing a few of the many actors and institutions on the supply side of the cigarette equation in the 1950s and 1960s leads to an understanding of how a multitude of social and physical injuries constituted blackness—race—in no simple way and through many struggles. The agentive moments of advertisers, consultants, editors, consumers, and commentators were as many as they were complicated, and, through these, a group called African Americans was identified in various and contradictory ways. Equality in advertising posed a way out of racist imagery and opportunities for respectable and lucrative jobs. Simultaneously, a movement that defined liberation in terms of cultural expression rose to challenge a model of freedom based in the consumption of sundry Americana. Among these spectra, as with other subcultures, groups of African Americans embraced the cigarette as a mode of expression, and tobacco companies seemed to know exactly how to guide this process.

Another commodity might have faded into a background of capitalist consumption. But the cigarette became a key actor in the making of blackness through its aggressive and explicit exertion of itself. This power to harm enrolled the industry in the defense of the cigarette, at first by disavowing its dangers altogether and then in *Brown* by claiming that it injures without discrimination. The cigarette's power to harm also led individual smokers to understand and inhabit injured bodies in complicated ways, one of which was to identify as an injured litigant and register a rights claim through law. Law was interpellated by these rights-claiming plaintiffs to arbitrate a new set of subjects (subjects that have been effected through the cigarette and its consolidating infrastructures) that the law will further secure. Law, then, rather than consumption, promises a new version of full citizenship.

Back to *Brown*

Brown, as a claim about racism in product distribution, allows us a particularly unique insight into how inequalities are constructed through products, law, and capital. My claim is not that products, the state, or businesses are in themselves racist but that terms such as racism and injury circulate in ways that both make visible and obscure structural inequalities that lead to physical injury. For if blackness is not only constituted but made meaningful through multiple sites of social and physical injury, how can a right not to be injured (and to be compensated) for a specific injury be claimed from that place—race—defined by a preceding injury, whether we take the preceding injury to be lodged in vulnerability to advertising, disenfranchisement from medical advice, or susceptibility to white violence?

The *Brown* claim can be read as an attempt to expand an essentially product liability law claim into a race-recognized context. Stripped to its bare bones, the complaint would read something like this: "We were injured by this product not only because it is dangerous, but because we—as a disenfranchised group (already considered a less than human group), were sold a version of the product that was designed to be both more addictive and more carcinogenic. We have suffered a great deal for this and we want you (the state) to stop allowing this to happen." This way of formulating the issue turned out to be remarkably easy to dismiss. As one of the three appellate court judges, Maryanne Trump Berry, said, "I have a very basic question about how encouraging the sale or even the preference for a legal product is intentional discrimination on the ground of race."[509] So, from a contractual perspective, if a product is legally available for purchase, how can a line be drawn around who gets to be the buyer? In other words, how does a group make a legible claim through stabilizing the meaningful and cross-secting semiotics of "race" and "injury"?

In a way, it is precisely since the law is not racist in understanding African Americans as fully sovereign contractual subjects that it addresses the complicated issues raised by *Brown* solely as contractual issues (menthols were offered to whites and blacks for the same price) with very particular sites of potential blame (tobacco corporations). But this formulation renders it unable to recognize—much less compensate—the race-based injuries and their multiple and nefarious physical and social expressions. Civil rights law holds an unfulfilled promise of linking social and physical injuries by going beyond an industry-smoker dialectic in which a liberal chooser-smoker later turns to a legal logic of a potentially repairable harm to gain compensation for a warrantable injury. But terms of difference, such as race, cannot be added to the contractual formulations implied by product liability legal frameworks. Race is integral to the form of the injury itself, just as all kinds of differences are always already present in human and nonhuman relations.

The background to this case exposes that race cannot be considered as an object or category with albeit contingent contents but needs to be traced as a process itself—and in that process, *Brown* is a key element. The consolidation of "race" in *Brown* clearly poses a strategy to make visible the ways that targeting had occurred. The dissenting opinion in the appeal offers a language to understand how civil rights law might have accepted this claim. Judge Shadur wrote, "[T]he reality of racial prejudice has unfortunately long outlived the reality of theory embodied in those [nineteenth-century] statutes." The statutes mandate "an equal playing field that is violated by conduct that imposes different and race-discriminatory conditions (however created) on the exercise of seemingly comparable contractual rights." He considered the deliberate and persuasive targeting as an impairment of the equality of rights, noting particularly that the chances would be only 1.28 in a trillion of such a high proportion of blacks choosing menthols compared to such a low proportion of whites.[510]

But *Brown*'s expressed contention was not only that cigarettes had been targeted to African Americans but that a more dangerous cigarette had been target marketed at them. The statistics on race and smoking I offered earlier are startling, but it is shocking to find that while on average African Americans attempt to quit more often than white Americans do, studies have shown their success rate is 34 percent lower than that of whites. A strong case exists that Kool and other mentholated brands were among the most dangerous cigarettes. By the 1960s, tobacco companies understood the cigarette as a drug delivery device, monitoring and managing the quantity of nicotine in the product. In one case, B&W's legal counsel issued a challenge to the charges of the surgeon general that cigarette smoking is extremely dangerous when he advised developing a cigarette that would remove the "unattractive side effects of smoking [that is, cancer]" and still deliver "a nice jolt of nicotine."[511] A Philip Morris (PM) scientist, Al Udow, contended in 1972 that Kool had the highest nicotine delivery of any king-size cigarette on the market. Udow wrote that this was its secret to success and recommended that PM also "pursue this . . . in developing a menthol entry."[512]

After initially denying that it bred plants for specific nicotine levels (and therefore understood the drug delivery nature of the cigarette), B&W admitted in 1994 that it had developed and imported (from Brazil) a tobacco plant that contained twice the amount of nicotine that was in regular American tobaccos.[513] Furthermore, recent studies suggest that menthol smokers have greater addiction rates because of the anesthetic and other physiological effects of menthol. Thus, African Americans, who tend to smoke menthols, would be more at risk, though they average fewer cigarettes (fifteen versus nineteen) per day. These facts on design predict a higher level of addiction for smokers of menthols, particularly B&W's Kool brand, than for smokers of other cigarettes.

Not to take away from the obvious dangers of mentholated cigarettes, medical researchers have presented varying reasons for the seemingly greater injuries suffered by African American smokers. For example, studies show that minority smokers are both less likely to participate in potentially expensive smoking cessation programs than is the general population and less likely to receive cessation advice from health care providers.[514] Other studies suggest that African Americans metabolize carcinogens and nicotine more slowly than white Americans do.[515] The class- and race-based explanations are at odds with the focus specifically on cigarette design and point to a broader corroborative effect that results in injury while they suggest a potential complication in bringing a "clean" case of proximate cause.

This difficulty hints at the deeper structural problems that *Brown* encountered. Claiming a right from the state conceals the ways in which African Americans were produced as a racialized group through the interacting forces of corporations, marketers, activists, and governments—and furthermore, how they are produced through the making of the claim. In a different context, Wendy Brown argues that developing "a righteous critique of power from the perspective of the injured . . . delimits a specific site of blame for suffering by constituting sovereign subjects and events as responsible for the 'injury' of social subordination." Such claims, she contends, cast "the law in particular and the state more generally as neutral arbiters of injury rather than as themselves invested with the power to injure."[516] Brown's point enables us to unpack several densely layered points here, given the multiple factors of education, medical access, targeting, and class that influence smoking practice. The heart of the issue here is that cigarettes are only legal—in virtually any articulation of product liability law—in their designed-commodity-product form because of intense industry and state collaboration since the 1950s. The simple fact is that when the health effects of smoking emerged in the 1950s, very few state actors took a stand against cigarettes, while many aggressively lobbied to have them separated from the grids that regulated other consumer products. Thus, tobacco companies have been able to successfully plead that the congressional intent has been to preempt them from civil injury claims.

The issues raised in *Brown* both reflect consumer culture more generally and zero in on the specificity of the cigarette. The *Brown* court could interrogate neither the nature of the product nor the contents of the choice (rather than the act of choosing). But beyond that, the claims in *Brown* extend so far beyond the specific dangers of menthol it is hard to know where they would end. The so-called rights that the group might claim, if they could, surely would include the right to equal access to education about products that are not advertised directly to them and the consequences of which are not written about in their magazines. It would include the "right" not to have inner-city African American communities plastered with billboard advertisements for alcohol and tobacco products. It would include the "right" to medical resources and access to research on smoking behavior and cessation that has "been conducted almost exclusively in white, middle-class populations."[517] It would include the recognition that a genetic pool as diverse as that which has been socially consolidated as "African American" presents serious difficulties to race-based genetic research, as biologists such as Joseph Graves and Stephen Jay Gould have shown.[518] All of these factors funneled the enhanced dangers of smoking toward

African Americans, and through them, an injured and racialized class was produced.

But even the analytic of making a claim breaks down as it carries further down the path of racial discrimination in tobacco use. For there might also be a right to have the cultural respect and self-esteem to not have started smoking in the first place. And then we have come full circle to three irresolvable aspects of the case. First, the basic fact remains that cigarettes seriously injure and kill people, and all kinds of people, and the state has corroborated for decades in these injuries. In the context of racialized injury, the dissenting appellate judge Milton Shadur pointed out that "it just will not do for the tobacco companies to argue that they are somehow equal opportunity deceivers—that they have betrayed Whites and Blacks alike by their deception."[519]

Second, African Americans were undeniably vulnerable (though perhaps no more vulnerable than other overlapping niche groups such as teens and women) throughout the 1950s and 1960s.[520] The complexity of the social and physical injuries neither started nor ended with cigarette design, targeting, lack of access to medical resources, or poverty. Third, the claims of enfranchisement for legal equality necessitate cultural or social equality, and yet these have to be made from a seemingly bad faith position. They have to be made from a position that claims an injured subjectivity and buys into a promise of repairable harm—one that can only be the flip side of the proposed liberal subject that "decided" to smoke in the first place.

Put most simply, I am developing two linked arguments. First, making rights claims, specifically the right to consume on an equal basis and the right not to be injured in consumption, blots out an understanding of the ways that commodities, such as cigarettes, circulate in economies to constitute human relations. The cause of physical injuries, particularly those based in multiple relations of subordination, simply cannot be traced solely to relations among (aberrant) corporations, a (neutral) government, and (sovereign) choosers. These adjectives will always already misread the power dynamics of consumer culture: that corporations are answerable to stockholders and therefore require smokers (drinkers, overeaters, drivers); that governments have their own investments in injury production that range from allowing dangerous products to exist and making "exceptions" for them (such as the case was with cigarettes); and that consumers make choices within contexts beyond their ken, or knowingly against their own and others' health.

Second, among agentive moments separated by time (consumer, litigant, juridical subject), race is mutually produced through the actions of humans and nonhumans, from advertisements to models, from advertising companies to civil rights claims, from nicotine to cancer. These mutual productions make the process of selecting a compensable point of injured status difficult indeed, as the failure of *Brown* demonstrates. This is precisely the anthropological point, and the one that has been relentlessly overlooked by the moralism that has tended to pervade both the pro- and anti-smoking debates. Whose injuries will count, and for what, in American injury culture? An alternative way to put this point would be by noting that, rather as Pasteur and his mold were mutually constituting, race and injury (as parallel but not equivalent to organism and the chemical compound of "smoke") were mutually constituted through a series of institutions that included corporations, magazine publication, and law. Within that, injury is a contingent category: at one point harnessed to imagine a new market as injury provided the impetus for the white middle classes to quit smoking, at another to write studies on nicotine metabilization, and at yet another, to make a legal claim. The cigarette floats as a collection of paper, tobacco, and other additives until its meaning is fixed by a social collective as cool, tacky, or dangerous. Product design can funnel these meanings through things like the use of menthol and high-nicotine tobaccos, but it cannot determine them.[521] Injury (the physical injury of cancer, the social injury of race) is about aligning these categories—this vast biological, legal, and technical collective—such that blame can be attributed. Thus, injury is not ultimately about the way that smoke destroys the organism or blackness creates the conditions for subordination. The liberal promise of reparable harm held so dearly in injury law maintains an integrity of the notion of "harm" and the value of "health," even as in practice it remains unattainable.

The continuing fascination with the cigarette lies precisely in the way it has so completely flaunted any question of responsibility or accountability to anything but itself. In that sense at least, the twentieth-century history of this product demonstrates that the cigarette has been a true American icon.

Conclusion

RUSSELL BANKS'S NOVEL *The Sweet Hereafter* begins when a school bus veers off a wintry road in upstate New York, killing most of the children in the community. The story of the crash and the aftermath is told in turns through the narration of four community members: the bus driver, Delores Driscoll; the father of two of the killed children, Billy Ansel; the attorney who flies from New York City and seeks to make a class-action tort claim, Mitchell Stephens; and a fourteen-year-old girl who has been paralyzed by the accident, Nichole Burnell. The complex narrative weaves themes of fatherhood, sexuality, memory, and mourning in a text that glitters with the violence of accidental loss.

If read through the role of the potential lawsuit and through Stephens's attempts to sign on clients and the communities' varied understandings and resistances to both Stephens and the suit, *The Sweet Hereafter* presents the complicated relations of social powers that consolidate around the suit as nearly a physical agent. While it would not be possible to miss the fact of the lawsuit in the novel, one might overlook the organizing effect it has in the post-accident community—its centrality in choreographing how the accident and the community members are understood by one another. Similarly, *Injury* has been written to better understand how the mechanisms of injury law and the cases that are brought before it shed light on what human wounding means. Law is only one of a number of complicated social powers that attempt to recognize wounding, but it centrally structures how accidents, product design, behaviors, safety, and progress are apprehended and valued.

An American audience immediately recognizes *The Sweet Hereafter*'s Mitchell Stephens, Esq. The lawyer describes his own stakes in the suit with a leftist masculine hunting fantasy trope. In describing the tribe of plaintiffs' lawyers, he says, "we're permanently pissed off, . . . and practicing law is a way to be socially useful at the same time. . . . [T]he real satisfaction, the true motivation, is the carnage and the smoldering aftermath and the trophy heads that get hung up on the den wall. I love it."[522] This characterization reverberates through both nonfiction and fictional accounts of injury law such as in the films *Class Action* (1991) and *A Civil Action* (1998), as well as through "real" TV, such as *Primetime* and *60 Minutes*. Indeed, law professor Richard Abel writes that "litigation is an important form of political activity: courts exercise political authority, modify substantive laws, and allocate resources. Litigation also affects the economy, conveys information, alters prices, and corrects market imperfections."[523] The potent character of the plaintiff's lawyer offers a political fusion of the moralistic, die-hard, and righteous.

   Complicated sets of interests in the lawsuit surface in the narrative, all of which need to be translated by Stephens into the language of the suit. For example, Stephens has to convert Mrs. Otto's desire for someone to "go to prison . . . and die there" into a desire for a kind of "punishment" that a civil payment could bring. Other parents carry unrelated debts and simply need money. For them, the suit is a convenience and a potential jackpot. Billy Ansel, a man who lost his wife to cancer a year prior, has carried a rage that cannot be converted to the terms of lawsuit. He offers to pay Nichole's hospital bills if her parents will drop it. While her parents do not drop it, the suit fizzles when Nichole, who had been sitting in the front seat of the bus, claims in a deposition that Delores, the bus driver, had been speeding. Nichole's own intentions are clearly to end the suit in an effort to both get back at and get back a father who had molested her before the accident. Through her teenage eyes, the suit refracts greedy parents trying to make good on a now defunct daughter: "I sat there for a minute, looking at my dumb worthless legs reflected in the window glass. They looked like they belonged to someone else. How much had they been worth a year ago, I wondered, or last fall. . . ? And to *whom*? That was the real question. To me, my legs were worth everything then and nothing now. But to Mom and Daddy, nothing then and a couple of million dollars now."[524] The candor of this statement, even in its slippages and stereotypical naiveté, captures the shifting import of worth, money, the material expense of disability, and the ease of ability.

   In derailing the suit, Nichole guilelessly tries to confirm that Delores will not be blamed for the accident as a result of her testimony—but the blame heaves through promises made to this disabled girl. A year later, after months of isolation, a Delores unaware of Nichole's testimony and the community's reproach attends the county fair. While Delores meets the hostile stares of other fairgoers, the crowds in the stadium cheer as Nichole enters. When asked by a stranger about why the crowds applauded Nichole, Delores thinks:

> It was a hard question for anyone to answer. Part of it, I knew, was that Nichole Burnell had survived the accident and had suffered terrible loss, loss made visible by the wheelchair, and . . . after many months away from us, she was at last returning to us, returning in a kind of triumph. Part of it

was that she was a beautiful young girl purified by her injury. . . . And part of it, I also knew, was me, Delores Driscoll. . . . If they could not forgive me, they could at least celebrate Nichole, and then maybe they would not feel so bad that I too, was one of them.[525]

I read this statement as one of a heartbreaking complexity of events that attenuate experience, despair, and community to the miserly terms of blame. What if Delores *had* been speeding (as Nichole claimed)? In Delores's own description of the accident she speaks of the necessity to travel fast at a place in the road where "the greatest danger was that I would be going too slow and a lumber truck or some idiot in a car would come barreling along at seventy-five or eighty, which you can easily do up there, once you've made the crest from the other side, and would come up on me fast and not be able to slow or pass and would run smack into me. . . . As a result, . . . I tended to drive that stretch of road at a pretty good clip."[526] How can her knowledge derived from twenty years of driving that mile compare to a nearly arbitrary posting of a state mandated speed limit? Why does the latter become the legal gauge in arbitrating blame?[527]

Delores's statement testifies to the way that blame circulates, always resting at a place where it can find its opposite: something to be blamed, and in blaming, to be othered. In this case, since the deposition found no other resting place, Delores became the outlet. And isolating blame is one way to make despair manageable; plucking at only a few faulty threads of a social fabric, the strategy leaves a certain integrity to the whole. Blame offers perhaps the easiest recourse. As Mary Ann Doane wrote in a different context, "The catastrophe, insofar as it is perceived as the accidental failure of technology (and one which can be rectified with a little tinkering), does not touch the system of commodity capitalism."[528] Tort law offers a tinkering mechanism.

It is not my goal here to speculate on which came first, the desire to isolate cause and blame or the structure of tort law that depends on that isolation. Billy Ansel puts it this way: "Who can we blame? Naturally, the lawyers fed off this need and cultivated it among people who should have known better."[529] Oliver Wendell Holmes traced the earliest instances of tort liability to "vengeance, not compensation, and vengeance on the offending thing."[530] Whether or not vengeance against objects strictly characterizes the early history of tort, product liability clearly revels in—as it requires—this purity. Product liability's mode narrows the focus of complicated accidents: did speed, drunkenness, seatbelts, faulty brakes, or highway design cause the given injury, and from there, was the driver, the bartender, the regulatory body, car manufacturer, or the highway engineer responsible?[531] Wherever fault tends to be located will have whole different sets of regulatory ramifications: pedestrian injuries in parking lots consistently traced to lot design rather than the bumper height of the striking vehicle will have everything to do with how future injuries register, continuing the momentum initiated by an initial complaint that selected the most legible way of citing blame. The legal method of stare decisis embeds this tendency.

Elaine Scarry has described the work of the trial as one in which the world is remade or in which intelligibility is recovered. She writes, "In the generic plot of a liability trial, the world has slipped from the ordinary to the extraordinary by the short path of a passive and unfathomable slippage that is resurrected into recoverable intelligibility by being subdivided into a sequence of discrete actions." By isolating and locating the slippage, the product liability trial can remake the world to resemble one in which the slippage did not occur. She writes that the trial in some sense materializes the belief that "the world can exist, usually does exist, should in this instance have existed, and may in this instance be 'remakable' to exist [through the material form of monetary compensation], without such slippage.[532] Recovering intelligibility, as Scarry demonstrates, necessitates specifying a site of actual reversal: the object. She illustrates this through a reading of a product liability trial that involved an odorless gas that ignited in a family kitchen and caused a young child's severe burns. And although the list of events that one can wish had not happened ranges from lighting the stove to the girl's having been in the kitchen, the only real place of restoration is in the communicative potential of the gas itself, which should have carried some warning signal such as smell or color. The "gas" is that which the jury can revisit and restore in the trial. As Scarry concludes, "This is, of course, the most crucial difference between the 'unifying plot action' of a play and the 'unifying plot action' of the trial. The action of the first is complete and cannot be altered; its audience must passively bear it. The action of the trial is incomplete and can be mimetically altered; its audience, the jury, is empowered to in some sense reverse it, and it is only because this possibility exists that the story is being retold."[533] Thus the community's varied stakes in the potential trial of *The Sweet Hereafter* concentrate in the promise of a site of reversal for the accident.

But *The Sweet Hereafter* offers as many sites for that reversal as potential plaintiffs. The nobility of the jury's potential to reverse events flips against the plaintiffs' churlish greed and insidious moralism. The suit itself acts in the open wound of the community. Thus, even as the law offered only a marginal, rudimentary mode of understanding the tragedy, it became the structuring principle of the community members' relations in the aftermath. In the same way as one could miss the organizing effect of law in the novel, the constitutive cultural role of injury in the understanding of human wounding in the United States has been overlooked.

Injury premises that the ubiquitous presence of personal injury claims in the United States can be analyzed as a social and material crystallization of alliances and contradictions among social and physical injuries, consumption and inequality, and economic and public health. The legal moment is a stabilizing one; it offers a place where interests are articulated and archived, objects are translated and stabilized. Within the legal moment, injury is a boundary term: contestations abound as to what will count as injury and how injury will be stabilized as a concept. When we cease to look at the law in isolation but rather put it into a history of present relations between persons and things, the social relations that make a set of arguments possible and sensical at a particular moment can expose how the material world and the politics of design harbor, even necessitate, inequality.[534] The question of how human wounding will matter in a political economy is a foundational one, and in the United States one that is difficult to grasp. This slipperiness is evident even between the legal meaning of injury, as meaning an infraction of property, and the vernacular use of the term as an everyday or serious hurt.

Despite the centrality of injury to everyday life, the law is ill-equipped to handle its crucial socioeconomic challenges. As the foregoing chapters have demonstrated, the law is far from an ideal public sphere where everyone comes with complaints and openly debates problems of health, injury, and design. These wider situations of injuries are usually left unspoken in the struggle to limit the specificities of injury causation. In that sense, *Injury* has presented an analysis of the ways that injury laws constitute the terms for understanding human wounding in the United States and continually reset the terms of its acceptability. I have argued that they narrow our modes of apprehension of what counts as injury, they divert attention away from other ways of understanding injury, and they miss the cultural implications of objects and the ways that objects are situated in networks of power. Understanding human unhealth in these narrow ways is a cultural phenomenon unique to the United States, given added cultural energy and centrality by the enormous expense of medical services—nearly ten times as much as any other industrialized nation—and the resulting desperation that parties may undergo after an accident. Injury is central to American citizenship.

Unequally distributed physical injury is a social fact deeply imbricated in the political economy of the United States. Because of this, various scholars and social movements have used injury law as one of a basket of strategies to bring about social justice. In many cases, appeals to law have been successful in bringing attention to cases of negligence and the politics of design. But as a political movement, the submission to law raises a crucial paradox. In American injury culture, the body operates on the one hand as the repository of culture and on the other as the imprimatur of its systems of social valuation. In other words, the body is required in the framework of injury law to precede its injury as "whole," reasonable, and objective even as citizens are made, and inevitably made unequally, through the material world.

Some of these specificities of product design, injury, and injury law fold within Foucault's notion of biopolitics. Foucault distinguished the biopolitical from the juridical functions of law by noting that the biopolitical adjudicates sets of norms that are created and deployed by statistical and actuarial practices. Alain Pottage summarizes the point by stating that "the impact which the norm has upon the 'outside world' is not directly visible to law or administration. The 'outside' world is experienced only as an opaque environment which constantly changes the administration into producing better and more finely adjusted normative programmes."[535] Thus, a biopolitical interpretation of American injury culture suggests that injury law apprehends questions of design only insofar as the normative equations used in the calculation of safety and risk need refocusing. Ford made a poor judgment and needs to recalibrate its equations. These equations may need to place a higher cash value on lives, as the court argued. Or they may simply need to better account for how a jury will react to the sight of a horribly burned young boy. Maybe McDonald's reformatted equations would lead to them to retire Ronald. Or perhaps they need only donate more money to tort reform lobby groups that would work to limit people's ability to sue corporations.

Biopolitically, injury culture teaches its subjects to identify as universal subjects for whom injury is exceptional. From this view, injury is understood as a compensatory state rather than one based in the categories and processes with which design, manufacturing, and marketing are initiated. For injury culture's subjects, compensation is not a trope but a means of recovery, a way to enact a right of citizenship. I have argued that while this denunciatory position has an important political role, analytically the advocacy position tends to obscure the cultural work done not only by injury law but by the material world, which distributes goods and bads (such as risk, health, mobility, and injury) and also naturalizes cross-secting relations of subordination. Thus, this position obviates the ways that norms are relied on by courts such that plaintiffs will have great difficulty in rendering intelligible the ways that product design mutates seemingly innocuous differences such as size, class, gender, mode of transportation, age, a variety of preferences, or class into inequities that carry burdens of risk.

For example, the CRLA's claims were made in the face of decades of assumptions that Mexicans had "the better body for the job." Or, as I analyze in chapter 4, in thinking about target marketing and wounding, a concept of equality was harnessed that claimed that groups were treated differently and thus suffered an increased harm. African Americans claimed that they were targeted for more dangerous cigarettes because they were African American. In the framing of the plaintiffs' argument, it did matter that a group of smokers was black because the product was specifically designed to attract (and harm) African Americans at a time when many white Americans were becoming aware of the dangers of smoking. I argued that the concept of race only makes sense within the circulating semiotics of objects, intentions, differences, and desires. Inequality does not precede or override relations with material objects; rather, that inequality constructs and is constructed by human wounding—a phenomenon that the law constructs as an artifact-body interface that sometimes translates into injury. Thus, one of my key premises has been that inequities presented to and through the law are not simply blind spots; they offer occasions to examine assumptions about subjectivity that sometimes fracture along familiar lines of race or gender, and other times require us to broaden the scope of how products and their capitalist distribution create new kinds of categories of inequity.[536] Certain of these categories will become morally abhorrent at different moments. Drunk driving or lung cancer offers examples of this, but one could imagine other kinds of injuries that could, in theory, join these types of moral insupportability on a broad scale, such as obesity or other cancers.

In this way, this book offers a contribution to the ways we can think about social and material culture and inequity. In another way, the evidence and arguments I have brought together force us down a different investigative route. Oliver Wendell Holmes, at the dawn of modern torts, claimed that the "law of torts abounds in moral phraseology."[537] If this statement seems self-evident, it is worth revisiting the nostalgia for human well-being and flourishing that is at the root of the moral claims in injury law in seeking alternative analytics for understanding human wounding and the material and rhetorical political work it does. This is not the place to launch this whole new inquiry, but to do it would require a better understanding of how an unanalyzed humanism underpins definitions of human sentience, since risk distributions, injuries, wounds, and deaths are good for the economy on many levels.

In the introduction I claimed that tort law can only be understood within an analysis of American injury culture, or the broad swath of injury production in the United States and the way it takes place within a web of economic interests. These range from the mass production of goods that do not fit everyone's bodies to the corporate mandate to elevate private profit over public safety concerns to the measurement of economics that puts costs aside into categories of "externalities." Legal theories that assume costs can be spread will miss the cultural ramifications of the means by which they are spread.

Accidents and human wounding provide a boost to the economy that is astonishingly undertheorized in economic and social theory. Elucidating the issues in this way raises the question of how human wounding counts, who "owns" health, and how it is to count as a social good. Thus, an analysis of injury within the broader context of the unique system of privatized health care and private litigation in the United States demonstrates that injury law can be more radically understood not in terms of who deserves compensation but rather in terms of how discourses of injury and compensation circulate as a rhetorical grounding for American moral economies underpinned by the ideologies of a consumer society. This has consequences for how citizenship carries meaning. A consumer culture by necessity maintains a division between the choosing subject-consumer and the object consumed. But these distinctions between subjects and objects are discursive formations that reproduce material inequity. In the case of injury law, not only do the dynamic complexities of human-artifact exchange continually overflow legal efforts to contain and stabilize them, but the very nature of the reasoning itself will leave beyond its purview the graspability of commonsense objects.

To return to the terms of the "rhetorical effect" of law and the "inequality effect" of material culture that I laid out in chapter 1, injury law does not create a better overall public health through encouraging sociomaterial progress. Rather, the law creates a rhetorical structure to simulate a moral economy in which egregious, and exceptional, corporate takings of human sentience will be understood as having been rectified. This was the logic at work in the *Grimshaw* opinion, which demonstrated the way in which calculations about the worth of life in an economy of scale led to the absurdity of design changes that equaled only a few dollars per car. Similarly, the CRLA was able to outlaw the short hoe but not other kinds of hurtful stoop labor, let alone pesticides and other agricultural practices.

This sits uneasily with the inequality effect of material culture, in which enabling and wounding are subtle, inevitable, and overlapping outcomes of everyday interactions, as examples such as fast food and the ubiquity of car crashes demonstrate. For exercising citizenship, this notion of reparable harm embedded in injury law's understanding and rectification of human wounding leaves few options. The citizen has to trace injury to narrow sets of causation; has to appeal to the states for reparation and thus, at the very least, play along with its posed neutrality; and finally, has to buy in with either the rights model of citizenship or a cynical individualist attempt to get-what-you-can from the system.

Yet consumption is simultaneously enabling *and* wounding; the products available for consumption always assume, encode, and simulate certain kinds of bodies. Part of what renders these relays both acceptable and logical is the basic discursive division between humans and nonhumans. Whether one considers this gap between the representation of the world through legal praxis (as in the "rhetorical effect" of injury law) and the distribution of wounding through material inequality a cultural mistake in need of revision depends on the extent to which one believes that injury law holds any hope for redressing injury, or whether, as I do, one holds that injury law inserts itself as a crucial discourse in rationalizing the distribution of the inevitable and integral costs of commodity culture.

Notes

I would like to acknowledge NSF grant number 22025–442612–HCDH: "Any opinions, findings, and conclusions or recommendations expressed in this material are those of the author(s) and do not necessarily reflect the views of the National Science Foundation."

1. The cartoon refers to a well-publicized lawsuit brought against McDonald's fast food restaurants by a group of overweight African American teenagers in late 2003 that was dismissed without a hearing in 2004. The plaintiffs claimed, in *Pelman*, that they had been misled as to the nutritional value of McDonald's food and had suffered the injury of obesity. In that sense the suit gave voice to the frustrations experienced by subjects of an economy that gains strength through tempting its citizens with unhealthy, cheap, and ubiquitous foods. *Pelman v. McDonald's Corporation*, 237 F. Supp. 2d 512; 2003 U.S. Dist. LEXIS 707, pp. 534–537. See also Roger Parloff, "Is Fat the Next Tobacco?" *Fortune*, Feb. 3, 2003, pp. 51–70. I discuss this issue further in chapter 1.

2. This representation of the litigious African American refers to *Pelman*. However, as legal anthropologists have well noted, communities in the United States have vastly different views of and engagement with American law.

3. Jeffrey Meikle, for example, writes of the domestication of plastic bags though massive advertising drives in the 1950s. When plastic dry cleaning bags were introduced in 1956, they were touted by Du Pont as being reusable. By 1959, after nearly one hundred children had died of suffocation and nearly twenty adults had adopted them for suicide, the industry blamed ignorant parents for keeping plastic bags (which they now claimed were disposable) within reach of children. Meikle reports that the contemporary press "aimed a barely contained fury at the plastic bags themselves as entities of near demonic malevolence." Meikle suggests that this simple new technology became the rhetorical outlet for more general anxieties about nuclear and industrial culture. Once the bags were rendered fully knowable—through a massive educational campaign by the plastics industry, redesign and standardization of the bag, and printed warnings that still appear—nationwide calls to "ban the bag" were appeased. Meikle, *American Plastic: A Cultural History* (New Brunswick, NJ: Rutgers University Press, 1995), 250–52.)

4. Richard Abel and Laura Nader argue that since studies show that nine out of ten people who become injured do not sue, the law cannot properly function in its role to publicize defective products and more adequately spread costs. They thus advocate more use of these laws. Laura Nader, *The Life of the Law: Anthropological Projects* (Berkeley: University of California Press, 2002), 203; Richard Abel, "The Real Tort Crisis—Too Few Claims," *Ohio State Law Journal* 48 (1997): 443, 447.

5. Peter A. Bell and Jeffrey O'Connell, *Accidental Justice: The Dilemmas of Tort Law* (New Haven: Yale University Press, 1997). See also Marshall S. Shapo, *Tort Law and Culture* (Durham, NC: Carolina Academic Press, 2003).

6. A variety of legal venues negotiate the drama of human wounding, and in the chapters that follow I examine several of them. I generally note these as the legal institutions addressed to the law of personal injury, or "injury law" for shorthand. Chapter by chapter I discuss each institution's relation to the more specific venues of tort and personal injury law; they overlap but do not fully encompass each other.

7. Donna Haraway writes in her chapter titled "A Cyborg Manifesto," "Our best machines are made of sunshine; they are all light and clean because they are nothing but signals, electromagnetic waves, a section of the spectrum, and these machines are eminently portable, mobile—a matter of immense human pain in Detroit and Singapore. People are nowhere near so fluid, being both material and opaque." Haraway, *Simians, Cyborgs, and Women: The Reivention of Nature* (New York: Routledge, 1991), 149–82, quote on p. 153.

8. The popular discourse that injury law has engendered tends to fracture along inherited rhetorics of politically powerful groups, particularly of business interests and of trial lawyers. In a nearly rote formula, corporate interests, generally under a header of "tort reform," employ a rhetoric of "frivolous cases" and "runaway juries" against U.S. individuals and their trial lawyers who believe they "truly have a good case." These sides correspond remarkably well to the two sides of the American political hegemony: the Republicans tend to support and collect lobby funds from the tort reform movement, while the trial lawyers ally themselves with Democrats. The tendency to ridicule the popular conception of lawsuits seems to be too much for anyone to resist. A recent parody published in *Utne* mimicked a company memorandum urging the use of more warnings. These warnings include, for example, "If the product uses an electric cord [*sic*], do not wrap the cord around your neck. Do not chew on the electrical cord." Douglas Jones, "Company Memorandum," *Utne*, Mar.–Apr. 2004, 93.

9. Elizabeth Povinelli, *The Cunning of Recognition: Indigenous Alterities and the Making of Australian Multiculturalism* (Durham: Duke University Press, 2002), 10.

10. The basic facts of the case are as follows: Stella Leibeck, an eighty-two-year-old woman, was severely burned when she opened a cup of coffee a few minutes after purchasing it at a drive-through, while the car was parked, and coffee spilled on her groin area. She suffered third-degree burns, was hospitalized for seven days, and underwent several painful skin grafts. While initially not wanting to launch a lawsuit, she also, as she wrote in a letter to McDonald's Restaurants, thought that "no person would find it reasonable to have been given coffee so hot that it would do the severe damage it did to my skin." (Quote from letter cited in Michael McCann, William Halton, and Anne Bloom, "Java Jive: Genealogy of a Juridical Icon," *Miami Law Review* 56 (2001): 120.) McDonald's offered $800 compensation, and Leibeck hired an attorney. During the trial, evidence was submitted that McDonald's had received about 700 complaints about the temperature of the coffee and resulting burns, and had

settled at least one case for severe coffee burns. A spokeswoman said that in accordance with company policy, coffee is served at 180–190 degrees—substantially hotter than that of home coffeemakers. Agreeing that the coffee was defectively designed and breached the Uniform Commercial Code's warranty of fitness for intended purpose, initially skeptical jurors decided on an award of $2.7 million in punitive damages. Recalling that the intent of a punitive damage award is to "punish" the wrongdoer, they used two days' worth of McDonald's coffee profits ($1.35 million daily) as a basis for setting the award. The judge later reduced this award, which was understood by him as being "excessive, as a matter of law," to $480,000. His rationale was based not in the punitive function of the law but rather as a "trebling of the $160,000 award of compensatory damages."Despite the reduction of the award, this suit was widely reported on and ultimately became the subject of a major tort reform campaign in the mid-1990s. In general, as scholars have detailed, "news coverage of civil tort disputes routinely parallel[ed] in form and substance the simplistic tort takes circulated by tort reformers to assail the explosion of frivolous lawsuits." (McCann, Halton, and Bloom, "Java Jive," 132. The authors make this claim based on a study of the media coverage of tort cases over the last twenty years.) This is not necessarily the result of a conspiracy but because of the manner in which the press tends to simplify narratives in ways that conflate complex problems to simple epithets such as "individual responsibility"; find large awards more spectacular than awards reduced on appeal (and so misrepresent the outcome of cases); misrepresent facts (many papers reported that Leibeck was in a moving vehicle); and simplify complicated legal structures. In this particular case, the misrepresentation in the press became the basis for the (mis)representation of the case in numerous comedy shows and corporate-funded advertising, both for products and as a basis for advertising tort reform. A widely aired radio ad featured this narration: "A jury awarded a woman $2.9 million in a lawsuit against McDonald's Corporation. She spilled coffee on her lap and claimed it was too hot. . . . Every day there is another outrageous lawsuit. Who pays? You do." (Jean Stefanic and Richard Delgado, *No Mercy: How Conservative Think Tanks Changed America's Social Agenda* [Philadelphia: Temple University Press, 1996], 105–6.) The reduction of the award was not mentioned. This typical radio ad gives neither the facts of the case, the truth about the ultimate award, or the details about how and why "we pay." See *Leibeck v. McDonald's Restaurants*, No. CV-93–02419, Sept. 16, 1994. Nevertheless, it is highly effective. Referring to that case, another plaintiff whose baby was killed in a cradle with a simple design flaw claimed, "I'd hate to call the shots on the McDonald's lawsuit. I personally believe there needs to be tort reform out there. But I don't believe [mine] is a frivolous case." (Jeanne Browkaw, "The Hand That Rocks the Cradle," *Mother Jones*, Sept./Oct. 1996, http://www.motherjones.com/news/special_reports/1996/09/chenowith.html.)

11. For an ethnography of the problems and paradoxes Americans face when they take issues to the courts, see Sally Engle Merry, *Getting Justice and Getting Even: Legal Consciousness among Working-Class Americans* (Chicago: University of Chicago Press, 1990). Counter to the stereotypes about litigious Americans, Merry found that "[p]eople hesitate to turn to court unless they

feel that important principles are at stake. The plaintiffs in this book endured problems for a long time before resorting to the court" (172). For a short ethnography of personal injury suits in a community in Illinois, see David M. Engel, "The Oven Bird's Song: Insiders, Outsiders, and Personal Injuries in an American Community," *Law and Society Review* 18, no. 4 (1984): 551–82. For an overview of the main players in the discipline of legal anthropology, see Sally Falk Moore, "Certainties Undone: Fifty Turbulent Years of Legal Anthropology, 1949–1999," *Journal of the Royal Anthropological Institute* 7 (2001): 95–116. See also Patricia Ewick and Susan S. Silbey, *The Common Place of Law: Stories from Everyday Life* (Chicago: University of Chicago Press, 1998); David Engel, Carol Greenhouse, and Barbara Yngvesson, *Law and Community in Three American Towns* (Ithaca: Cornell University Press, 1994); and Susan Bilber Coutin, "Smugglers or Samaritans in Tucson, Arizona: Producing and Contesting Legal Truth," *American Ethnologist* 22, no. 3: 549–71.

12. Richard Abel has stated that in a lifetime, 60 percent of Americans will have an injury for which they could rightly sue (cited in Abel, "The Real Tort Crisis"). While statistics such as these certainly hint at the depth of the injury problem in the United States, they also mislead with their solidity. Are we to include pesticide injuries, which cause serious injuries but for which no clear legal strategy for litigation has emerged? What about cancer caused by increased use of plastics—certainly an injury, but again, how would we begin to locate a proximate cause? Whom would one sue? What does it mean to define injury as that which could "rightly" be litigated?

13. While I do want to argue with this book that legal trials tend to reproduce hegemonic cultural assumptions, I also think that the various actors, human and nonhuman, perform their roles in trials in ways that cannot be completely explained. They exceed the conditions of their production, and in this excess much of the interest of lawsuits is derived. To take a clear example, legal opinions will often harbor unexpected logics, and dissents can act as "placeholders" to set the intelligibility for future majority decisions. For an outline of some of the key questions about how "law uses the resources of the larger culture precisely in order to establish its own particular kind of discourse," see Robert Post, "Introduction: The Relatively Autonomous Discourse of Law," in *Law and the Order of Culture*, ed. Robert Post (Berkeley: University of California Press, 1991), quote on p. viii. For a brief sociolegal studies treatment of injury in law, which compares three cases of injury at three different historical moments in three different cultures, see David M. Engel, "Injury and Identity: The Damaged Self in Three Cultures," in *Between Law and Culture: Relocating Legal Studies*, ed. David Theo Goldberg, Michael Musheno, and Lisa C. Bower (Minneapolis: University of Minnesota Press, 2001), 3–21. Engel argues that "differing perspectives on injury [have] significant implications for the role and meaning of law" (3).

14. Dick Pels, Kevin Hetherington, and Frederic Vandenberghe, "The Status of the Object: Performances, Mediations, and Techniques," *Theory, Culture, and Society* 19, no. 5/6 (2002): 1–21, quote on p. 9.

15. Sarah Jain, "Dangerous Instrumentality (Bystander as Subject in Automobility)," *Cultural Anthropology* 19, no. 1 (Feb. 2004): 61–94.

16. Cited in Webb Keane, "Semiotics and the Social Analysis of Material Things," *Language and Communication* 23, no. 3–4 (July–Oct. 2003): 409–25. Haraway's "Cyborg Manifesto" was the landmark text in cultural studies to push an examination of humans and nonhumans using analytic terms that remain constantly in motion. She writes, "Why should our bodies end at the skin, or include at best other beings encapsulated by the skin? From the seventeenth century til now, machines could be animated—given ghostly souls to make them speak or move or to account for their orderly development and mental capacities. Or organisms could be mechanized—reduced to body understood as resource of mind. These machine/organism relationships are obsolete, unnecessary. . . . We don't need organic holism to give impermeable wholeness" (178). See also Sarah Jain, "Prosthetic Pathology: Enabling and Disabling the Prosthesis Trope," *Science, Technology, and Human Values* 24, no. 1 (winter 1998): 31–54.

17. *Words and Phrases*, permanent edition, vol. 21A, *Industrial—Innkeepers* (St. Paul, MN: West Publishing, 2003), 238–39. In the legal literature, care is also taken to distinguish injury from accident. See, for example, *Judicial and Statutory Definition of Words and Phrases*, coll., ed., and comp. members of the editorial staff of the *National Reporter System*, vol. 4, *Freeze—Kept* (St. Paul: West Publishing, 1904), 3616. An earlier citation takes care to distinguish injury from damage, the latter in which "no manner of *right* is concerned." See Alexander M. Burrell, *Law Dictionary and Glossary: Terms of the Common and Civil Law*, 2nd ed., vol 2 (New York: John Voorhies, 1859). The slippage among wounding, intent, incidental, accidental, negligent, and unavoidable is exactly the stuff of the debates in legal literature.

18. In the vernacular use of the term, bodies—as themselves material objects—are subject to injury as a matter of course. Arguably, time itself is a prolonged injury process. Consider the aging woman's disfigured, painful, and swollen feet that are dismissed by doctors as the effects of aging. Are they less important than the young basketball player's fallen arch? How is the "importance" of these signs of pain to be objectified or measured? Furthermore, an application of the term "injury" to describe subjective phenomena is both inexact to begin with and vastly open to rhetorical manipulation. High stakes can make it easy to appeal for fiduciary gain or time off from an unsatisfying job: certain claims of whiplash may not be exactly feigned but may remain painful until the application of what doctors call the "green poultice." Like "need," injury is a term open to interpretation and not easy to objectively measure. Injury, when put in the terms that the law requires, must also have a certain resting place. An act of god, such as a heat wave that causes several hundred deaths, does not injure in a compensable form—even when those injuries may be traced to government regulations on energy supply and air conditioners— but a medical device with a poorly designed wick may translate directly into proximate cause. For a book-length study of the decisions that culminated in several deaths in the Chicago heat wave of 1995, see Eric Klinenberg, *Heat Wave: A Social Autopsy of Disaster in Chicago* (Chicago: University of Chicago Press, 2002).

19. Even as Bill Maurer pointed out to me, consumer capitalism also attempts to absorb parts of the subject—particularly labor—into its logic. Still,

on the consumer side, even in instances of body parts, cell lines, and so on, a subject-consumer is required, by definition.

20. "Governmentality," in *Michel Foucault: Power*, ed. James D. Faubion, *Essential Works of Foucault, 1954–1984* (New York: The New Press, 1994), 201–22, quote on pp. 208–9.

21. Bruno Latour, "The Berlin Key or How to Do Words with Things," in *Matter, Materiality and Modern Culture*, ed. P.M. Graves-Brown (New York: Routledge, 2000), 10–21, quote on p. 18.

22. Latour, "Berlin Key," 18. Latour seems to shy away from analysis of either the stakes or the consequences of the distinctions he explains so lucidly.

23. This theorization of the animation of matter can be traced back through anthropological theory to Evans-Pritchard, who discussed the way in which the spear was an animate aspect of the Nuer male, extending his strength, vitality, and virtue. Similarly, Gregory Bateson wrote that the blind man's "stick is a pathway along which differences are transmitted under transformation, so that to draw a delimiting line across this pathway is to cut off a part of the systematic circuit which determines the blind man's locomotion" (Bateson, "The Cybernetics of "Self": A Theory of Alcoholism," *Psychiatry* 34 [1971]: 1–18, quote on p. 7). For more on his related work on prostheses, see Jain, "Prosthetic Pathology."

24. His research question is rather different from those I broach here. He asks, "What is the concept of history embedded in the accident investigation that begins while crushed aluminum is still smoldering?" Peter Galison, "An Accident of History," in *Atmospheric Flight in the Twentieth Century*, ed. P. Galison and A. Roland (Dordrecht: Kluwer, 2000), 3–43, quote on p. 3; quote in text on pp. 38–39 (emphasis original).

25. Elaine Scarry writes perhaps more thoughtfully and more complexly of the implications of "object awareness." She writes that a door with its "design is a material registration of the awareness that human beings both need the protection of solid walls and need to walk through solid walls at will. The door not only seems capable of transforming itself back and forth between the two states of wallness and nonwallness but, more remarkably, seems capable of understanding which of the two states the man wants it to be at any given moment." Scarry, *Bodies in Pain: The Making and Unmaking of the World* (New York: Oxford University Press, 1985), especially 296–304, quote on p. 296. For a demonstration of a variety of science and technology studies (STS) approaches to these questions, see Nelly Oudshoorn and Trevor Pinch, eds., *How Users Matter: The Co-Construction of Users and Technologies* (Cambridge, MA: MIT Press, 2003). See also Karin Knorr Cetina, "The Market as an Object of Attachment: Exploring Postsocial Relations in Financial Markets," *Canadian Journal of Sociology/Cahiers canadiens de sociologies* 25, no. 2 (2000): 141–68.

26. Jacques Derrida, "Force of Law: The 'Mystical Foundation of Authority'," *Cardozo Law Review* 11 (1990): 919–1045, quote on p. 949.

27. This market research in a way is self-fulfilling as markets and marketing become more homogeneous. One example of this is in the difficulty that game designers have had in building computer games that are more appealing to girls. Making the games pink and based less in violence and more in communi-

cation serves only to fold into the same forces that do the girling in the first place. In other words, people identified as girls are taught from birth to identify with pink and not with computer games—these identifications are what make this subset of people girls.

28. A number of scholars concerned with the social roles of technology have launched deep critiques of mid-twentieth-century design theory that contended that design should be interpreted in light of its combination of craftsmanship, utility, and intuition. Langdon Winner lay the groundwork for understanding how artifacts invariably have politics of all kinds built into them, from underpasses that do not allow public buses to pass through them to nuclear programs that demand centralized control and decision-making centers. (Winner, "Do Artifacts Have Politics?" in *The Whale and the Reactor: A Search for Limits in an Age of High Technology* [Chicago: University of Chicago Press, 1986], 19–39.) Scholars such as Adrian Forty have demonstrated that design is simply not just an aesthetic exercise but highly contingent on political economics. (Forty, *Objects of Desire: Design and Society since 1750* [New York: Thames and Hudson, 1992].) Ellen Lupton has illustrated that technologies such as telephones have delighted in their cultural suffusion with gender stereotypes— and that we ignore these object semiotics at our peril. (Lupton, *Mechanical Brides: Women and Machines from Home to Office* [New York: Cooper-Hewitt, National Museum of Design, Smithsonian Institution; Princeton: Princeton Architectural Press, 1993].) Furthermore, historians such as Joy Parr, Edward Tenner, and Ruth Schwartz Cowan have vividly examined the ways that technology can too easily "bite back" in the form of "more work for mother" and other unintended consequences. (Parr, *Domestic Goods: The Material, the Moral, and the Economic in the Postwar Years* [Toronto: University of Toronto Press, 1999]; Tenner, *Why Things Bite Back: Technology and the Revenge of Unintended Consequences* [New York: Knopf, 1996]; Schwartz Cowan, *More Work for Mother: The Ironies of Household Technology from the Open Hearth to the Microwave* [New York: Basic Books, 1983].) All of these commentators have worked to embed a notion now well accepted in STS that objects and communities are co-constituted; designed "things" unleashed in the world thereafter produce and shape future possible worlds and ways of imagining them. This observation leaves open the perennial question of unintended consequences: unintended by whom? Who notices structural inequalities such as gender or size, and who gets to materially encode these? How does this process work, and how can it be challenged?

29. The purpose of an "award of damages to a person injured by the negligence of another is to compensate the victim. . . . The goal is to restore the injured party, to the extent possible, to the position that would have been occupied had the wrong not occurred." *McDougald v. Garber*, 73 N.Y. 2d 246, 253–54, 538 N.Y.S. 2d 937, 536 N.E. 2d 372, 374 (1989).

30. Mary Douglas has noted that the social comprehension and reaction to risk is based in "a fixed repertoire of possible causes among which a plausible explanation is chosen," rather than any truly objective risk calculus. (Douglas, *Risk and Blame: Essays in Cultural Theory* [New York: Routledge 1992], 5.) Douglas critiques the notion of objective risks and the search for them by experts in risk analysis, noting that "the risk perception analysts say practically nothing

about intersubjectivity, consensus making, or social influences on decisions" (12). Furthermore, she writes, "Resort to the law in itself engenders mistrust. We have to get used to these anxieties, this mathematics of probability intruding into our intimate concerns, this bogus objectivity, this coding of risks in our present culture. If anyone ever thought that the complex coding of taboos was more restrictive, the work of the modern safety officer should give them pause" (16).

31. The Canadian government, however, has recently legislated far more stringent warnings, which take up half of the packages with graphic images and information that are at once instructional and admonitory. The Canadian warning labels appeal to the rational consumer-chooser in a radically different way, assuming in fact that no rational chooser would decide to smoke and asserting a much greater stake in ensuring that people do not smoke. The government's warnings seem to meet the potential addictive behavior with the irrational elements of disgust and fear of the consequences. The Canadian government has had both a greater stake and a greater legitimacy in its involvement in debates about seatbelt and helmet use, product warnings, and informational campaigns because of its role in providing public health care. As lawyers are very aware, the decision to add warnings can be a very dicey thing, as they can also imply retroactive liability. This was the debate in the late 1960s with the issue of cigarette warnings. David Rempel, who advised on the warning that Compaq added to computer keyboards in the mid-1990s, said that for manufacturers this concern with retroactive liability was also at issue. Rempel, phone interview, May 6, 2004.

32. Or a social network will notice a social structure—law—that may enable him to benefit from this "injury."

33. Friends of mine recall that in the 1960s deaths resulting from drunk driving were perceived simply as accidental and no charges were filed.

34. This circulation and bundling of an object's meaning is a condition required for the biography of things approach of material culture studies. See, for example, Arjun Appadurai, "Introduction: Commodities and the Politics of Value," in *The Social Life of Things: Commodities in Cultural Perspective* (New York: Cambridge University Press, 1986), 3–63.

35. But furthermore, it is one through which so many of the actors are back-boxed, or removed from the equation. What about the engineers and business administrators who made certain decisions? Their public accountability is made manifest only through the corporate stock prices, not through the consumers of their products with only few notable exceptions such as the civil rights boycotts of the 1960s or the boycott of Nestle products in the 1970s. How these interests play out is not at all self-evident.

36. For a direction toward a more subtle analysis of how object intentions might be said to translate linguistically, see Keane, "Semiotics and the Social Analysis of Material Things."

37. Francois Ewald, "Insurance and Risk," in *The Foucault Effect: Studies in Governmentality*, ed. Graham Burchell, Colin Gordon, and Peter Miller (Chicago: University of Chicago Press, 1991), 197–210, quote on p. 205.

38. Scarry, *The Body in Pain*, 301.

39. Eve Kosofsky Sedgwick, "Epidemics of the Will," in *Incorporations*, ed. J. Crary and S. Kwinter (New York: Zone Books, 1992) 582–95, quote on p. 594.

40. Another example through which behaviors and design came directly into conflict was in the 1960s when the notion of the negligent motor vehicle driver took on a very different valence. Until 1966, courts reasoned that since automobiles were not "intended" to crash, injuries that occurred as a result of the "second collision," the collision of occupants with interior knobs or other hard surfaces, were not the responsibility of manufacturers. Courts sided with the manufacturers in deciding that they were under no obligation to make cars "crashworthy." This changed radically with *Larsen v. General Motors*, when the court found that cars crash regularly and as a matter of course and therefore should be expected to be reasonably crashworthy. Though certainly *Larsen* has to be contextualized within a broader cultural shift that, at the highest political echelons, started to treat car deaths and injuries as a political issue, the case marks a key moment in the social model for a complete revision of how crash injuries would be understood by engineers, lawyers, and politicians who worked to have NHTSA instituted on the premise that automobiles were murderously unsafe. (*Larsen v. General Motors Corporation*, 391 F.2d 495; 1968 U.S. App. LEXIS 7766 Mar. 11, 1968.) The opinion stated:

> Automobiles are made for use on the roads and highways. . . . This intended use cannot be carried out without encountering in varying degrees the statistically proved hazard of injury-producing impacts. . . . The manufacturer . . . can easily foresee . . . that [a car] will be involved in some type of injury-producing accident. Jeffrey O'Connell in his article "Taming the Automobile," *58 Nw.U.L.Rev. 299, 348 (1963)* cites that between one-fourth to two-thirds of all automobiles during their use at some time are involved in an accident producing injury or death. . . . We think the "intended use" construction urged by General Motors is much too narrow and unrealistic.

Compare this case to one decided only two years earlier: *Evans v. General Motors Corporation*, in which the "court held that a manufacturer is not under a duty to make his automobile accident-proof or fool-proof; nor must he render the vehicle "more" safe where the danger to be avoided is obvious to all. Defendant had a duty to test its frame only to ensure that it was reasonably fit for its intended purpose" (359 F.2d 822 [7th Cir. 1966]).

41. Quoted in Susan Buck-Morss, "Envisioning Capital: Political Economy on Display," *Critical Inquiry* 21, no. 2 (1995): 434–76, quote on p. 448. The division of labor in pin manufacture had already been well established by 1772, and the manual process was illustrated in Denis Diderot's *L'Encyclopedie*. See Henry Petroski, *The Evolution of Useful Things* (New York: Vintage Books, 1992), 53.

42. "With the wave of a hand, the victim of the division of labor becomes its beneficiary." Buck-Morss, "Envisioning Capital," 448–50.

43. Scarry, *The Body in Pain*, 263.

44. Thomas O. McGarity and Sidney A. Shapiro, *Workers at Risk: The Failed Promise of the Occupational Safety and Health Administration* (Westport, CT: Praeger, 1993), 3. Current rates are between 4,650 and 12,000 per year, and nonfatal injuries are between two and eleven million per year, far above other in-

dustrialized nations. Underreportage rates are extremely high, ranging from 30 to 40 percent (4–6).

45. McGarity and Shapiro, *Workers at Risk*, 17.

46. Anthony F. Bale, "Compensation Crisis: The Value and Meaning of Work-Related Injuries and Illnesses in The United States, 1842–1932" (Ph.D. diss., Brandeis University, 1987), 103.

47. Charles Noble, *Liberalism at Work: The Rise and Fall of OSHA* (Philadelphia: Temple University Press, 1986), 43.

48. Bale, "Compensation Crisis." See also John Fabian Witt, *The Accidental Republic: Crippled Workingmen, Destitute Widows, and the Remaking of American Law* (Cambridge, MA: Harvard University Press, 2004).

49. About 87 percent of employees are currently covered by workers' compensation. Only railroad workers and seamen—whose unions have consistently preferred the higher damage awards (paid when negligence can be proven) available through tort law to the lower payments of workers' compensation—are universally excluded. Agricultural workers are covered by workers' compensation in twenty states. As poorer laborers and often as immigrants, they have less access to the tort law system and typically work with high-risk pesticides. Injuries caused by these pesticides are difficult to prove and often are not evident immediately.

50. In order to qualify for workers' compensation an employee "must have received (1) a personal injury (2) as the result of an accident (3) which arose out of and (4) in the course of employment." (Marc A. Franklin and Robert L. Rabin, *Tort Law and Alternatives: Cases and Materials*, 5th ed. [Westbury, NY: Foundation Press, 1996], 723.) The "accident" requirement has been difficult for people with repetitive strain injuries to meet.

51. McGarity and Shapiro, *Workers at Risk*, 24. Workers' compensation systems do not have a built-in incentive, as safe employers are not given reduced rates on payments, which are standardized across vocation categories according to risk, ranging from 0.1 to 25 percent of payroll.

52. Benefits are paid according to established schedules and will cover medical expenses and some combination of temporary, partial, or permanent disability. Benefits are calculated from combinations of financial loss and physical impairment and amount to a capped percentage of wages. Franklin and Rabin, *Tort Law and Alternatives*, 726.

53. Robert L. Rabin, "The Quest for Fairness in Compensating Victims of September 11," *Cleveland State Law Review* 49 (2001): 573–89, quote on p. 580.

54. State-level work regulations began with the 1867 Department of Factory Inspection in Massachusetts, followed by the first workers' safety law in 1877. Since then, state regulatory programs have been notoriously inadequate. Charles Noble's research indicates that before 1970, state regulation programs were starved for resources, spending an average of 48 cents per nonagricultural worker on occupational health and safety regulation. Restricted by legal and administrative problems, agencies had little power to enforce regulations. In addition, there were vast differences among states, and even states with sound programs depended on voluntary compliance. Twenty-one states did not allow inspectors to shut down machinery in imminent danger situations;

sixteen states had no criminal sanctions against deliberate violations of the law; and five states did not give inspectors the legal right to enter the premises without the permission of the employer. Most states relied on outdated standards. Noble, *Liberalism at Work*, 56–57.

55. Even the most conservative commentators recognize this. See Cass R. Sunstein, Reid Hastie, John W. Payne, David Schakade, and W. Kip Viscusi, *Punitive Damages: How Juries Decide* (Chicago: University of Chicago Press, 2002). For a full study, see Michael Rustad, "In Defense of Punitive Damages in Products Liability: Testing Tort Anecdotes with Empirical Data," *Iowa Law Review* 78 (1992): 1.

56. G. Edward White, *Tort Law in America: An Intellectual History* (New York: Oxford University Press, 1985), xx.

57. Thanks to Janet Halley for pointing out her theory of the "sandwich maker."

58. *MacPherson v. Buick Motor Co.*, Court of Appeals of New York, 217 N.Y. 382, 111 N.E. 1050 (1916).

59. *Escola v. Coca-Cola Bottling Co. of Fresno*, 24 Cal. 2d 453, 461, 150 P.2d 436, 440 (1944).

60. *Escola*, 24 Cal. 2d 453, 150 P2d 436.

61. *Escola*, 24 Cal. 2d 453, 462, 150 P.2d 436, 440.

62. Edward H. Levi, *An Introduction to Legal Reasoning* (Chicago: University of Chicago Press, 1949), 27. C. Edward White argues that torts emerged from a diverse series of writs to answer for society's need for a generalized standard of care toward strangers. He argues, "Negligence provided that unity; it also provided a workable standard—a limiting principle—for the numerous inadvertent injuries involving strangers that had come to be a characteristic late 19th-century tort action." White, "The Intellectual Origins of Torts in America," *Yale Law Journal* 86, no. 671 (1977): 593.

63. Levi, *An Introduction to Legal Reasoning*, 10–27.

64. Ibid., 15, citing *Loop v. Litchfield*, 42 N.Y. 351, 359 (1870).

65. Jain, " 'Dangerous Instrumentality,' " xx.

66. Andrew L. Kaufman, *Cardozo* (Cambridge, MA: Harvard University Press, 1998), 279–80.

67. Ibid.

68. Susan Stewart, *Crimes of Writing* (New York: Oxford University Press, 1991), 21.

69. Jamie Cassels, "(In)equality and the Law of Tort: Gender, Race and the Assessment of Damages," *Advocates' Quarterly* 17 (1995): 158–98. See also Barbara Welke's painstaking and insightful analysis of the gender implications of streetcar alighting injuries in the early twentieth century in *Recasting American Liberty: Gender, Race, Law, and the Railroad Revolution, 1865–1920* (New York: Cambridge University Press, 2001), and Leslie Bender, "Feminist (Re)torts: Thoughts on the Liability Crisis, Mass Torts, Power, and Responsibilities," *Duke Law Journal* (1990) 848–912.

70. White, *Tort Law in America*, 41.

71. Duncan Kennedy, *A Critique of Adjudication* (Cambridge, MA: Harvard University Press, 1997), 4.

72. Ewald, "Insurance and Risk," 202. See also Durkheim's discussion of suicide and statistics in *Suicide: A Study in Sociology,* trans. John A. Spaulding and George Simpson (New York: Free Press, 1997). See Jonathan Simon, "The Ideological Effects of Actuarial Practices," *Law and Society Review* 22, no. 4 (1988): 771–800.

73. Indeed, Elaine Scarry argues that the jury's role is to "take back" the injury.

74. For a legal realist take on types of jurisprudential logic, see, for example, John Dewey, "Logical Method and Law," *Cornell Law Quarterly,* 10 (1925): 17–27. Dewey also discusses the incongruity between logic and good sense.

75. Many of these cases are masterful at isolating causative events as well as simply disregarding certain facts that are irrelevant to the actual injury suffered: for example, where a trespasser dives into a pool and is injured by the rubber bottom, or a drunk person crashes and the seatbelt is faulty; trespassing and drunkenness are extra-legal matters in cases of strict liability.

76. Risk-benefit standards offer a definition of "defective" that is considerably different from that of strict liability (which serves more of an insurance role) or of consumer expectation (which bases built-in safety as a measure of what a reasonable consumer ought to be able to expect). In risk-benefit, the jury is asked to consider "the gravity of the danger posed by the challenged design, the likelihood that such danger would occur, the mechanical feasibility of a safer alternative design, the financial cost of an improved design, and the adverse consequences to the product and to the consumer that would result from an alternative design." *Barker v. Lull Engineering Co.,* 20 Cal. 3d 413 (1978).

77. See Scott S. Sagan, *The Limits of Safety: Organizations, Accidents and Nuclear Weapons* (Princeton: Princeton University Press, 1992).

78. Guido Calabresi, *The Cost of Accidents: A Legal and Economic Analysis* (New Haven: Yale University Press, 1970), 24. This book provides an overview and analysis of the key theories of accident law and their strengths and weaknesses rather than strongly arguing for any particular model. It is not my intention here to outline or discuss in any detail the pros and cons of the many theories and possible goals of the law.

79. Peter Huber, *Galileo's Revenge: Junk Science in the Courtroom* (New York: Basic Books, 1993), 22.

80. Other commentators have addressed the "junk science" issue with more finesse and rigor. See particularly Sheila Jasanoff, *Science at the Bar: Law, Science, and Technology in America* (Cambridge, MA: Harvard University Press, 1995).

81. I say "by its very structure" while acknowledging the theorists, such as Calabresi, who believe that accidents are inevitable because I think the structure and the Calabresian theory of cost-sharing are at odds. I am proposing with this book that the structure of the law, its case-by-case method, its way of training and selecting judges, and the power of the medical and other cultural institutions overshadow the cost-sharing possibilities.

82. The Bronco II case won an appeal to the California Court of Appeals. "The evidence supports the jury's conclusion that Ford willfully and consciously ignored the dangers to human life inherent in the 1978 Bronco as de-

signed," appellate Judge Steven Vartabedian said. Punitive damages were calculated as "1.2 percent of Ford's net worth or nine days of profits at the time of
trial." (Eric Freedman, "Punitive Damages Upheld in Rollover Suit," *Automotive
News*, Sept. 9, 2002. See *Juan Ramon Romo v. Ford Motor Company*, 113 Cal. App.
4th 738; 6 Cal. Rptr. 3d 793; 2003 Cal. App. LEXIS 1736; 2003 Cal. Daily Op.
Service 10150; 2003 Daily Journal DAR 12739.) The U.S. Supreme Court subse-
quently sent the case back to the California court claiming that the punitive
damages should be of a single-digit multiple of the compensatory damages.
(See *Ford Motor Company v. Juan Ramon Romo*, 538 U.S. 1028; 123 S. Ct. 2072; 155
L. Ed. 2d 1056; 2003 U.S. LEXIS 3680; 71 U.S.L.W. 3721; 2003 Daily Journal DAR
5278.) Vartabedian did reduce the punitive damage awards, but not before
some recalcitrant working through of the philosophy and purpose of punitive
damages. The opinions in this series of trials make for fascinating reading.

83. This factoring was the primary bone of contention in the Ford Pinto case
when evidence was presented showing that Ford neglected to make simple
design changes on the basis that the lives saved would not be worth it. The
Pinto story "broke" in *Mother Jones* with a Pulitzer Prize–winning article in
August 1977 by Mark Dowie titled "Pinto Madness." Dowie's prose is incendi-
ary, but no more so than Ford's: "If we can't meet the standards when they are
published, we will have to close down. And if we have to close down some
production because we don't meet standards we're in for real trouble in this
country" (31). The Pinto fires were also covered by *60 Minutes* and extensive
newspaper reportage. See Francis T. Cullen, William J. Maakestad, and Gray
Cavender, *Corporate Crime under Attack: The Ford Pinto Case and Beyond* (Cincin-
nati: Anderson, 1987).

84. *State Farm Mutual Automobile Insurance Company v. Inez Preece Campbell
and Matthew C. Barneck*, 538 U.S. 408; 123 S. Ct. 1513, Dec. 11, 2002, Argued,
Apr. 7, 2003, Decided. It would be difficult to fathom what "malice" might
mean in terms of corporate behavior. *Cammack v. Ford Motor Co. and Max Ma-
haffy Ford Inc.*, June 1995, Harris, Texas, provides one example of an Explorer
rollover in which jury damages were decreased because of lack of malice on
Ford's part. The press widely covered the initial jury award (punitive) of $22.5
million, even though it was reduced immediately by the judge to four times
the compensatory award of $2.5 million and eventually settled for under $4
million (how much under is proprietary knowledge) when Ford countersued,
claiming that the parents of the deceased had no legal standing on which to
sue. These and more details or rollover suits are accounted in Adam L. Penen-
berg, *Tragic Indifference: One Man's Battle with the Auto Industry over the Dangers
of SUVs* (New York: HarperBusiness, 2003), 41–48.

85. If, as Robert Proctor argues, Americans are going to accept, first, that
chemicals dumped into the environment (either as part of the production process or as a disposed of consumable) and, second, that food and consumer
items are safe until proven otherwise, they also trade in futures. The company
making money as a side effect of the chemical use will have more resources to
"prove" that a chemical was and remains safe. Johns-Manville and RJR proved
that asbestos and tobacco were safe for decades. (Proctor, *Cancer Wars: How
Politics Shapes What We Know and Don't Know about Cancer* [New York: Basic

Books, 1995].) In a similar vein, Ulrich Beck examines in detail the multiple ways that risks in industrial economies have been consistently legitimized and unequally distributed as a latent side effect of other activities such that *everyone* can claim that no one either "saw or wanted their consequences." (Beck, *Risk Society: Towards a New Modernity,* trans. Mark Ritter [Newbury Park, CA: Sage, 1992].)

86. Steven Lee Myers, "Russians Become Litigious: Survivors of Theater Siege Sue," *New York Times,* Dec. 6, 2002.

87. Frank Bardacke, personal communication with the author, Mar. 3, 1999.

88. See the work of Robert C. Post, who writes on looks and discrimination. Robert C. Post, with K. Anthony Appiah, Judith Butler, Thomas C. Grey, and Reva Siegel, *Prejudicial Appearances: The Logic of American Antidiscrimination Law* (Durham: Duke University Press, 2001).

89. Cassels, "(In)equality and the Law of Tort."

90. While some theorists posit an insurance system or "cost-spreading" notion of the function of law, these ideals ultimately cannot connect with the structures of law that require plaintiffs to recoup their losses.

91. Legal theorists seek to balance how the importance of the body will be weighed in terms of economic and technological notions of progress and profit, such that manufacturers will ensure that their products are reasonably safe, and they use a variety of theories that vary from cost-benefit "tests" to theories based in insurance models. Reallocation, when these equations have caused "unjust" losses, takes place through compensatory damages, which cover the costs of the injury (medical, loss of consortium, pain and suffering, and so on). In the case of egregious misconduct, such as premarket knowledge of a serious defect or fraudulent advertising, a court may decide to award punitive damages as way of literally "punishing" a company. The law requires the physical body to come to the table as a preceding artifact being reclaimed after having been unjustly altered. This reclamation presents an act of citizenship both in the individuated terms of literally reclaiming the body through compensation and in the ways referred to by certain tort scholars as fulfilling one's social duty to keep corporations honest.

92. Jonathan Parry writes that it was the "Christian world which developed the theory of pure utility, and that—as Mauss indicated—is perhaps no accident. Since the things of this world are seen as antithetical to the person's true self, his soul, an ethicised salvation relation is I think likely to encourage that separation of persons from things which is an ideological precondition of market exchange." Parry, "The Gift, the Indian Gift, and the 'Indian Gift,' " *Man* 21 (Sept. 1986): 453–73, quote on p. 468.

93. Ivan Illich, *Energy and Equity* (New York, Harper and Row, 1974).

94. One standard anecdote is that as a nation gets richer, its population gets fatter. However, it is certainly worth noting that highly educated populations have only "half the level of obesity of those with a lower education." (Craig Lambert, "The Way We Eat Now," *Harvard Magazine* [May/June 2004]: 49–58 [quote on p. 51].) Furthermore, while about 60 percent of the general population is overweight, low-income African American groups have a rate closer to 80 percent.

95. Celeste Langan "Mobility Disability," *Public Culture* 13, no. 3 (2001): 459–83, quote on p. 468.

96. Airbags provide an excellent way to see how bodies are built into both social and technological systems. The airbag poses the classic example of a product that was calculated to fit men of average height and weight without seatbelts on. Airbags are designed to "deploy in front of an average adult male's chest." They are designed not to save the largest percentage of drivers but the largest percentage of male drivers. (Associated Press, "Small Women Vulnerable to Air Bags, Data Show," *Star Tribune* [Minneapolis- St. Paul], Oct. 26, 1996, 11A.) Though overall credited with saving lives, inflating at 200 miles per hour from a little cubbyhole in the steering wheel, airbags also cause a number of injuries, including severe cuts caused by the plastic cover flying off the steering wheel, the amputation of hands and arms caught in the way of the inflating bag, broken bones, tearing of heart and internal organs, and fatal head injuries. (Keith Harper, "Car Air Bag Design Could Be Fatal to Children, Tests Show," *The Guardian*, Feb. 17, 1997, 5.) Consequently, as a correlate of height, 42 percent of women compared to 24 percent of men received facial injury from the airbags. While 50 percent of drivers under 5'5" received facial injury, only 18 percent of drivers 5'11" and over did. (Associated Press, "Two-thirds in Air Bag Study Suffered Injury," *Buffalo News*, Apr. 1, 1997, A5.) The "shortness-bias" is also built into seatbelt designs. Because of body size differences that tend to fall along gendered lines and the one-size-fits all attitude of the Big Three manufacturers, airbags were, post-market, found to be excessively dangerous to smaller women. (For an explanation of attempts and failures to set regulations that would locate automotive controls within reach of smaller people, see Jerry L. Mashaw and David L. Harfst, *The Struggle for Auto Safety* [Cambridge, MA: Harvard University Press, 1990], 75–76.) This disconnect between mass production of the same design and mass consumption of consumers with different kinds of bodies is not atypical; indeed, it is absolutely predictable. How are we to describe these injuries? (See Andrew M. Pope and Alvin R. Tarlov, *Disability in America: Toward a National Agenda for Prevention* [Washington, DC: National Academy Press, 1991] for an overview of the scope of disability in the United States, and Susan Wendell, *The Rejected Body: Feminist Philosophical Reflections on Disability* [New York: Routledge, 1996], for a thoughtful discussion on setting disability "standards," and of definitional problems in general.)

97. Thomas Koenig and Michael Rustad, "His and Her Tort Reform: Gender Injustice in Disguise," *Washington Law Review* 70 (1995): 1–89. This article reports that in early tort law, injured women did not receive compensation for harms they suffered; compensation was awarded for "damaged goods" to the man who was perceived to own the woman. Eleanor D. Kinney et al., "Indiana's Medical Malpractice Act: Results of a Three-Year Study," *Indiana Law Review* 24 (1991): 1275–1428. demonstrates that women are less likely to be able to show that their bodies are as valuable as men's bodies.

98. As I argue in detail elsewhere, the automobile comes with a complex semiotic organization of social difference, space, and community. I here call it

double-injury to vastly oversimplify. See my *Commodity Violence* (Durham: Duke University Press, forthcoming).

99. "More than 60% of citizen-respondents in our surveys and experiments exhibited a zero-risk mentality by endorsing the statement 'If everyone tries as hard as they can, the risk of environmental damage from industrial accidents like train derailments, oil spills, and toxic waste problems can be reduced to zero.' " Sunstein et al., *Punitive Damages*, 230.

100. Grey had had returned the car to the dealer a number of times since the vehicle's purchase. It's problems included "excessive gas and oil consumption, down shifting of the automatic transmission, lack of power, and occasional stalling." *Grimshaw v. Ford Motor Co.* App., 174 Cal.Rptr. 348, 359, May 29, 1981.

101. *Grimshaw*, 174 Cal.Rptr. at 358.

102. Ford did not issue a "voluntary" recall until May 1978 under threat of NHTSA action.

103. Schwartz, "The Myth of the Ford Pinto Case," 1020.

104. The plaintiff presented the expert evidence of a former engineering executive who had been terminated from Ford on the basis of his interest in safety, as well as the cost of an alternative design ($4–8/car). He testified that Ford had "decided to defer corrective measures to save money and enhance profits" (*Grimshaw*, 174 Cal.Rptr. at 351). The plaintiff also produced a motion picture and a report of crash tests showing the faulty design of the fuel tank. Dowie notes that even this document underestimated the likely number of burn injuries, which were listed as equal in number to burn deaths. This has no statistical value, as burn injuries are much more prevalent that burn deaths. In addition, Dowie reports that one of the delay tactics Ford used on NHTSA was to try to diminish the importance of burn deaths in autos. In its further research, NHTSA found, on the contrary, that "40,000 cars were burning up every year, burning more than 3,000 people to death. . . . Forty per cent of all fire department calls in the 1960s were to vehicle fires—a public cost of $350 million a year, a figure that, incidentally, never shows up in cost-benefit analyses" ("Pinto Madness," 30). Not until 1977 did NHTSA impose a rear-end collision standard on fuel leakage.

105. Gary T. Schwartz, "The Myth of the Ford Pinto Case," *Rutgers Law Review* 43 (Summer 1991), 1033.

106. Ibid., 1025.

107. Ibid., 1040.

108. Ibid., 1060.

109. Marcia Angell expresses some outrage at the way that the FDA handled the breast implant recall, claiming that it behaved as a political rather than a regulatory agency. (Angell, *Science on Trial: The Clash of Medical Evidence and the Law in the Breast Implant Case* [New York: W.W. Norton, 1996], especially 50–68.) However, regulation (and its lack) in the United States has always been a highly political issue. For one example, whose title can only be seen as tongue-in-cheek, see Philip J. Hilts, *Protecting America's Health: The FDA, Business, and One Hundred Years of Regulation* (New York: Knopf, 2003). He traces the history of the FDA, precisely as a political body.

110. Mashaw and Harfst, *The Struggle for Auto Safety*, 233.

111. Studies have consistently shown that improved energy efficiency will have major benefits in terms of thousands of dollars saved in fuel over the life of the car. This seems like a straightforward cost-benefit calculation but again, whose costs? Whose benefit?

112. The court found that the fact "that defendant manufacturer fired [a] high ranking engineering executive for advocating automotive safety was indicative of the industrial management's attitude towards safety in automobile production and was thus relevant to the issue of malice in this products liability suit since it has tendency . . . to prove that manufacturer's failure to correct automobile's fuel system design defects, despite knowledge of their existence, was deliberate and calculated." The finding of malice was key in the issuance of punitive damages. (*Grimshaw v. Ford Motor Co.*, App., 174 Cal.Rptr. 348, at 350, May 29, 1981.)

113. After six months of offering seatbelts, Ford caved to pressure by General Motors and stopped offering them for fear that they would focus attention on design and that cars would have to meet federal safety standards "as trains, ships and aircraft have been required to do for decades." (Ralph Nader, *Unsafe at Any Speed: The Designed-In Dangers of the American Automobile* [New York: Pocket Books, 1966], 88.) Consumers Union recommended seatbelts, but found that of 39 brands tested, 26 failed. (Norman Isaac Silber, *Test and Protest: The Influence of the Consumers Union* [New York: Holmes and Meier, 1983], 91.) The National Safety Council's attitude toward seatbelts was noted in an article by its president. (Howard Pyle, "Automobile Seat Belts: What They Can Mean for Safety," *State Government* 35 (winter 1962): 24–29.) Advocating lap belts, Pyle notes that 80 percent of Swedish drivers use a lap and shoulder belt: "We encourage motorists to choose what is best for themselves, and emphasize always that the seat belt is no substitute for good driving" (26), and "We at the National Safety Council believe that everyone working toward the same end will achieve the same results as accomplished in Sweden through more voluntary actions" (28). While some manufacturers added anchors so that buyers could purchase and install belts, the fact was that they were extremely difficult to install and, furthermore, associated with dangerous driving. The CBS documentary *The Great Holiday Massacre* (aired Dec. 26, 1960) shows the difficulty of installation and societal perspective on the belts. One gentleman I interviewed told me that in the early 1960s his girlfriend's parents treated him with suspicion when they found out he had installed seatbelts, which indicates the level to which people believed in behaviors over design at that time. For an excellent overview of auto safety debates, see Joel W. Eastman, *Styling vs. Safety: The American Automobile Industry and the Development of Automotive Safety, 1900–1966* (Lanham, NY: University Press of America, 1984).

114. *Food and Drug Administration, et al. v. Brown and Williamson Tobacco Corporation, et al.*, No. 98–1152 Supreme Court of the United States, 529 U.S. 120; 120 S. Ct. 1291; 146 L. Ed. 2d 121; 2000 U.S. LEXIS 2195; 68 U.S.L.W. 4194; 2000 Cal. Daily Op. Service 2215; 2000 Daily Journal DAR 2987; 2000 Colo. J. C.A.R. 1435; 13 Fla. L. Weekly Fed. S 161 Dec. 1, 1999, Argued, March 21, 2000, Decided.

115. The majority wrote: "[T]he court must be guided to a degree by common sense as to the manner in which Congress is likely to delegate a policy

decision of such economic and political magnitude to an administrative agency." On cigarettes being too dangerous to be regulated, the majority wrote: "Various provisions in the [Food, Drug, and Cosmetic] Act require the agency to determine that, at least for some consumers, the product's therapeutic benefits outweigh the risks of illness and serious injury. This the FDA cannot do, because tobacco products are unsafe for obtaining any therapeutic benefit." Thus, the agency would have to ban cigarettes, which the majority found inconceivable. On the other hand, the dissent argues that regulation, rather than an outright ban, would be possible. See Richard Klugar, *Ashes to Ashes: America's Hundred-Year Cigarette War, the Public Health, and the Unabashed Triumph of Philip Morris* (New York: Vintage, 1993), for an account of the ways in which the industry has lobbied to exclude itself from all regulatory agencies.

116. A provision in the United States Code put it this way: "[T]he marketing of tobacco constitutes one of the greatest basic industries of the United States with ramifying interests which directly affect interstate and foreign commerce at every point, and stable conditions are necessary, therefore, to the general welfare." *FDA et al.*, US LEXIS 2195 (2002).

117. For more on the FDA's collection of information to build their case, see David Kessler, *A Question of Intent: A Great American Battle with a Deadly Industry* (New York: Public Affairs, 2000).

118. Significantly, states only moved into litigation after tobacco injury had become a legible issue. Shifts in government interests resulted in a similar issue with the Firestone/Ford debacle. Plaintiffs' lawyers did not file reports of injury with NHTSA, since the agency had been so lax in setting regulations in their past analysis of Blazer rollovers. Thus, attorneys feared that if an investigation was launched and closed without regulatory action, preemption would not allow their plaintiffs to make claims successfully. Keith Bradsher, *High and mighty: SUVs—The World's Most Dangerous Vehicles and How They Got That Way* (New York: Public Affairs, 2002). See also *Geier v. Honda Motor Company*, 529 U.S. 861; 120 S.Ct. 1913; 146 L.Ed 2d 914, 2000 LEXIS 3425, where the U.S. Supreme Court ruled that federal regulations on airbags preempt civil recovery.

119. Timothy Mitchell, *Rule of Experts: Egypt, Techno-Politics, Modernity* (Berkeley: University of California Press, 2002), 79.

120. Structurally, the paradox I am outlining here has tended to resolve on the side of economic health for several key reasons. In brief: (1) the privatization of health care that marks its success not by public health but by profit; (2) the way that accidents churn money into the economy; (3) the ability of corporations to lobby government officials; (4) the contradictory mandates of several key governmental organizations, which are supposed to encourage both public health and private industrial development; (5) laws about corporations that understand them to be "persons," rather than complex organizations; (6) a separation of moral and economic logics; and, as I suggested above, (7) the very rudimentary understandings of how injury costs work and are spread.

121. U.S. General Accounting Office, 1998, cited in Eric French and Kirti Kamboj, "Analyzing the Relationship between Health Insurance, Health Costs, and Heath Care Utilization" (Chicago: Federal Reserve Bank, Third Quarter, 2002,

Economic Perspectives), *http://www.chicagofed.org/publications/economicperspectives/ 2002/3qepart4.pdf*, 60. Another study found that "In 2003, premiums for job-based health benefits rose by 13.9%. This is the third consecutive year of double-digit premium increases, and a higher rate of growth than any year since 1990. Premium increases in 2003 exceeded the overall rate of inflation by nearly 12 percentage points." Kaiser Family Foundation, *Employer Health Benefits 2003 Annual Survey*, The Kaiser Family Foundation and Health Research and Educational Trust, information provided by the *Health Care Marketplace Program*, publication number 3369 (Menlo Park, CA: Kaiser Family Foundation, 2003), 1–152, quote on p. 18.

122. "National Health Expenditures, 2003, "Virginia Centers for Medicare and Medicaids Services (CMS)," *http://www.cms.hhs.gov/statistics/nhe/historical/high-lights.asp*. This marks an increase of 9.3 percent from 2001–5.7 percent faster than the overall economy "as measured by growth of the gross domestic product." The article further reports that the "healthcare share of the GDP increased from 14.1% in 2001 to 14.9% in 2002." This includes private insurance, out-of-pocket, Medicaid, and government health spending (workers, veterans, public health, schoolchildren). Health care expenditures have nearly doubled since 1992, as reported in the Kaiser Family Foundation, *Trends and Indicators in the Changing Health Care Marketplace, 2004*, update, Health Care Marketplace Project, publication number 7031 (Menlo Park, CA: Kaiser Family Foundation, 2004).

Medicare costs are not dissimilar, having reached $5,400 per beneficiary in 1996. David Cutler, "What Does Medicare Spending Buy Us?" in *Medicare Reform: Issues and Answers*, ed. Andrew J. Rettenmaier and Thomas R. Saving (Chicago: University of Chicago Press, 1999), 131–52, quote on p. 135.

123. Uwe E. Reinhardt, Peter S. Hussy, and Gerard F. Anderson, "U.S. Health Care Spending in an International Context: Why Is U.S. Spending So High, and Can We Afford It?" *Health Affairs* 23, no. 3 (2004): 10–25, quote on p. 14.

124. Robert J. Mills and Shailesh Bhandari, "Health Insurance Coverage in the United States: 2002," U.S. Census Bureau, September 2003, 1, *http:// www.census.gov/prod/2003pubs/p60–223.pdf*. Reinhardt, Hussy, and Anderson, "U.S. Health Care," give the following comparison for total health spending per capita for 2001: United States, $4,887; Canada, $2,792; Switzerland $3,322; Germany $2,808; Australia, $2,513.

125. This difference in medical systems is reflected in national behaviors. Wendy Waters has found that Canadians were much more likely to wear seatbelts than Americans were, largely because they understood health and safety as communal concerns. Wendy Waters, Michael Macnabb, and Betty Brown, "A Half Century of Attempts to Re-Solve Vehicle Occupant Safety: Understanding Seatbelt and Airbag Technology," Insurance Corporation of British Columbia, Canada, Paper No. 98–56-W-24, Jan. 2003, *http://www.nhtsa.dot.gov/ esv/16/98S6W24.pdf*.

126. To give an example, the current premiums for the Alberta Health Care Insurance Plan (public) are $44 per month for single coverage and $88 per month ($1,056/year) for family coverage. Subsidized rates are charged to qualifying low-income earners. For more on the debates in Canada over public and

private health care, see Kevin Taft and Gillian Steward, *Clear Answers: The Economics and Politics of For-Profit Medicine* (Edmonton: Duval House, 2000).

127. In the United States, studies have demonstrated that for-profit hospitals are more expensive than not-for-profit ones in every category of service, echoing on a local level this comparison between the American and Canadian health care systems. Elaine M. Silverman, M.D., M.P.H., Jonathan S. Skinner, Ph.D., and Elliott S. Fisher, M.D., M.P.H., "The Association between For-Profit Hospital Ownership and Increased Medicare Spending," *New England Journal of Medicine* 341, no. 6 (Aug. 5, 1999): 420–26.

128. In the United States, administration costs $1,059 per person, compared to $307 per capita in Canada, which translates in the United States to 31 percent of health care expenditures compared to 16.7 percent in Canada. Steffie Woolhandler, M.D., M.P.H., Terry Campbell, M.H.A., and David U. Himmelstein, M.D., "Costs of Health Care Administration in the United States and Canada," *New England Journal of Medicine* 349, no. 8 (Aug. 21, 2003): 768–75, *http://content.nejm.org/cgi/content/full/349/8/768*: "In 1999 U.S. private insurers retained $46.9 billion of the $401.2 billion they collected in premiums. Their average overhead (11.7 percent) exceeded that of Medicare (3.6 percent) and Medicaid (6.8 percent). Overall, public and private insurance overhead totaled $72.0 billion—5.9 percent of the total health care expenditures in the United States, or $259 per capita. The overhead costs of Canada's provincial insurance plans totaled $311 million (1.3 percent) of the $23.5 billion they spent for physicians and hospital services. An additional $17 million was spent to administer federal government health plans. The overhead of Canadian private insurers averaged 13.2 percent of the $8.4 billion spent for private coverage. Overall, insurance overhead accounted for 1.9 percent of Canadian health care spending, or $47 per capita."

129. "A recent price comparison of a U.S. Internet pharmacy with a Canadian Internet pharmacy, for example, found that the price of 60 capsules of 100-mg celecoxib is $92 in the United States and $54 in Canada; the price of fluticasone propionate nasal spray is $60 versus $40; 90 tablets of 20-mg atorvastatin is about $276 versus $205, and 180 tablets of 10-mg generic tamoxifen is about $140 versus $45 (in U.S. dollars based on an exchange rate of $1.34)." (Jennifer Fisher Wilson, "Cheaper Drugs in Foreign Markets Increase the Focus on Domestic Drug Prices," *Annals of Internal Medicine* 140, no. 8 [Apr. 20, 2004]: 677–80, quote on p. 677.) Furthermore, "In a recent report comparing prices in 8 countries relative to the United States, Danzon determined that Japan paid more for prescription drugs than U.S. consumers, while the other countries— Canada, Chile, France, Germany, Italy, Mexico, and the United Kingdom— paid 6% to 33% less." This is corroborated in study after study. For example, "a 30-day supply of clozapine (Clozaril, Novartis), costs $51.94 in Spain, $294.93 in the UK, $271.08 in Canada, and $317.03 in the USA. The newest antipsychotic, olanzapine (Zyprexa, Eli Lilly), costs $76.87 in Spain and $324.08 in the USA. If prices for clozapine and Lilly's fluoxetine (Prozac) were reduced to the average European price, US purchasers would save $1.1 billion, said HRG." (Alicia Ault, "Call for Tightening of U.S. Drug Price Controls," *Lancet* 352, no. 9124 [July 25, 1998], 299).

130. Bureau of Labor Statistics, Current Employment Statistics Survey, 2002.

131. Jonathan Oberlander, *The Political Life of Medicare* (Chicago: University of Chicago Press, 2003).

132. When my child was in the hospital for four months and I watched my paychecks evaporate, I checked the Stanford Web site for ways to "lower my medical expenses." The benefits page suggested exercising more, eating better, and some other unfathomably ridiculous things. Around that time Stanford faculty and staff also received an email from the dean explaining the rising costs of medical care as a result of the increase in technological progress. These rhetorics about personal responsibility (exercise) and technology (progress) completely miss the way in which expenses grow in corporate-based medical insurance.

133. For the latter estimate, see Elizabeth Warren, Teresa A. Sullivan, and Melissa B. Jacoby, "Medical Problems and Bankruptcy Filings" (April 2000), *Norton's Bankruptcy Adviser*, May 2000, *http://ssrn.com/abstract=224581*. See also Elizabeth Warren, Teresa A. Sullivan, and Melissa B. Jacoby, Harvard Law School Public Law working paper, No. 8, and University of Texas Law, Public Law Research Paper No. 9. This article furthermore notes that "households without a male present were nearly twice as likely to file for bankruptcy giving a medical reason or identifying a substantial medical debt as households with a male present." And, "[o]f debtors 65 or older, 47.6% listed a medical reason, as compared with 7.5% of debtors under 25."

134. National Economic Accounts, Bureau of Economic Analysis, Department of Commerce, *http://www.bea.doc.gov/bea/dn2/gpoc.htm#1994–2001*. Reflecting consumer spending in 2003, "Medical Care" is the largest category of services.

135. National Highway Traffic Safety Administration, "The Economic Impact of Motor Vehicle Crashes 2000" (U.S. Department of Transportation, DOT HS 809 446, May 2002), also reported in "Cost of Crashes Has Increased Dramatically, NHTSA Reports," *Insurance Institute for Highway Safety Status Report* 37, no. 7 (Aug. 17, 2002): 6. It is not clear in the article how far these statistics go in including costs.

136. In 1999, pharmaceutical companies spent $1.8 billion on direct-to-consumer advertising. Andrew Ellner, "Rethinking Prescribing in the United States," *http://bmj.bmjjournals.com/cgi/content/full/327/7428/1397?eaf*.

137. Marcia Angell, "The Pharmaceutical Industry—To Whom Is It Accountable?" *New England Journal of Medicine* 342 (2000): 1902–4. Indeed, it is very difficult to ascertain spending patterns on advertising and research. Kurt Brekke and Michael Kuhn write that "the pharmaceutical industry is one of the most advertising intensive industries" (1). They cite Schweitzer, saying "the marketing expenses for three of the largest US pharmaceutical companies—Merck, Pfizer, and Eli Lilly—ranged from 21 to 40% of annual sales, while the R&D expenses varied between 11 and 15%. Similar figures are reported from Novartis and Aventis, the largest pharmaceutical companies in Europe" (1). (Brekke and Kuhn, "Direct-to-Consumer Advertising in Pharmaceutical Markets," working paper 9, 2003 [Program in Health Economics, Department of Economics, University of Bergen], 1–23. See also S. O. Schweitzer, *Pharmaceuti-*

cal Economics and Policy [New York: Oxford University Press, 1997].) On the other hand, the Pharmaceutical Research and Manufacturers Association (PhRMA) states in their 2004 annual report that member companies spent $2.5 billion on research and development in fiscal year 2003, while $13.9 billion was spent on promotion of pharmaceuticals to doctors and consumers during the same period. (PhRMA, May 23, 2001; *http://www.phrma.org/mediaroom/press/ releases/23.05.2001.225.cfm.*) PhRMA member institutions include among them such "big pharma" companies as AstraZeneca, Bayer, Biogen Idec, Bristol-Myers Squibb, GlaxoSmithKline, Hoffman LaRoche, Johnson & Johnson, Ortho, Eli Lilly, Merck & Co., Novartis, Pfizer, Schering-Plough, and Wyeth Pharmaceuticals.

PhRMA's reports on industry spending have been roundly criticized. A report by the American Medical Student Association ("Issue Forum on the Pharmaceutical Industry") sums up these critiques as follows:

> In 2000, an analysis of 11 Fortune 500 pharmaceutical companies showed that 30% of their revenues went to marketing while only 12% went to research and development. Promotional spending on prescription drugs rose from $9 billion in 1996 to $15.7 billion in 2000 . Of that $15.7 billion, 26% or $4 billion was spent on detailing to doctors. Promotion to health care professionals accounts for 80% of pharmaceutical marketing expenses. It increased from $8.4 billion to $13.2 billion between 1996 and 2000. (*http://www.amsa.org/hp/COCForum_Pharm.doc*)

138. Nader, *Unsafe at Any Speed*, vi. See also William Haddon Jr., Edward A. Suchman, David Klein, *Accident Research: Methods and Approaches* (New York: Harper and Row, 1964), who note that medical research is funded at 300 times the amount of accident prevention (4). They trace this to a folklore of accidents that says they just happen, and also that prevention is a threat to industry since it implies responsibility. Furthermore, they write that "health and safety has become one of the basic needs in modern life."

139. Proctor, *Cancer Wars*, 266–67.

140. Peter S. Green, "Czechs Debate Benefits of Smokers' Dying Prematurely," *New York Times*, July 21, 2001, Sect. C, p. 2.

141. For an insightful analysis of the historical purification of economic passions, see Sylvia Junko Yanagisako, *Producing Culture and Capital: Family Firms in Italy* (Princeton: Princeton University Press, 2002).

142. See Bell and O'Connell, *Accidental Justice*, for an outline of how quickly even a wealthy family can become destitute after the serious injury of a breadwinner—and how this desperation leads even initially disinclined people to find a deep pocket and sue.

143. Scarry, *Bodies in Pain*, 20.

144. Ibid., 122–23.

145. Marion Nestle, *Food Politics: How the Food Industry Influences Nutrition and Health* (Berkeley: University of California Press, 2002), 4.

146. The endless desire on the part of producers to create new niche markets has recently introduced the market of girl "tweens." I recently attended a talk by a corporate anthropologist (Intel, Feb. 2002) in which the vulnerabilities of

this group were carefully analyzed to understand how they might more effi-caciously be targeted as a market. One notes here first the injurious intent of using people's vulnerabilities for the sole purpose of making money (using a potential vulnerability to advertise in such a way as to capitalize on that vul-nerability such that the person will purchase products that make her think she is assuaging that vulnerability), and in doing so, in this case, invariably leading to further injury in a sort of prosthetic circularity. But second, what it is about the culture of U.S. capitalism that makes good—or at least normal, social be-ings—people do this kind of work, and that makes this kind of work so highly remunerative? Like the cigarette industry representative I sat beside on a flight from San Francisco to Toronto who simultaneously claimed that he did not want his teenage daughter to smoke and obsessively talked about the massive sushi bill that he and his colleagues had racked up the previous evening. Cor-porate branding has somehow been able to interpellate white-collar workers into aligning their identities with the corporation, even as citizens hold con-flicting demands of parent and worker. Part of the way this can happen is through the remuneration gained through this kind of work: the anthropolo-gist and the tobacco executive knowingly promote injurious products that they do not want for their own "tweens," but in doing the work they are able to provide private educations, health care, and other goods to their families.

147. Paco Underhill, *Why We Buy: The Science of Shopping* (New York: Touch-stone Books, 2000).

148. Ralph Nader analyzes the nag factor as one facet of the "corporatiza-tion" of kids that is intended to prepare them for a life of brand consumption. Ralph Nader, Alternative Radio, "Corporate Power: Profits before People," lec-ture and interview, September 1, 1994, #RNAD3b.

149. In 2001 corporations spent over $230 billion in advertising. (McCann-Erickson U.S. Advertising Volume Reports and Bob Coen's Insider's Report for December 2001 [*web.archive.org/web/20011202101952/http://www.mccann.com/insight/bobcoen.html*].) The 2000 census reported 105 million households in the United States. (U.S. Census Report, Sept. 2001, Households and Families: 2000.)

150. Cheryl Idell, Lucy Hughes, and Dick Huston, "MarketResearch C'mon, Mom! Kids Nag Parents to Chuck E. Cheese's, Selling to Kids," May 12, 1999 (c) Phillips Publishing International, Inc., *http://www.findarticles.com/p/articles/mi_m0FVE/is_9_4/ai_54631243*.

151. For $3,325, reduced from $3,500, one can have instant online delivery of *The U.S. Kids Market*, 6th ed. (2004), which analyzes the consumer behavior of kids aged 3–12 and their parents. Available at *http://www.packagedfacts.com/pub/928713.html*.

152. J. DiFranza and T. McAfee, "The Tobacco Institute: Helping Youth Say 'Yes' to Tobacco," *Journal of Family Practice* 34, no. 6 (1992), *http://www.findarticles.com/p/articles/mi_m0689/is_n6_v34/ai_12348520*.

153. L. Bird, "Joe Smooth for President," *Adweek's Marketing Week*, May 20, 1991.

154. Paul M. Fischer, Meyer P. Schwartz, John W. Richards Jr., Adam O. Goldstein, and Tina H. Rojas, "Brand Logo Recognition by Children Aged Three to Six Years," *Journal of the American Medical Association* 266, no. 22 (1991): 3145–48. At the beginning of the campaign, the brand had less than 1 percent of the under age eighteen market. Within three years, it had a one-third share of the youth market—and nearly one-half billion dollars in annual sales. Joseph R DiFranza, John W. Richards, Paul M. Paulman, Nancy Wolf-Gillespie, Christopher Fletcher, Robert D. Jaffe, and David Murray, "RJR Nabisco's Cartoon Camel Promotes Camel Cigarettes to Children," *Journal of the American Medical Association* 266 (1991): 3154–58; Karen Lewis, "Addicting the Young: Tobacco Pushers and Kids," *Multinational Monitor* 44, no. 1–2, Jan./Feb. 1992, *http://www.multinationalmoniter.org/hyper/issues/1992/01/mm0192_07.html*.

155. "In 2000, the most common actual causes of death in the United States were tobacco (435,000) and poor diet and physical inactivity (400,000)." Alcohol consumption came in third, with an estimated 85,000 deaths. Center for Disease Control, "Fact Sheet: Actual Causes of Death in the United States, 2000," *http://www.cdc.gov/nccdphp/publications/actual_causes.htm*.

156. James McNeal and Chyon-Hwa Yeh, "Born to Shop," *American Demographics*, June 1993, pp. 34–39.

157. For older children, one might mention toy guns, violent computer games, sexualized girls' underwear, and Barbie dolls—all products that arguably contain violent and injurious underbellies in the ways that they create and normalize gender identities.

158. *Pelman*, 237 F. Supp. 2d at 534–37.

159. Carol Sanger, "Girls and the Getaway: Cars, Culture, and the Predicament of Gendered Space," *University of Pennsylvania Law Review* 144, no. 2 (Dec. 1995): 705–56, quote on p. 712.

160. For a more detailed analysis of automobility and identity, see Sarah Jain, "Violent Submission," in *Cultural Critique*, forthcoming.

161. Lizabeth Cohen, *A Consumers' Republic: The Politics of Mass Consumption in Postwar America* (New York: Knopf, 2003).

162. Ibid., 141.

163. Ibid., 146.

164. Social activist groups such as anti-fur organizations have at times successfully repartnered violent means of production to the act of consumption. In other ways, violence may become part of the "fetish" quality products. I analyze this in *Commodity Violence*.

165. Cohen has a fascinating discussion of recent notions of citizenship and identity politics—notions that both Democrats and Republicans have been able to use in their advertising, whereas in the 2000 election Nader depended on a notion of citizenship represented by his flagship organization Public Citizen. (See Cohen, *Consumers' Republic*, chapter 8, pp. 345–98.)

166. Excellent reviews of the history of the consumer's movement are provided by Cohen, *A Consumer's Republic*, and Silber, *Test and Protest*.

167. Cited in Greg Critser, *Fat Land: How Americans Became the Fattest People in the World* (Boston: Houghton Mifflin, 2003), 3.

168. Adriana Petryna, *Life Exposed: Biological Citizens after Chernobyl* (Princeton: Princeton University Press, 2002), 14–15. See also Jake Kosek, *Understories: The Political Life of Forests in Northern New Mexico* (Durham: Duke University Press, 2006).

169. Lauren Berlant, "The Subject of True Feeling: Pain, Privacy, and Politics," in *Left Legalism/Left Critique*, ed. Wendy Brown and Janet Halley (Durham: Duke University Press, 2002), 105–33, quote on pp. 107–8.

170. Duncan Kennedy argues this point in "The Critique of Rights in Critical Legal Studies," in *Left Legalism/Left Critique*, ed. Wendy Brown and Janet Halley (Durham: Duke University Press, 2002), 178–228.

171. Anthropologist Aiwa Ong has rewritten the notion of citizenship from a completely different angle to mean, rather than a particular identification with a nation-state, "the cultural logics of capitalist accumulation, travel, and displacement that induce subjects to respond fluidly and opportunistically to changing political-economic conditions." Ong, *Flexible Citizenship: The Cultural Logics of Transnationality* (Durham: Duke University Press, 1999), 6.

172. Berlant, "The Subject of True Feeling," 108.

173. Wendy Brown, *States of Injury: Power and Freedom in Late Modernity* (Princeton: Princeton University Press, 1995). Brown, *States of Injury*, 27.

174. See James C. Scott, *Seeing Like a State: How Certain Schemes to Improve the Human Condition Have Failed* (New Haven: Yale University Press, 1998).

175. Therefore we might valuably think about injury as a boundary object, how it carries stakes for various parties reflected through the ways that it is represented. Adele Clarke and Theresa Montini use this approach in their study of RU486; see "The Many Faces of RU486: Tales of Situated Knowledges and Technological Contestations," *Science, Technology, & Human Values* 18, no. 1 (winter 1993): 42–78.

176. Koenig and Rustad, "His and Her Tort Reform."

177. "The Fund provides an alternative to the significant risk, expense, and delay inherent in civil litigation by offering victims and their families an opportunity to receive swift, inexpensive, and predictable resolution of claims. The Fund provides an unprecedented level of federal financial assistance for surviving victims and the families of deceased victims." September 11th Victim Compensation Fund of 2001, Lexsee 67 FR 11233, Federal Register, vol. 67, no. 49, Rules and Regulations, Department of Justice, Office of the Attorney General, 28 CFR Part 104 (CIV 104F; AG Order No. 2564–2002), RIN 1105-AA79. See also Elizabeth Kolbert, "The Calculator: How Kenneth Feinberg Determines the Value of Three Thousand Lives," *The New Yorker*, Nov. 25, 2002.

178. Sheila Jasanoff has traced the changes in court systems in dealing with these new mass class action suits in "Science and the Statistical Victim: Modernizing Knowledge in Breast Implant Litigation," *Social Studies of Science* 32, no. 1 (Feb. 2002): 37–69, quote on p. 42.

179. What if the *New York Times* published car accident deaths on its back page each day, as it did with the deaths resulting from the attacks on the World Trade Center? We would see, as we did then, images of good people (over 100 each day) and the testimony of those who loved them. The contradictory

mandates among state interests in consumption, injury, and protection are a total social fact in the state and corporate management of injury.

180. And in each of these cases, the moral judgments on injury seem to differ. Consider Wendy Brown's observations of neo-liberalism in this light:

> In making the individual fully responsible for her/himself, neo-liberalism equates moral responsibility with rational action; it relieves the discrepancy between economic and moral behaviors by configuring morality entirely as a matter of rational deliberation about costs, benefits, and consequences. In so doing, it also carries responsibility for the self to new heights: the rationally calculating individual bears full responsibility for the consequences of his or her action no matter how severe the constraints on this action, e.g., lack of skills, education, and childcare in a period of high unemployment and limited welfare benefits. . . . The model neo-liberal citizen is one who strategizes for her/himself among various social, political and economic options, not one who strives with others to alter or organize these options."

(Brown, "Neo-liberalism and the End of Liberal Democracy," *theory and event* 7, no. 1 [2003], article available at *http://muse.jhu.edu/journals/theory_and_event/*.

181. The Personal Responsibility in Food Consumption Act is referred to in the vernacular as the "cheeseburger bill." It is described as a "bill to prevent frivolous lawsuits against the manufacturers, distributors, or sellers of food or non-alcoholic beverage products that comply with applicable statutory and regulatory requirements." Lexsee 108 H.R. 339: "To prevent legislative and regulatory functions from being usurped by civil liability actions brought or continued against food manufacturers, marketers, distributors, advertisers, sellers, and trade associations for claims of injury relating to a person's weight gain, obesity, or any health condition associated with weight gain or obesity." At the time of this writing the bill had passed the House but not the Senate.

182. Marilyn Strathern, "Losing (out on) Intellectual Resources," in *Law, Anthropology, and the Constitution of the Social: Making Persons and Things*, ed. Alain Pottage and Martha Mundy (New York: Cambridge University Press, 2004), 201–33, quote on p. 221, citing M. Minnegal and P. Dwyer, "Women, Pigs, God, and Evolution: Social and Economic Change among Kubo People of Papua New Guinea," *Oceania* 68, no. 47 (1997): 47–60 (emphasis original).

183. Strathern, "Losing (out on) Intellectual Resources," 201–33, quote on pp. 221–22.

184. Michel Callon, "An Essay on Framing and Overflowing: Economic Externalities Revisited by Sociology," in *The Laws of Markets*, ed. Michel Callon (New York: Blackwell, 1999), 255.

185. Mitchell, *Rule of Experts*, 292.

186. The file on the short-handled hoe at the CRLA in Salinas includes all of the transcriptions of the Division of Industrial Safety's hearings on the hoe, newspaper clippings, the studies and correspondence related to the studies done on the use of the hoe across the United States, letters that were written to the CRLA in support of its work, petitions and briefs written by the CRLA attorneys, and the notes of attorneys who worked on the case. When specific documents are not directly cited, future notes will cite this file. See also Mau-

rice Jourdane, *The Struggle for the Health and Legal Protection of Farm Workers El Cortito* (Houston: Arte Publico Press, 2004).

187. Transcript of the Salinas hearing, Mar. 27, 1975, 29.

188. Bart Goldie, "Study of Soledad and Orange Cove," senior thesis, Community Studies, UCSC, May 31, 1971, 10.

189. Ibid., 13.

190. Alma Rose, Transcript of the Salinas hearing, Mar. 27, 1975, 37. Another worker testified, "I came to the U.S. five years ago, and that is the first time I saw the short-handled hoe. I looked at it and not listening to what others said, I said that instrument cannot hurt me. But after using the short hoe for a few months it sure did change my mind, because it hurt so much I have decided never to use the short hoe again. I don't care if I am ridiculed by my friends that I was not a man and afraid to use the short hoe." (Jose Marks, eighteen years old, Transcript of the Salinas hearing, Mar. 27, 1975, 35.) The quality of the transcription varies for each hearing. Many of the farm workers testified in their second language. I have made minor editorial changes in the cases where there has been an obvious translation or transcription error.

191. Douglas Murray, "The Abolition of El Cortito, The Short-Handled Hoe: A Case Study in Social Conflict and State Policy in California Agriculture," *Social Problems* 30, no. 1 (Oct., 1982): 28.

192. Carey McWilliams, *Factories in the Field: The Story of Migratory Farm Labor in California* (Boston: Little, Brown, 1939). This book appeared the same year as *The Grapes of Wrath*, and both created an uproar among growers of California.

193. Transcript of the Salinas hearing, May 3, 1973.

194. Most of the doctors who worked on the case are deceased or no longer practicing. Dr. Oakley Hewitt, the one doctor who testified for the defenders of the short hoe and is still in practice at this writing at the Palo Alto Medical Clinic, refused to talk to me. His nurse reported that he "doesn't want anything to do with it."

195. Much of this was found in the file of the Salinas branch of the CRLA. I asked both of the attorneys working on the side of the growers for their records (Richard Maltzman and Asher Rubin). Although they seemed willing to giving them to me, they were unable to locate their files.

196. Michel-Rolph Trouillot, *Silencing the Past: Power and the Production of History* (Boston: Beacon Press, 1995), 52.

197. Murray, "The Abolition of El Cortito," 37. The goal of Murray's paper is to explore an example of "how social problems are solved within the state arena and how state policy affects the sources of social conflict" (27).

198. Although the victory "belonged" to the CRLA, a strategic decision was made to attribute the work on the short-handled hoe to Chavez and the United Farm Workers. Martin Glick, interview by the author, San Francisco, June 1, 1998; Maurice Jourdane, interview by the author, San Diego, Dec. 10, 1998.

199. For a highly readable account of California farming and land ownership history and irrigation, see John Opie, *The Law of the Land: Two-Hundred Years of American Farmland Policy* (Lincoln: University of Nebraska Press, 1987), especially chapter 9, "The California Difference," 133–49. For a far more de-

tailed account, see Robert C. Fellmeth, *Politics of Land: Ralph Nader's Study Group Report on Land Use in California* (New York: Grossman, 1973).

200. In 1870, 1/500 of the population owned one half or more of all agricultural land in the state. McWilliams, *Factories in the Field*, 23.

201. Ernesto Galarza, *Merchants of Labor: The Mexican Bracero Story* (Santa Barbara: McNally and Loftin, West, 1978), 25.

202. Lawrence J. Jelinek, *Harvest Empire: A History of California Agriculture*, 2nd ed. (San Francisco: Boyd and Fraser, 1982), 52.

203. They were also hired to reclaim five million acres of swamp in San Francisco Bay and the Sacramento-San Joaquin River delta and produced $60–90 million in wealth annually, according to a congressional committee estimate. Theo J. Majka and Linda C. Majka, *Farm Workers, Agribusiness, and the State* (Philadelphia: Temple University Press, 1982), 20.

204. Organized opposition to Chinese immigration began as early as 1859. Majka and Majka, *Farm Workers*, 22. See also Jelinek, *Harvest Empire*, 53.

205. Maxine Hong Kingston, *China Men* (New York: Vintage Books, 1977), 153, quoting a congressman. Her chapter "The Laws" (153–59) outlines the laws relating to Chinese immigration and exclusion from the 1868 Burlingame Treaty to 1978 immigration quotas. The California referendum on Chinese exclusion turned up a vote of 154,638 for and 833 against (Majka and Majka, *Farm Workers*, 24).

206. Majka and Majka, *Farm Workers*, 24–25. For an account of how the Chinese were reinscribed as "friendly" during World War II, see Ronald Takaki, *Strangers from a Different Shore: A History of Asian Americans* (Boston: Little, Brown, 1989), 370–79.

207. Majka and Majka, *Farm Workers*, 5.

208. Ibid., 12.

209. Between 1880 and 1910, 15,000 miles of railways were built through uninhabited land to export gold, silver, and copper from Mexico to the United States (Galarza, *Merchants of Labor*, 27.) The Mexican Civil War of 1911 caused a wave of immigration and provided a new set of agricultural laborers.

210. For more on Mexican American deportation during the depression, see Camille Guerin-Gonzales, *Mexican Workers and American Dreams: Immigration, Repatriation and California Farm Labor, 1900–1939* (New Brunswick, NJ: Rutgers University Press, 1996). She argues that the "failure of the federal government to protect farm workers during the 1930s had tremendous consequences for the entrenchment of Mexican immigrants as a reserve labor force constructed as foreign and temporary" (134). Another author who focuses on migrant workers in the early century is Don Mitchell, *The Lie of the Land: Migrant Workers and the California Landscape* (Minneapolis: University of Minnesota Press, 1996).

211. Jelinek, *Harvest Empire*, 67.

212. Galarza, *Merchants of Labor*, 39.

213. The price of California's lettuce, for example, can range from $2.50 to $15.00 a carton. William H. Friedland, Amy E. Barton, and Robert J. Thomas, *Manufacturing Green Gold: Capital, Labor, and Technology in the Lettuce Industry* (New York: Cambridge University Press, 1981), 44.

214. Jelinek, *Harvest Empire*, 68.

215. Quoted in Galarza, *Merchants of Labor*, 39.

216. Ibid., 42–44. The program was first run through the Farm Security Administration (a department of the New Deal), but after industry complaints it was switched to the War Manpower Commission in 1943. Galarza, *Merchants of Labor*, 51.

217. Quoted in Galarza, *Merchants of Labor*, 55.

218. Patrick H. Mooney and Theo J. Majka, *Farmers' and Farm Workers' Movements: Social Protest in American Agriculture* (New York: Twayne, 1995), 152.

219. Lee G. Williams, quoted in ibid., 152.

220. Richard B. Craig, *Bracero Program: Interest Groups and Foreign Policy* (Austin: University of Texas Press, 1971), 14–15.

221. Jelinek, *Harvest Empire*, 84.

222. Guerin-Gonzales writes that "the Bracero Program resuscitated and helped to perpetuate the perception of Mexicans as foreign, temporary, male workers, although renewed immigration from Mexico was anything but temporary" (*Mexican Workers*, 135).

223. Jelinek, *Harvest Empire*, 84–85.

224. Mooney and Majka, *Farmers' and Farm Workers' Movements*, 154.

225. Glick interview.

226. Fred J. Heistand, "The Politics of Poverty Law," in *With Justice for Some: An Indictment of the Law by Young Advocates*, ed. Bruce Wasserstein and Mark J. Green (Boston: Beacon Press, 1972), 160–89, quote on p. 163. Because of the seasonal nature of farm work, the average Mexican American family income in 1970 was $4,000. Mexicans were excluded from unemployment insurance and virtually excluded from public assistance (only 7 percent of Mexican American families received public assistance in 1965).

227. Heistand, "The Politics of Poverty Law," 180.

228. Ibid.

229. Michael Bennett and Cruz Reynoso, "California Rural Legal Assistance (CRLA): Survival of a Poverty Law Practice," *Chicano Law Review* 1, no. 1 (1972): 78–79.

> For years and years Chicano and other farm workers had no representation while their large corporate employers had plenty—in the State Legislature and Congress, the Governor's mansion, and before the courts. And these facts shaped the laws of agricultural employment: Agribusiness became accustomed to legal *rights* called the bracero program (subsidized labor supply), federal and state water projects (subsidized irrigation), and the Agricultural Extension Service (subsidized research and technical assistance . . .), and the national Soil Bank (subsidized non-use of land). Each cost the tax payer billions, and each cost the farm workers jobs, wages, and dignity. On the other hand, farm workers were the only Americans that Congress specifically *excluded* from the statutory right to a minimum wage, collective bargaining, and unemployment insurance. . . . [When worker housing, wage, and labor conditions codes were legislated,] enactments were rarely enforced and violators never punished. (78)

230. Heistand, "The Politics of Poverty Law," 184.

231. Despite the official end to bracero labor importation at the end of 1964, the practice continued until 1967 through a loophole in the law. The CRLA lawsuit challenged the fact that growers' claims of labor shortages (if they demonstrated this they could import labor through a clause in the ban) were never verified by the Department of Labor. As a result, 1968 was the first year that bracero labor was not imported (although by 1970, 50,000 commuter aliens were admitted into the state and over 180,000 illegal immigrants entered). Heistand, "The Politics of Poverty Law," 164–66; Bennett and Reynoso, "California Rural Legal Assistance," 8–10.

232. Heistand, "The Politics of Poverty Law," 182.

233. *America's War on Poverty*, film series; Hector de la Rosa, interview by the author, Salinas, CA, May 11, 1998; Jerome B. Falk and Stuart R. Pollak, "Political Interference with Publicly Funded Lawyers: The CRLA Controversy and The Future of Legal Services," *Hastings Law Journal* 24 (1973): 607; "Diana File" at CRLA office in Salinas.

234. For a description of the ways in which the welfare department's attorney's depositions were used to press criminal fraud charges against welfare recipients, see Heistand, "The Politics of Poverty Law," 169.

235. Heistand, "The Politics of Poverty Law," 183. See Bennett and Reynoso, "California Rural Legal Assistance," for an account of the biased ways in which information on the CRLA was collected by Lewis K. Uhler. The practice of hiring illegal immigrants "cost northern California farm workers approximately $2.7 million in lost wages in 1969 and costs to the public increased annual welfare expenditures of not less than $1.4 million for the support of domestic farm workers and their families" (166). With state expenditures so high, it is no wonder that Reagan wanted to cut welfare and medical care and, rather than ensuring decently paid work for farm workers, try to have them disappear from statistics and other information by erasing them from any state registration.

236.

The origin of certain measures designed to cripple or kill legal services belied their purported purpose. Thus, when [Republican senator] George Murphy moved to give a line item veto to state governors over legal services, it was less likely intended, as claimed, to decentralize legal service than, as he acknowledged on the floor of the Senate, to permit governors to stop litigation against the growers hiring illegal entrants. When the Justice Department resorts to collecting dossiers on legal service attorneys—a clandestine activity, so there is no rationale provided by the department as yet—it is logical to infer that they are resentful of defending, and losing, numerous cases in which the federal government is sued by legal service attorneys. (Heistand, "The Politics of Poverty Law," 175–76)

237. Quoted in Falk and Pollak, "Political Interference," 641. "The California Farmer estimated that growers' newspaper and magazine ads, radio and TV spots, billboards, and other organizational efforts netted Reagan 800,000 votes." *California Farmer*, June 17, 1967, 14, quoted in Bennett and Reynoso, "California Rural Legal Assistance," 10n. 38.

238. De la Rosa interview; Jourdane, interview.

239. Jourdane interview.

240. Murray reports the year as 1973, although the petition I found in the CRLA archives is dated Sept. 20, 1972. Murray, "The Abolition of El Cortito."

241. California Labor Code, Section 6306 (a).

242. Jourdane and the other main attorney on the case, Martin Glick, realized that when this clause had been challenged it was for tools that had been individually faulty or broken but believed it to be their only option. (Jourdane interview.) Jourdane's petition included affidavits from eight injured and disabled farm workers; the statements of five physicians; the results of a study comparing back injuries of workers using the short-handled hoe to farm workers not using the short-handled hoe in Orange Cove (Bart Goldie); the results of a nationwide study examining different states' crops and how they were thinned (finding that all other states used the long-handled hoe for the same and similar crops corroborated by farm worker statements on working in other states); a declaration by a labor contractor who claimed that he started using the long-handled hoe and it was better all around; and a list of a number of sections in the California Labor Code that he argued should be applied to create a safe working space for farm workers, including the abolition of the short-handled hoe. He also noted that section 142 imposes "the duty to enforce its safety orders" on the Division of Industrial Safety.

243. Murray, "The Abolition of El Cortito," 33.

244. Ibid.

245. Transcript of the San Diego hearing, Mar. 24, 1975, 15.

246. Ibid., 32.

247. De la Rosa interview.

248. Jourdane interview.

249. The short-handled hoe was manufactured in Virginia and Sacramento, and cost between $2.50 and $2.85 and was heavier than the long hoe (CRLA files).

250. Transcript of the Imperial (El Centro) hearing, May 1, 1973, 53.

251. Ibid., 55–56.

252. Transcript of the Salinas hearing, Mar. 27, 1975, 27.

253. Ibid., 16.

254. Robert Granger, quoted in "Two Views on Short Handled Hoe," editorial, *Salinas Californian*, May 3, 1973. Also in Granger, transcript of the Salinas hearing, May 3, 1973, 14.

255. Transcript of the Salinas hearing, Mar. 27, 1975, 22.

256. Paul Englund, transcript of the Salinas hearing, May 3, 1973, 44.

257. George Betz from Bruce Church, quoted in "Two Views on Short Handled Hoe," editorial, *Salinas Californian*, May 3, 1973.

258. Mervyn Baily, transcript of the Salinas hearing, May 3, 1973, 33.

259. Hector de la Rosa, a community worker for the CRLA, claims that labor contractors would pay them for the afternoon of work if they testified that short hoe was not injurious while telling them that without hoes there would be no jobs. De la Rosa, interview.

260. Transcript of the Salinas hearing, May 3, 1973, 9.

261. CRLA file; de la Rosa interview.

262. For more on the gender presumptions of the wording of "workmen's compensation," see Penny Kome, *Working Wounded* (Toronto: University of Toronto Press, 1998). Although in the 1970s workmens' compensation was still the term in use, I use the current, more gender representative workers' compensation.

263. Transcript of the Imperial (El Centro) hearing, May 1, 1973, 12–22, testimony of Dr. Robert W. Murphy (discussed by other doctors as well).

264. Dr. Murphy, transcript of the Imperial (El Centro) hearing, May 1, 1973, 20.

265. Ibid., 22.

266. Transcript of the Salinas hearing, Mar. 27, 1975, 28.

267. Michael Rucka, interview by the author, Salinas, CA, June 4, 1998.

268. Dr. Robert Thomson, transcript of the Imperial (El Centro) hearing, May 1, 1973, 29.

269. Ibid., 31. Thomson argued that farm workers did not know about workers' compensation.

> But also I fill out workmen's compensation forms, and there are a couple of reasons for this. One is that the patient I typically see is a man who comes in complaining of an acute onset of back pain which occurred while he was lifting an irrigation ditch, or jumping over the edge, or lifting a piece of pipe. . . . And I know the man has worked off and on for a number of years using the short-handled hoe in a bent position. What I fill out on this form that we get from Pan American Underwriters is that he has acutely injured his back, for example, while lifting an irrigation ditch [*sic*]. Now, if he doesn't tell me that, if I don't have something specific I can tie that to, I don't bother to fill out the workmen's compensation form. What I do is fill out a State disability insurance form, and frequently send the man down to the welfare department.

270. Transcript of the Imperial (El Centro) hearing, May 1, 1973.

271. Rucka interview.

272. David Flanagan, transcript of the Salinas hearing, May 3, 1973, 62.

273. Ibid.

274. Michael Rucka, transcript of the Salinas hearing, May 3, 1973, 23.

275. Ibid., 25. Rucka told me that once it became clear that the hoe was going to go, doctors were much more willing to diagnose the hoe-related injuries. Rucka interview.

276. Transcript of the Salinas hearing, May 3, 1973, 8.

277. Jose Cavazos argues this in relation to lettuce cutting. Transcript of the Salinas hearing, Mar. 27, 1975.

278. Transcript of the Salinas hearing, Mar. 27, 1975, 29.

279. Transcript of the Imperial (El Centro) hearing, May 1, 1973, 47.

280. Ibid.

281. Hisaura Garza, sociology Ph.D. student, ex-farm worker testifying in Salinas, May 3, 1973, 61. Another worker suggests that "primarily it's a question of riders. They're the guys that are pushing the crew, and if the people are standing you can't tell whether they're really working at a steady pace or not. When they're bending over you know they're working. It's not a question of having a better productivity or a better quality of work, it's just a matter of having all the people down at the same time so you know they're working." Manuel Olvidas, transcript of the San Francisco hearing, Mar. 6, 1973, 31.

282. Transcript of the Salinas hearing, Mar. 27, 1975, 25.

283. Transcript of the Imperial (El Centro) hearing, May 1, 1973, 4.

284. Ibid., 39.

285. Transcript of the Salinas hearing, Mar. 27, 1975, 31.

286. Otis Glendenning, transcript of the Imperial (El Centro) hearing, May 1, 1973, 24.

287. Glick interview.

288. Edward White, memo, May 3, 1975, CRLA file.

289. Press release, "Industrial Safety Board Denies Petition against Short Hoe," July 13, 1973, CRLA file.

290. The CRLA filed a petition for rehearing in August 1973 that primarily addressed the medical proof issue. Jourdane claims that a rehearing was denied, and they then took the issue to the California Supreme Court (CRLA file).

291. Glick interview.

292. *Sebastian Carmona et al. v. Division of Industrial Safety*, Jan. 13, 1975. The California Supreme Court in general, and Justice Tobriner specifically, were known to be extremely pro-plaintiff in cases of product liability law. Whether or not the court was swayed by the crowd of farm workers in the audience, who, Asher Rubin claims, were planted to garner sympathy for the cause, remains a question. (Asher Rubin, telephone conversation with the author, June 4, 1998.)

293. Glick was appointed as head of the State Employment Department and Rose Bird became agricultural secretary. A number of anti-hoe advocates were now "insiders." (Glick interview.) Administrative edict, Administrative Interpretation No. 62, Division of Industrial Safety, Apr. 7, 1975.

294. The popular folk singer Malvina Reynolds sent a copy of her song "El Cortito" to Jourdane. The chorus reads, "Bend down Ronnie Handsome / And manicure the land / Bend down / Mister Governor / How I'd love to see you bend / Moving along the endless rows with the short hoe in your hand." (c) 1973, Schroder Music Co. (ASCAP) Berkeley, 94704 (CRLA file).

295. Several authors have pointed out that growers were only spurred to embrace new technologies when they could no longer exploit labor. The mechanical tomato harvester provides one such example. While it had been developed by the mid-1950s, it was adopted for use only after the end of the bracero program. (Carroll Pursell, *The Machine in America: A Social History of Technology* [Baltimore: Johns Hopkins University Press], 293–94; R. Douglas Hurt, *Agricultural Technology in the Twentieth Century* [Manhattan, KS: Sunflower University Press, 1991], 88–98; and Langdon Winner, "Do Artifacts Have Politics?" *Daedalus* 109, no. 1 [winter 1980]: 121–36.) After the short-handled hoe was abolished, massive state funding was given to the University of California–Davis in 1975 to develop new methods of seeding and new seeds, which were at first wrapped in strips of plastic to protect them from pests. As stronger seeds were developed, hoe work on the starts became altogether unnecessary. (De la Rosa interview.) A strip of the plastic-enclosed seeds is on file at the Salinas office of the CRLA.

296. "Praise for Long Hoes," *San Francisco Chronicle*, Apr. 15, 1975, 20.

297. For example, California growers groups, including the Grower-Shipper Vegetable Association, the Western Growers Protective Association, and the

California Farm Bureau Federation, were particularly vocal about interning the Japanese. The Grower-Shipper Vegetable Association claimed in the *Saturday Evening Post* in May 1942: "We've been charged with wanting to get rid of the Japs for selfish reasons, we might as well be honest. We do. It's a question of whether the white man live on the Pacific Coast or the brown man. They came into this valley to work, and they stayed to take over. . . . If all the Japs were removed tomorrow, we'd never miss them in two weeks, because the white farmers can take over and produce everything the Jap grows." Takaki, *Strangers from a Different Shore*, 389.

298. Transcript of the San Diego hearing, Mar. 24, 1975, 8–9. Dr. Hewitt still works at the Palo Alto Medical Clinic, but he chose not to speak to me about his involvement in this case.

299. Transcript of the Salinas hearing, May 3, 1973, 33.

300. For more on the control of pain as a crucial aspect of power, see Scarry, *Bodies in Pain*.

301. Guerin-Gonzales, *Mexican Workers*, 135.

302. Scarry, *Bodies in Pain*, 122. See also Hortense J. Spillers, "Mama's Baby, Papa's Maybe: An American Grammar Book," *Diacritics* 17, no. 2 (summer 1987): 65–81, for a related argument on slaves, in which she distinguishes "flesh" from "body" as central to the difference between captive and liberated subject positions.

303. Robert Jay Lifton, *Home from the War: Learning from Vietnam Veterans* (New York: Beacon Press, 1992), 198. It may seems anachronistic to compare the Vietnam War to capitalist mass production in this way. There are clear and present differences, such as the fact that American soldiers were constantly under the threat of death themselves. A key point Lifton makes is that the Americans, "themselves under constant threat of grotesque death," needed to find, "in a real sense create, a group more death tainted than themselves, against whom they [could] reassert their own continuity of life" (197) However, one of my primary goals in this book is to examine the ways in which everyday technologies imbricate with lives to create the everyday conditions of trauma, while the broader literature that has recently coalesced under the rubric of "trauma studies" has focused more distinctly on discretely violent events of war.

304. Lifton, *Home from the War*, 199. For a different but related reading of the ways in which racial slurs cite histories of trauma and thus reiterate trauma "through the linguistic substitution for the traumatic event," see Judith Butler, *Excitable Speech: A Politics of the Performative* (New York: Routledge, 1997), 36.

305. Transcript of the San Diego hearing, Mar. 24, 1975. Affidavit of Dr. Berkeley Huett (Oakley Hewitt) read into the record by Richard Maltzman, 8–9.

306. Maltzman, transcript of the San Diego hearing, Mar. 24, 1975, 12.

307. Transcript of the Salinas hearing, May 3, 1973, 42–43.

308. Lloyd Heger, transcript of the Imperial (El Centro) hearing, May 1, 1973, 8.

309. Otis Glendenning, transcript of the Imperial (El Centro) hearing, May 1, 1973, 25.

310. Transcript of the San Diego hearing, Mar. 24, 1975, 35.

311. In his analysis of the relationship between reason and violence in the state, Michael Taussig distills the key facets of Max Weber's account of the way in which political domination legitimates itself into two points: first, through the "monopoly on the legitimate use of violence within a given territory," and second, through the "State's embodiment of Reason, as in bureaucratic forms." Taussig adds, however, that "[w]hat we are missing here . . . are the intrinsically mysterious, mystifying, convoluting, plain scary and arcane cultural properties and power of violence to the point where violence is very much an end in itself—a sign . . . of the existence of the Gods." Taussig, "*Maleficium*: State Fetishism," in *Fetishism as Cultural Discourse*, ed. Emily Apter and William Pietz (Ithaca: Cornell University Press, 1993), 223.

312. Scarry, *Bodies in Pain*, 14.

313. Ibid., 17.

314. De la Rosa interview.

315. Michael Taussig examines the social significance of the devil in the folklore of plantation workers and miners in South America in *The Devil and Commodity Fetishism in South America* (Chapel Hill: University of North Carolina Press, 1980).

316. This account is based on personal communication with Michael Rucka, workers' compensation attorney, Feb. 10–19, 1999.

317. California Labor Code, section 5412.

318. Rucka, Personal communication.

319. Ibid.

320. Trouillot, *Silencing the Past*, 16.

321. Mark Twain, "The First Writing Machines," in *The $30,00 Bequest and Other Stories"* (New York: Harper and Brothers, 1906), available at *wysiwyg:// 291/http://www.boondocksnet.com/twintexts/writing_machines.html*.

322. For more on Australia, see Andrew Hopkins, "The Social Recognition of Repetition Strain Injuries: An Australian/American Comparison," *Social Science and Medicine* 30, no. 3 (1990): 365–72.

323. In the United States alone there are an estimated 230,000 carpal tunnel surgeries a year, each with a 54–56 percent success rate and a minimum of two to six months loss of hand use. By the mid-1990s RSI accounted for 56 percent of the illnesses reported to OSHA (double the amount reported in 1984). The American Academy of Orthopedic Surgeons estimated that RSI costs $27 billion annually in medical treatment and lost income. In 1989, 3.2 million cases of RSI were serious enough to take time away from jobs, adding up to 57 million lost workdays. These statistics do not, of course, include writers and students who are not considered laborers, nor do they include people who, due to the nature of the injury and labor relations, do not report it. See Kate Montgomery, "The Body Is Not a Robot," *Massage* 57 (Sept./Oct. 1995): 58.

The difficulties of collecting injury data are reported in A. Olenick J.D., M.D. et al., "Current Methods of Estimating Severity for Occupational Injuries and Illnesses: Data for the 1986 Michigan Comprehensive Compensable Injury and Illness Database," *American Journal of Industrial Medicine* 23 (1993): 231–2. The authors argue that the present federal and state systems for estimating occupational injury underestimate the problem by as much as a factor of eight. See also H. N. Diwaker and J. Stothard, "What Do Doctors Mean by Tenosynovitis and Repetitive Strain Injury?" *Occupational Medicine* 45, no. 2 (1995): 97–104. I use medical establishment in this essay as an umbrella term that includes doctors, physical therapists, nurses, and other practitioners of medicine.

324. Denis Paul Judge et al., "Cumulative Trauma Disorders—'The Disease of the 90's': An Interdisciplinary Analysis," *Louisiana Law Review* 55 (1995): 895–96. Laura Punnett explains that computer-induced disorders fall in a grey area between injuries (which refer to acute onset pain attributable to a "moment in time") and illnesses, which have more gradual onset. This distinction is used by the Bureau of Labor Statistics, yet, as she claims, it is an arbitrary distinction that affects the way that statistics are collected.

325. Theresa A. Cortese, "Cumulative Trauma Disorders: A Hidden Downside to Technological Advancement," *Journal of Contemporary Health Law and Policy* 11 (1995): 479–504; Russell Leibson and Danny Wan, "Statutes of Limitations and Repetitive Strain Injuries: Winning Strategies," *Defense Counsel Journal* 61 (1994): 399; J. Stratton Shartel, "Defense Litigators Should Not Relax after Early Wins in Computer Keyboard Trials," *Inside Litigation* 8 (1994): 2; Lawrence Chesler, "Repetitive Motion Injury and Cumulative Trauma Disorder: Can the Impending Wave of Products Liability Litigation Be Averted?" *New York State Bar Journal* 64 (1992): 30–35.

326. *Shirl Jeanne Howard v. Digital Equipment Corporation and Honeywell, Inc.*, C.A. No. 95–905, 1998 U.S. Dist, LEXIS 18795; CCH Prod. Liab.Rep. P15, 418. The court granted the manufacturers' motion for summary judgment and entered the judgment against the user (quote on p. 20).

327. Phil Waga, "The Threat of Repetitive Stress—Keyboard Injuries Are a Legal Time Bomb," *Seattle Times*, May 3, 1995, D1; Steve Lohr, "Vigorous Defense Stalls Injury Claims on Repetitive Strain," *New York Times*, May 29, 1995, 37.

328. Tom Jackman, "IBM Not Responsible for Injuries, Jury Says," *Kansas City Star*, Oct. 24, 1996, C1.

329. N. Khilji and S. Smithson, "Repetitive Strain Injury in the UK: Soft Tissues and Hard Issues," International Journal of Information Management 14 (1994): 95–108; H. Jacubowicz and Andrew Meekosha, "Repetition Strain Injury: The Rise and Fall of an 'Australian' Disease," *Critical Social Policy* 11, no. 1 (1991): 18–37; A. Hopkins, "The Social Construction of Repetitive Strain Injury," *Australian and New Zealand Journal of Sociology* 25 (1988): 239–59.

330. Steven Phillips, phone interview by the author, June 15, 2004.

331. Cortese, "Cumulative Trauma Disorders," 496. Katia Hetter, "Closing Arguments in $6 Million RSI Suit," *Newsday*, June 12, 1998, A71, reports that there are, at present, over 1,000 RSI suits pending.

332. "Jury Awards $5.3 Million to Carpal Tunnel Plaintiff; First Time Keyboard Maker Liable in RSI Case," *Washington Post*, Dec. 10, 1996, D1; Hetter, "Closing Arguments in $6 Million RSI Suit.".

333. Laura Punnett, phone interview by the author, July 5, 2004.

334. Proximate cause in an RSI case would be evidence that directly linked keyboard and/or mouse use to the injury. I spoke to one sufferer in Toronto

who was told repeatedly by her doctor that her RSI was computer keyboard induced, yet when she asked him to testify on her behalf in court he refused.

335. Reynolds Holding, "RSI Suits May Finally Catch up with Apple," *San Francisco Chronicle*, Jan. 19, 1997, 6/Z1.

336. Phillips interview.

337. David Thompson, phone interview by the author, Apr. 23, 2004.

338. David A. Thompson, "ergonomic Analysis of a DEC Keyboard, Portola Associates," p. 9. This report was written by the request of Ms. MaryBeth Scarcello in the case of *Linda Doll v. Digital Equipment Corporation*, 1995 (on file with author).

339. Ibid.

340. Ibid.; Restatement (Third) of Torts, sec. 2(c) (draft adopted at May 1997 meeting of American Law Institute).

341. Waga, "The Threat of Repetitive Stress"; Lohr, "Vigorous Defense Stalls Injury Claims on Repetitive Strain."

342. The basic content of this statement has been repeated by Cerussi time and time again in newspaper articles on RSI product liability litigation.

343. *Blanco v. American Telephone and Telegraph Co., et al.* (unpublished decision and order of the Supreme Court of New York, Appellate Division, First Department, Aug. 1, 1996; on file with author).

344. *Blanco*, 6. "Toxic tort" extends the statute of limitations for certain chemical injuries for which the injury was not evident until long after the statute of limitations had passed. "Latent Harms and Risk-Based Damages," *Harvard Law Review* 111 (1998): 1505–22.

345. *Blanco*, 7–8.

346. Gary Spencer, "Filing of Keyboard Claims Limited; Statute of Limitations Middle Ground Taken," *New York Law Journal*, Nov. 26, 1997, 1.

347. Since the lion's share of the cases settled, few can be traced through published legal venues. In part I have been able to get around this by interviewing lawyers involved in the cases.

348. *Howard*, 1.

349. *Creamer v. IBM Corp.*, 877 F.2d 54.

350. Citing *Reiff v. Convergent Technologies*, 957 F Supp. 573 (D.N.J. 1997).

351. *Howard*, 16, emphasis added.

352. *Howard*, 16–17, emphasis added.

353. Ibid., 16, emphasis added.

354. *Howard*, 17.

355. John Larner, *Culture and Society in Italy, 1290–1420* (New York: Charles Scribner's Sons, 1971), 157.

356. Bernardini Ramazzini, *De Morbis Artificum* (1713), trans. Wilmer Cave Wright (Chicago: University of Chicago Press, 1940), 420–25.

357. Allard Dembe, *Occupation and Disease: How Social Factors Affect the Conception of Work-Related Disorders* (New Haven: Yale University Press, 1996), 29–35.

358. James H. Lloyd, *The Diseases of Occupations*, (1895), 45, quoted in Dembe, *Occupation and Disease*, 32; Stephen Tyrer, "Repetitive Strain Injury," editorial, *Journal of Psychosomatic Research* 38, no. 6 (1994): 493.

359. Michael H. Adler, *The Writing Machine: A History of the Typewriter* (London: Allen and Unwin, 1973); and George Carl Mares, *The History of the Typewriter: Being an Illustrated Account of the Origin, Rise, and Development of the Writing Machine* (London: Guilbert Pitman, 1909; reprinted as *The History of the Typewriter, Successor to the Pen* [Arcadia, CA: Post-Era Books, 1985]).

360. Terry Abraham, "Charles Thurber: Typewriter Inventor," *Technology and Culture* 21, no. 3 (1980): 430–34. Similarly, Charles Thurber and his brother-in-law, Ethan Allen, also early typewriter inventors, manufactured firearms. "Because of the mechanical skills and techniques involved, many firearms firms became involved in the manufacture of precision machined devices" (431).

361. George Nichols Engler, "The Typewriter Industry: The Impact of a Significant Technological Innovation" (Ph.D. diss., University of California–Los Angeles, 1969).

362. James W. Cortada, *Before the Computer: IBM, NCR, Burroughs, and Remington Rand and the Industry They Created, 1865–1956* (Princeton: Princeton University Press, 1993), 85.

363. London also writes in that book: "sitting at my machine, in the stifling, shut in air, repeating, endlessly repeating, at top speed, my series of mechanical motions." Mark Seltzer, *Bodies and Machines* (New York: Routledge, 1992), 15, quoting Jack London's *John Barleycorn* (1913).

364. QWERTY is the standard key layout. The letters QWERTY appear as the first five keys on the top left row. Jan Noyes, "The QWERTY Keyboard: A Review," *International Journal of Man-Machine Studies* 18 (1983): 265–81. This explanation is also commonly given in the vast literature on RSI in popular magazines.

365. Noyes, "The QWERTY Keyboard" (discussing various explanations and a detailed bibliography of the keyboard ergonomic literature throughout the century).

366. Wilfred A. Beeching, *Century of the Typewriter* (New York: St. Martin's, 1974), 41.

367. R. C. Cassingham, *The Dvorak Keyboard: The Ergonomically Designed Typewriter Keyboard, Now an American Standard* (Arcata, CA: Freelance Communications, 1986), 24.

368. Dvorak found, for example, that from a sample of 3,000 words, 300 were typed by the right hand alone, and 2,700 by the left. Noyes, "The QWERTY Keyboard," 267, 270–72.

369. Dembe, *Occupation and Disease*, 35–43.

370. By 1907 there were nearly 16,000 telegraphic systems in use in Great Britain. Dembe, *Occupation and Disease*, 36.

371. Departmental Committee on Telegraphists' Cramp, *Report of the Departmental Committee on Telegraphists' Cramp* (London: His Majesty's Stationery Office, 1911) (hereafter Committee on Telegraphists' Cramp).

372. A 1984 Australian study found that 56 percent of keyboard users had symptoms of keyboard injuries, 8 percent serious enough to need medical help. Winn L. Rosch, "Does Your PC—Or How You Use It—Cause Health Problems?"

PC Magazine, Nov. 25, 1991, 493. The hand positioning necessary to use the mouse is almost exactly the same as that required to use a telegraph machine.

373. Margery W. Davies, *A Woman's Place Is at the Typewriter: Office Work and Office Workers, 1870–1930* (Philadelphia: Temple University Press, 1982), 54.

374. Margery Davies, "Women Clerical Workers and the Typewriter: The Writing Machine," in *Technology and Women's Voices: Keeping in Touch,* ed. Chris Kramarae (New York: Routledge, 1988), 29; Bruce Bliven Jr., *The Wonderful Writing Machine* (New York: Random House, 1954), 15. Davies's work was the first feminist examination of the typewriter; previous histories are misogynist indeed—either tangentially discussing the enabling facets of the typewriter for women, praising the wonderful and profitable lives of secretaries, or eliding gender altogether.

375. In 1870, women accounted for 4.5 percent of the 154 people employed as stenographers and typists; by 1900, they accounted for 76.7 percent of 112,699, and by 1930, 95.6 percent of 811,200. Margery Davies, "Woman's Place Is at the Typewriter: The Feminization of the Clerical Labor Force," *Radical America* 8 (1974): 10. In 1968, 40 percent of women in the workforce were employed as clerical and sales workers. For important histories of this shift in the gender of clerical workers, see Gregory Anderson, ed., *The White-Blouse Revolution: Female Office Workers since 1870* (Manchester: University of Manchester Press, 1988); H. Braverman, *Labor and Monopoly Capital* (New York: Monthly Review Press, 1974); Lisa M. Fine, *The Souls of the Skyscraper: Female Clerical Workers in Chicago, 1870–1930* (Philadelphia: Temple University Press, 1990); Rosemary Pringle, *Secretaries Talk: Sexuality, Power, and Work* (New York: Verso, 1988).

376. Davies, "Women Clerical Workers," 29.

377. The main skill of clerical work was literacy, and in the last decades of the nineteenth century the number of female high school graduates significantly exceeded that of male graduates. Davies, "Women Clerical Workers," 56.

378. Bliven, *The Wonderful Writing Machine,* 13.

379. Forty, *Objects of Desire.*

380. Davies, *A Woman's Place,* 54 (quoting statement made by U.S Treasurer General Francis Elias Spinner in 1869).

381. Forty, *Objects of Desire,* also noting that by the 1950s factory wages were higher than clerical wages.

382. Cockburn, "The Material of Male Power," in *The Social Shaping of Technology,* ed. Donald MacKenzie and Judy Wajcman (Philadelphia: Open University Press, 1999), remains one of the standard texts on this phenonenon.

383. Frederick Taylor, author of *The Principles of Scientific Management* (1911), is considered to be the main proponent of the popularization of scientific management. Taylorism is typically understood to mean the "rationalization through the analysis of work (time and motion studies to eliminate wasteful motions) and the 'scientific selection' of workmen for prescribed tasks." David A. Hounshell, *From the American System to Mass Production, 1800–1932: The Development of Manufacturing Technology in the United States* (Baltimore:

Johns Hopkins University Press, 1984), 249. Hounshell discusses Taylor's influence on the development of factories at the turn of the century.

384. Forty, *Objects of Desire*, 123 (citing W. H. Leffingwell, *Scientific Office Management* [1917]).

385. The word ergonomics was developed in World War II by the British.

386. Forty, *Objects of Desire*, 122–39.

387. Fine, *The Souls of the Skyscraper*, analyzes films such as *The Stenog* (1918), *His Secretary* (1925), *Summer Bachelors* (1926), *The Trespasser* (1929), and *The Office Wife* (1930). Novels addressing clerical work include: Booth Tarkington, *Alice Adams* (1921); Sinclair Lewis, *The Job* (1917); John Dos Passos, *U.S.A.* (1937); Christopher Morley, *Kitty Foyle* (1937); Christopher Morley, *Human Beings* (1935); and Ruth Suckow, *Cora* (1929).

388. Fine, *The Souls of the Skyscraper*, 140.

389. *The Lyre and the Typewriter* (1913), cited in Friedrich A. Kittler, *Discourse Networks, 1800/1900* (Stanford: Stanford University Press, 1990), 359.

390. Kittler, *Discourse Networks*, 359.

391. Homi Bhabha expressed his views on anxiety at a presentation given at the American Anthropological Association meeting, San Francisco, Nov. 1996. "Affect" is defined in psychoanalytic terms as an "expression or instigation of a general mood," a "psychical energy attached to an idea or group of ideas." Jean LaPlanche and J-B. Pontalis, *The Language of Psycho-Analysis*, trans. Donald Nicholson-Smith (New York: Norton, 1973).

392. Wendy Brown argues that women are constitutively excluded from the eroticization of power through violence and discusses the warrior in terms of Weber's "prestige of domination." She writes, "The problem . . . is one most feminists can recite in their sleep. Historically, women have been culturally constructed and positioned as the creatures to whom this pursuit of power and glory for its own sake stand in contrast: women preserve life while men risk it; women tend the mundane and the necessary while men and the state pursue larger than life concerns. . . . The distinction between daily existence preserved by women and the male pursuit of power or prestige through organized violence simultaneously gives a predatory, rapacious, conquering ethos to prerogative power and disenfranchises women from this kind of power" (*States of Injury*, 190). I argue here that it is not only power from which women are disenfranchised but the way of eroticizing control and power as evident in the quote from the young man.

393. Pictured in Lupton, *Mechanical Brides*, 42.

394. Abigail Solomon-Godeau, "The Other Side of Venus: The Visual Economy of Feminine Display," in *The Sex of Things: Gender and Consumption in Historical Perspective*, ed. Victoria De Grazia and Ellen Furlough (Berkeley: University of California Press, 1996), 113.

395. On the one hand, the point can in part be demonstrated by the semiotic conflation of typewriter and type writer, one referring to the machine and the other to the user. On the other, inventions such as the Lazy Susan, Tin Lizzy, and Spinning Jenny have been inscribed with girls' names.

396. Solomon-Godeau, "The Other Side of Venus," 113. In this essay she traces the preconditions for the "connotative linkage of the erotics of femininity with the commodity" and the "homology between the seductive, possessable feminine and the seductive, possessible commodity" (114).

397. Lupton, *Mechanical Brides*, 43–44.

398. Pringle, *Secretaries Talk*, quoted in Lupton, *Mechanical Brides*, 48.

399. The opinion of this committee was: "the nervous breakdown known as telegraphists' cramp is due to a combination of two factors, one a nervous instability on the part of the operator, and the other repeated fatigue during the complicated movements required for sending messages by hand on a telegraph instrument . . . a person of average health can suffer fatigue again and again indefinitely without becoming affected with cramp; but if a nervous instability exists, fatigue cannot be prolonged beyond a certain point without causing cramp. This point depends on the nervous constitution of the subject, and varies not only in different persons but in the same person at different times according as the nervous 'tone' is affected by general health or other conditions." Committee on Telegraphists' Cramp, 9.

400. S. Freud and J. Bruer, *Studies in Hysteria*, trans. A. A. Brill (Boston: Beacon Press, 1961).

401. Dembe, *Occupation and Disease*, 47.

402. Ibid., 52.

403. Ibid., 53. Dembe concludes his section of low reportage by stating: "[A] major increase in cases did not take place until the mid-1980s. At that point, in the course of a few years, a new surge of public, legal, and medical attention was directed at occupationally-induced hand and wrist disorders. The reported incidence of these disorders began to rise and has increased substantially each year since. During this period, new medical terms—*cumulative trauma disorders* and *repetitive stress injuries*—became part of the common lexicon of occupational safety and health" (66). It is precisely this medical and legal attention that materializes, or brings into being, the injury in the social consciousness.

404. Forty, *Objects of Desire*, 133.

405. Noyes, "The QWERTY Keyboard," 267, 270–72; Cassingham also notes that a U.S. report titled, "A Practical Experiment in Simplified Keyboard Retraining" (July 1944), was classified for several years after its production for no apparent reason.

406. Ergonomics was developed to facilitate the coding and manipulation of body and machine design to splice and exact an elegant cybernetic loop. Donna Haraway writes, "Ergonomics is . . . rigorously directed to studying labor in terms of technical systems design, especially attending to the operational breakdown of any factor under stress. Ergonomics seeks answers to questions like: What information does an operator need? What are the most efficient channels for getting information to the receiver-operator? What communication loads are tolerable for each component? Stress, a psychiatric and medical concept crucial to postwar ideology and practice, is intimately linked to these communications theoretical questions about system potential and de-

sign limits" (Haraway, "The High Cost of Information in Post–World War II Evolutionary Biology: Ergonomics, Semiotics, and the Sociobiology of Communication Systems," *The Philosophical Forum* 13 [1982]: 250.) Ergonomics in contemporary computer use hygiene literature, for example, is precisely about locating stress breakdown in the human components of the man-machine system. What exercises should the office worker do? How many breaks are necessary? What type of chair maintains correct posture?

407. Kroemer keyboard, studied in 1972 but based on a 1926 keyboard design.

408. K. H. Eberhard Kroemer, "Human Engineering the Keyboard," *Human Factors* 14, no. 1 (1972): 51–63.

409. Kroemer, "Human Engineering the Keyboard"; David G Alden, Richard W. Daniels, and Arnold F. Kanarick, "Keyboard Design and Operation," *Human Factors* 14, no. 4 (1972): 274–93, and Noyes, "The QWERTY Keyboard." For other work of keyboard design and injury see J. Buesen, "Product Development of an Ergonomic Keyboard," *Behavior and Information Technology* 3, no. 4 (1984): 387–90; Joan Duncan and D. Ferguson, "Keyboard Operating Posture and Symptoms in Operating," *Ergonomics* 17, no. 5 (1974): 651–62; D. Ferguson and Joan Duncan, "Keyboard Design and Operating Posture," *Ergonomics* 17, no. 6 (1974): 731–44; Stephen K. Jones, Michael J. Gerard, Leo A. Smith, Robert E. Thomas, and Tai Wang, "An Ergonomic Evaluation of the Kinesis Ergonomic Computer Keyboard," *Ergonomics* 37, no. 10 (1994): 1661–67; Elaine Serina, Paul Smutz, and David Rempel, "A System for Evaluating the Effect of Keyboard Design on Force, Posture, Comfort, and Productivity," *Ergonomics* 37, no. 10 (1994): 1649–60.

410. George Phalen recognized the physiological etiology of carpal tunnel syndrome and developed the surgical techniques to partially remedy it. Dembe, *Occupation and Disease*, 69–77.

411. Dembe, *Occupation and Disease*, 74. Dembe notes that although inattention to the details of discrete job risk factors was not rare, other physicians did conduct careful studies of hand and arm use in occupations. For example, Radford C. Tanzer organized studies in the 1950s that involved collecting occupational histories and details about manual activities required during daily work.

412. Dr. George Phalen, interview by Allard Dembe, Sept. 29, 1993, and July 18, 1994, quoted in Dembe, *Occupation and Disease*, 74.

413. The founder of the company that later became IBM made his first major breakthrough in the development of a punch card machine that would collate census data in the 1890s. A critical flaw in the equipment was painfully revealed to Herman Hollerith during the tests in Baltimore. To punch holes in the cards, he had used a small handheld punch of the type employed by trade conductors. Although the conductors' punch was satisfactory for intermittent use, it was not suitable for punching thousands of holes in cards. Hollerith's hand and arm became nearly paralyzed after spending a day continually punching holes in cards. Emerson Pugh, *Building IBM* (Cambridge, MA: MIT Press, 1995), 10.

414. Diana Brahms, "Medicine and the Law: Keyboard Operators' Repetitive Strain Injury," *Lancet* 339 (Jan. 25, 1992): 237.

415. Lisa Gitelman, *Scripts, Grooves, and Writing Machines: Representing Technology in the Edison Era* (Stanford: Stanford University Press, 1999), 39–41.

416. In a series of interviews I did as another part of this research on RSI, I spoke to a number of people who lost jobs because of their struggles with the injury and who were unable, once injured, to switch to other work. See the publication of the Association for Repetitive Motion Syndromes (P.O. Box 47193, Aurora, CO 80047–1973).

417. Jonathan Goldberg, *Writing Matter: From the Hands of the English Renaissance* (Stanford: Stanford University Press, 1990), 24.

418. Goldberg, *Writing Matter*, 236.

419. J. I. Whalley, *Writing Implements and Accessories: From the Roman Stylus to the Typewriter* (Newton Abbott, England: David & Charles, 1975), 60.

420. Forty, *Objects of Desire*, 137, quoting W. H. Leffingwell, *The Office Appliance Manual* (1926), 344. With this analysis of advertisements I do not mean to imply that users immediately accepted marketing rhetoric as "truth." On the contrary, much of the facade and aesthetisization was, and remains, an attempt to displace anxieties over new technologies. In some cases this is all too obvious. An ad for Fujistsu ("built for humans") illustrates a huge skeletal hand beside which it claims "the human HAND also known as: the 'CRUSHER.' Able to inflict massive amounts of damage when confronted with a poorly designed notebook. In extreme cases, it is quite capable of putting a hole in the wall." The "design" of the notebook is not considered in terms of hardware at all—indeed, the notebook is very conventional in its shape and size. The Fujitsu advertisement appears in *Wired*, Jan. 1997, 28–29, and *Wired*, Feb. 1997, 42–43. An integrated communications software program (FocalPoint) advertisement takes a full-page spread to claim: "We've changed the dreaded, backbreaking, mind-numbing, painful task of communicating through your computer." Again, the silhouette of a fellow seated with his hands on his lap, facing a computer screen only implies a change to the internal designs aspects of computing. *Wired*, May 1996, 106–7.

420. Gary Lee Downey, *The Machine in Me: An Anthropoligist Sits among Computer Engineers* (New York: Routledge, 1998), 151.

421. Of the fourteen computer ads that appear in four arbitrarily chosen issues of *Wired* Magazine, ten show images of bodies juxtaposed with the machines. Seven of those bodies are male, three are female, and three are children. All except two are white. None of the bodies is actually using the machines. Indeed, most are not even depicted on the same scale as the machines; they are shown doing another activity altogether, or in the background. *Wired*, Jan. 1996, 2–3, 36–37; *Wired*, Mar. 1996, 27, 34–35; *Wired*, May 1996, 38–39, 75; *Wired*, Apr. 1997, 74–75. I am not including here ads for computer components or software, which were even less likely to show people at the keyboard. The one image of a black man is accompanied by text that claims, "I marched on Washington and never left home." The copy continues, by saying that the Acer computer allows one not just to "talk change and betterment" but to "make it happen." *Wired*, May 1996, 75.

422. The first computers were marketed more like cars, with heterosexually available looking young women standing suggestively beside them. See illustrations in Pugh, *Building IBM*.

423. *Wired*, Dec. 1995, 18–19.

424. On voice overuse, see Tenner, *Why Things Bite Back*.

425. This advertisement has appeared in several magazines. *Wired*, May 1996, 38–39.

426. Microsoft Natural Keyboard advertisement (on file with author).

427. This increase in keyboard use is documented in several occupations in Barbara Garson, *The Electronic Sweatshop* (New York: Penguin, 1988); J. Gregory and K. Nussbaum, "Race against Time: Automation of the Office," *Office: Technology and People* 1 (1982): 197–236.

428. Lohr, "Vigorous Defense Stalls Injury Claims."

430. Thompson, "Ergonomic Analysis of a DEC Keyboard, Portola Associates."

431. Frank R. Wilson, *The Hand: How It Shapes the Brain, Language, and Human Culture* (New York: Vintage Books, 1998).

432. Barendsen, "Light at the End," 41–42.

433. Lee Balefsky, personal communication with the author, June 30, 2004.

434. Punnett interview.

435. The complaint that people never even knew about the possibility of the injury until they got it is made time and time again, for example, on the "sorehand" email list, *http://www.ucsf.edu/sorehand/*, shared by hundreds of RSI sufferers. There are local and national chapters of organizations for RSI sufferers that offer support and information as well as lobby on their behalf. For a list, see Emil Pascarelli, M.D. and Deborah Quilter, *Repetitive Strain Injury: A Computer User's Guide* (New York: Wiley, 1994), 205–9.

436. *Greenman v. Yuba Power Products, Inc.*, 59 Cal. 2d 57 (1963). This is the case that is typically referred to for the key articulation of strict liability. Marshall Shapo, *Products Liability and the Search for Justice* (Durham: Carolina Academic Press, 1993); and Franklin and Rabin, *Tort Law and Alternatives*.

437. *Greenman*, 59 Cal. 2d at 64.

438. Punnett interview.

439. Many of the major mass torts relating to women have had to do with reproductive medications and implants. It has also been noted that the compensation for women's injury compared to men's injury of reproductive organs is about 10 percent less. Kerith Cohen, "Truth and Beauty, Deception and Disfigurement: A Feminist Analysis of Breast Implant Litigation," *William and Mary Journal of Women & Law* 1, no. 149 (1990): 153. The medical establishment has generally acknowledged that drugs are usually tested on men, and that therefore female patients can be in effect "marketplace guinea pigs." Malcolm Gladwell, "Women's Health Research to Be New Priority at NIH," *Washington Post*, Sept. 11, 1990, A17. Kinney et al., "Indiana's Medical Malpractice Act," demonstrates that women are less likely to be able to show that their bodies are as valuable as men's bodies.

440. *Brown v. Philip Morris, Inc.*, 1999 U.S. Dist Lexis 14495 (1999).

441. Second Amended Class Action Complaint, section A.5.

442. Michael D. Basil, Caroline Scooler, David G. Altman, Michael Slater, Cheryl L. Albright, and Nathan Maccoby, "How Cigarettes Are Advertised in Magazines: Special Messages for Special Markets," *Health Communication* 3 (1991): 75–91. Menthol has only very recently been studied for potential carcinogenic compounds, and the issue is still controversial.

443. Karen Ahijevych and Mary Ellen Wewers, "Factors Associated with Nicotine Dependence among African American Women Cigarette Smokers," *Research in Nursing and Health* 16 (1993): 283–92.

444. Laurie Hoffman-Goetz, Karen K. Gerlach, Christina Marino, and Sherry L. Mills, "Cancer Coverage and Tobacco Advertising in African-Americans' Popular Magazines," *Journal of Community Health* 22 (1997): 261–71. This study, which was conducted on adult women, found that women read popular magazines in order to acquire information rather than from habit.

445. U.S. Department of Health and Human Services, *Health Status of Minorities and Low-Income Groups* (Washington, DC: U.S. Department of Health and Human Services, 1990), 17.

446. Brown found documents from the Minnesota lawsuit that led him to conclude that the industry knew that menthol, "even in small doses, destroys mucus membranes." Sabrina Rubin, "Holy Smokes!" *Philadelphia Magazine*, Feb. 1999, 23. Web version at *http://www.naaapi.org/documents/justice.asp*. The article reports further dangers of mentholated cigarettes.

447. Claims of breach of warranty or fraud and misrepresentation were interpreted by the court as state law claims, not civil rights claims, and were therefore dismissed by the U.S. District Court for the Eastern District of Pennsylvania. *Brown*'s other claims, brought under section 1983, were dismissed since *Brown* was unable to show that tobacco companies should be understood as "state actors." Similarly, charges brought under section 1985(3) were dismissed on statutory grounds. Judge Padova's opinion of September 21, 1999, is posted on the Brown and Williamson Web site, *http://www.brownandwilliamson.com*.

448. Gene Borio, "Tobacco Timeline," *Tobacco BBS, http://www.tobacco.org*, 2001.

449. B&W document cited in Times News Service, "Tobacco Industry's Ad Assault on Blacks Is Detailed in Records Newly Released," *St. Louis Post-Dispatch*, Feb. 8, 1998, A14.

450. In 1974 B&W sold 56.1 billion units of Kool after spending $15 million for advertising the cigarette in 1973. "Brown & Williamson Tobacco Co.," *Advertising Age*, Aug. 26, 1974, 76. R. J. Reynolds Tobacco Company (RJR) introduced Salem in 1956, the first filter-tip menthol, which by 1960 outsold Kool three to one. By the late 1960s, however, B&W's Kool was again the best-selling mentholated brand. Klugar, *Ashes to Ashes*, 93.

451. Michael Omi and Howard Winant, *Racial Formation in the United States: From the 1960s to the 1990s*, 2nd ed. (New York: Routledge, 1994), 99.

452. The possibly apocryphal story is that Lloyd "Spud" Hughes's mother insisted he inhale menthol crystals for his asthma. He soon noticed that when he stored his menthol and cigarettes in a tin container, the cigarette was pleasantly flavored.

453. Kluger, *Ashes to Ashes*, 93.

454. Ibid.

455. Ad is on file at Archive of Cigarette Advertising, University of British Columbia, Vancouver, curated by Richard Pollay.

456. Shannon P. Duffy, "Court Urged to Dismiss Menthol Cigarette Class Action," *Law News Network*, Apr. 8, 1999.

457. Adam Hochberg, "Menthol Suit," National Public Radio's *All Things Considered*, Nov. 2, 1998.

458. R. Eccles, "Menthol and Related Cooling Compounds," *Journal of Pharmacy and Pharmacology* 46 (1994): 618–30. Menthol can also be extracted or synthesized from other essential oils such as citronella, eucalyptus, and Indian turpentine oils. Eccles cites a number of studies demonstrating that menthol inhalation causes "a subjective nasal decongestant effect without any objective decongestant action" (622). Thanks to Stuart Anderson of the London School of Hygiene and Tropical Medicine; Katie Eagleton, assistant curator of the London Science Museum; and George Twigg for email communication on the issue of menthol's history and tobacco.

459. Robert E. Weems, *Desegregating the Dollar: African American Consumerism in the Twentieth Century* (New York: New York University Press, 1998), 34. In 1963 Dave Berkman found forty-nine ads for patent medicines and other health aids in *Ebony* compared to only fourteen in *Life*. He notes that this "was not an unexpected finding in a magazine whose readership contains such a high proportion of people engaged in work demanding heavy physical exertion (and a race whose memberships' deaths occur, on the average, about eight years earlier than among the White population)." Berkman, "Advertising in *Ebony* and *Life*: Negro Aspirations vs. Reality," *Journalism Quarterly* 40 (1963): 43–64, 54–55.

460. "Documents about the Kool brand showed that the company sought to 'capitalize upon the erroneous consumer perception that their [*sic*] is a health benefit to smoking mentholated cigarettes.'" Richard Pollay, "Getting Good and Being Super Bad: Chapters in the Promotion of Cigarettes to Blacks," working paper, History of Advertising Archives, University of British Columbia, 1993, 18.

461. "Merit Ethnic Research," Jan. 1980, Bates: 2047167333–2047167497. Report is available online at *http://tobaccodocuments.org/pm/2047167333–7497.html*. See also Tibor Koeves Associates for Philip Morris Inc., "A Pilot Look at the Attitudes of Negro Smokers toward Menthol Cigarettes," Sept. 1968. Posted on *Philip Morris Incorporated Document Site, http://www.pmdocs.com*. (Search using Bates number, 1002483819/3830.) This study concludes, "here was a product [menthols] which by some virtue was especially suited to the needs, desires, and tastes of Negro consumers."

462. Warren Mitchell quoted in Tracey Reeves, "A Targeted Payback: Black Communities in Md. Want More Tobacco Money," *Washington Post*, Feb. 16, 2000, B1.

463. Editorial, *Ebony*, Aug. 1967.

464. Paul M. Hirsch, "An Analysis of *Ebony*: The Magazine and Its Readers," *Journalism Quarterly* 45 (1968): 267–68. In 1966, circulation was 926,644. *The Negro Handbook* (Chicago: Johnson, 1966), 384.

465. Hirsch, "An Analysis of *Ebony*, 261–70, 292.

466. Other 1960s ads for mentholated cigarettes are collected in the Archive of Cigarette Advertising at the University of British Columbia.

467. Stuart Ewen, *PR!: A Social History of Spin* (New York: Basic, 1996), 53–54.

468. Hirsch reports that by 1966, "CORE, SNCC, and the Southern Christian Leadership Conference were out of favor with *Ebony* and its readers" ("An Analysis of *Ebony*," 267).

469. Purposefully resisting the middle-class assimilationist African American identity that attended the menthol image, professor and activist Angela Y. Davis, for example, told me that she smoked unfiltered Pall Malls in the mid-1960s rather than mentholated cigarettes.

470. Many thanks to Deborah Bright, who offered me substantial written feedback on a very early draft.

471. John H. Johnson with Leone Bennett Jr., *Succeeding against the Odds: The Inspiring Autobiography of One of America's Wealthiest Entrepreneurs* (New York: Warner, 1989), 90.

472. As described in *The Negro Handbook*, compiled by the editors of *Ebony*. This compilation of facts and statistics on the African American community was, suggests Robert Weems, possibly a guide to the black community for white corporations—with a distinct bias against black-owned businesses. Weems, *Desegregating the Dollar*, 74–75.

473. Johnson, *Succeeding against the Odds*, 161.

474. Ibid., 230.

475. "Admans' Guide to Negro Media," *Sponsor* (*Negro Market Supplement*) 21 (1967): 42–45, 48–51.

476. Weems, *Desegregating the Dollar*, 26.

477. Grace Elizabeth Hale, *Making Whiteness: The Culture of Segregation in the South, 1890–1940* (New York: Pantheon, 1998), especially chap. 4.

478. Weems, *Desegregating the Dollar*, 26.

479. David J. Sullivan, "Don't Do This—If You Want to Sell Your Products to Negroes!" *Sales Management* 52 (1943): 46–51.

480. In a 1952 article in *Advertising Age*, Johnson advised would-be advertisers not to "use the term 'nigger,' 'negress,' 'darky' or 'boy.'" John H. Johnson, "Does Your Sales Force Know How to Sell the Negro Trade? Some Do's and Don'ts," *Advertising Age*, Mar. 17, 1952, 73–74.

481. Arnold M. Barban and Edward W. Cundiff, "Negro and White Responses to Advertising Stimuli," *Journal of Marketing Research*, Nov. 1964: 53–56.

482. "*Ebony* Survey Reveals Negro Buying Habits," *Advertising Age*, Aug. 28, 1950, 16–17.

483. Marcus Alexis, "Pathways to the Negro Market," *Journal of Negro Education* 28 (1959): 114–27.

484. Johnson, "Negro Trade," 74.

485. "The Forgotten 15,000,000 . . . Three Years Later," *Sponsor* 6 (1952): 76–77.

486. "Because of the psychological considerations involved, Negroes are extremely desirous of being identified as customers who recognize and demand quality merchandise" ("*Ebony* Survey," 17).

487. T. J. Jackson Lears, "From Salvation to Self-Realization: Advertising and the Therapeutic Roots of Consumer Culture, 1880–1930," in *The Culture of Consumption: Critical Essays in American History, 1880–1980*, ed. Richard Wightman Fox and T. J. Jackson Lears (New York: Pantheon, 1983), 1–38.

488. Henry Allen Bullock, "Consumer Motivations in Black and White—I," *Harvard Business Review* 38 (May/June 1961): 99.

489. Bullock, "Consumer Motivations I," 102.

490. William Leiss, for example, discusses how in consumer culture "class" is about learning to consume at a particular level in *The Limits to Satisfaction: An Essay on the Problem of Needs and Commodities* (Toronto: University of Toronto Press, 1976).

491. Berkman, "Advertising in *Ebony* and *Life*," 62.

492. Henry Allen Bullock, "Consumer Motivations in Black and White—II," *Harvard Business Review* 39 (July/August 1961): 113.

493. "Adman's' Guide," 42, quoting Moss H. Kendrix, African American owner of a Washington consulting firm (emphasis original). The article goes on to note that "although the Negro no longer wants to be white, he most certainly wants to have the same things and do the same things as white people."

494. E. Franklin Frazier, *Black Bourgeoisie* (Glencoe, IL: Free Press, 1957), 56.

495. Ibid., 173.

496. "Clients Seek Advice on Negro Market," *Sponsor (Negro Market Supplement)* 20 (1966): 40–43. The article notes that RJR ranks first and Liggett & Myers seventh for advertisers providing the most business on "Negro-appeal" radio stations.

497. "Yule Boycott Is Senseless, Johnson Says," *Advertising Age*, Oct. 21, 1963, 3, and "No Christmas Boycott," *The Crisis* 70 (1963): 555–56.

498. Ramona Bechtos, "Ads in Negro-Market Media Do Double Duty with Negro Buyers, Zimmer Says," *Advertising Age*, Jan. 13, 1964, 72. Jackie Robinson advocated the use of prominent African Americans who were affiliated with the civil rights movement in advertising ("Be Sure Negroes Featured in Ads Are Identified with Civil Rights Effort: Robinson," *Advertising Age*, Apr. 10, 1967, 12).

499. "Ads Alone Won't Win Negro Market: Russell," *Advertising Age*, Oct. 21, 1963, 3, 130.

500. Ibid.

501. "Clients Seek Advice," 43.

502. Ironically, the growth of a white middle class and its attendant white flight enabled the high-density inner-city neighborhoods to become crucibles for high-density advertising (billboards, buses, bus stops).

503. See, for example, John H. Pierce, Lora Lee, and Elizabeth Gilpin, "Smoking Initiation by Adolescent Girls, 1944 through 1988: An Association with Targeted Advertising," *Journal of the American Medical Association* 271 (1994): 608–11. The effectiveness of targeting is also linked to education, and smoking rates are about twice as high for adults with less than a high school diploma compared with those with four or more years of college. David Koepke, Brian R. Flay, and C. Anderson Johnson, "Health Behaviors in Minority Families: The Case of Cigarette Smoking," *Family and Community Health* 13

(1990): 35–43. See also Gilbert J. Botvin, Eli Baker, Catherine J. Goldberg, Linda Dusenbury, and Elizabeth M. Botvin, "Correlates and Predictors of Smoking among Black Adolescents," *Addictive Behaviors* 17 (1992): 97–103.

504. Tomas E. Novotny, Kenneth E. Warner, Juliette S. Kendrick, and Patrick L. Remington, "Smoking by Blacks and Whites: Socioeconomic and Demographic Differences," *American Journal of Public Health* 79 (1988): 1187–89. Fourteen percent of cancers in white males are cancer of the lung, and cancer increased 85 percent in white men between 1950 and 1985. Henry Weinstein and Alissa J. Rubin, "Tobacco Firms Targeted Blacks, Documents Show," *Los Angeles Times*, Feb. 6, 1998, A1.

505. R. C. Smith, "The Magazines' Smoking Habit: Magazines That Have Accepted Growing Amounts of Cigarette Advertising Have Failed to Cover Tobacco's Threat to Health," *Columbia Journalism Review* Jan./Feb. 1978, 29–31; Philip H. Dougherty, "Advertising: RJR Flap Not the First in Ad History," *New York Times*, Apr. 7, 1988.

506. "Nor did *Ebony* editors express any interest in covering the historic conference on the Realities of Cancer in Minority Communities." Alan Blum, "The Targeting of Minority Group by the Tobacco Industry," in *Minorities and Cancer*, ed. L. A. Jones (New York: Springer Verlag, 1989), 153–62.

507. Richard Pollay, "Separate But Not Equal: Racial Segmentation in Cigarette Advertising," *Journal of Advertising* no. 1 (1992): 52.

508. Thomas W. Laqueur, "Smoking and Nothingness," *The New Republic*, Sept. 18 and 25, 1995, 39–48.

509. Joseph A. Slobodzian, "Black Smokers Try to Revive Menthol Targeting Claim," *Fulton County Daily Report*, Feb. 9, 2001. Berry's statement begs the question of the legality of cigarettes, taking that to be the main premise of the contract, whereas *Brown* is trying to point out the extremely disparate results of this already questionable legality.

510. Shadur wrote, "It is surely unreasonable to ascribe such an enormous disparity to chance rather than to the purposeful steering that has been alleged by Black Smokers—at a minimum, they should be allowed their day in court." United States Court of Appeals for the Third Circuit No. 99–1931, *Rev. Jesse Brown v. Philip Morris*. Opinion and dissent available online at *http://law.findlaw .com/3rd/991931.html*.

511. Addison Yeaman, cited in Stanton A. Glantz, *The Cigarette Papers* (Berkeley: University of California Press, 1996), 54. Nicotine was always known to be the central ingredient in cigarettes. A senior scientist for PM wrote this in a confidential document released in a 1988 trial: "Think of the cigarette as a storage container for a day's supply of nicotine." Jerry Carroll, "Killing Us Softly: Women, a Prime Target of Cigarette Advertisers, Are About to Overtake Men as the Tobacco Industry's Best Customer," *San Francisco Chronicle*, Sept. 1, 1996, B4.

512. Borio, "Tobacco Timeline."

513. *Brown*, section 170. At that time, four million pounds of the imported high-nicotine tobacco, which was used in five brands, were found in B&W's warehouses. Tobacco companies also add several ammonia compounds to cigarettes in order to increase the efficiency of nicotine transfer.

514. "Appendix: A Brief History of Tobacco Advertising Targeting African Americans," in *Tobacco Use among U.S. Racial/Ethnic Minority Groups African Americans, American Indians and Alaska Natives, Asian Americans and Pacific Islanders, and Hispanics: A Report of the Surgeon General* (Atlanta: Department of Health and Human Services, Centers for Disease Control and Prevention, National Center for Chronic Disease Prevention and Health Promotion, Office on Smoking and Health, U.S. Department of Health and Human Services, 1998), 240–44. For a discussion of discriminatory intent and effect, see Henry Louis Gates, "Statistical Stigmata," *Cardozo Law Review* 11 (1990): 1275–89.

515. For studies that show a possible genetic difference between African Americans and whites in the metabolism of nicotine, indicating that black smokers have a higher exposure to cigarettes' carcinogenic components even when they smoke fewer cigarettes, see the editorial, "Pharmacogenics and Ethnoracial Differences in Smoking," *Journal of the American Medical Association* 280 (1998): 170–80; Ralph S. Caraballo, Gary A. Giovino, Terry F. Pechecek, Paul D. Mowery, Patricia A. Richter, Warren J. Strauss, Donald J. Sharp, Michael P. Eriksen, James L. Pirkle, and Kurt R. Maurer, "Racial and Ethnic Differences in Serum Cotinine Levels of Cigarette Smokers," *Journal of the American Medical Association* 280 (1998): 135–39; J. Eliseo Perez-Stable, Brenda Herrera, Peyton Jacob III, and Neal L. Benowitz, "Nicotine Metabolism and Intake in Black and White Smokers," *Journal of the American Medical Association* 280 (1998): 152–56; and Karen Ahijevych and Lea Ann Parsley, "Smoke, Constituent Exposure and Stage of Change in Black and White Women Cigarette Smokers," *Addictive Behaviors* 24 (1999): 115–20. None of these studies questions a generic use of genetic categories as "black" or "white." William Feigelman and Bernard Gorman found that class and stress differences, rather than race, account for variations in smoking behavior and that race is primarily a correlate of other demographic features. See Feigelman and Gorman, "Toward Explaining the Higher Incidence of Cigarette Smoking among Black Americans," *Journal of Psychoactive Drugs* 21 (1989): 299–305. For the importance of "cultural" as opposed to "socioeconomic" factors, see Geoffrey C. Kabat, Alfredo Morabia, and Ernst L. Wyner, "Comparison of Smoking Habits of Blacks and Whites in a Case-Control Study," *American Journal of Public Health* 81 (1991): 1483–86.

516. Brown, *States of Injury*, 27.

517. Kolawole S. Okuyemi, Jasjit S. Ahluwalia, and Kari J. Harris, "Pharmacotherapy of Smoking Cessation," *Archives of Family Medicine* 9 (2000): 270–81.

518. Joseph L. Graves Jr., *The Emperor's New Clothes: Biological Theories of Race at the Millennium* (New Brunswick, NJ: Rutgers University Press, 2001).

519. United States Court of Appeals for the Third Circuit No. 99–1931.

520. Nan Goodman shows how in the nineteenth century, "the law of the Good Samaritan helped significantly to designate African Americans as a class of expendable accident victims—a class defined by its existing marginality and by its actual or imagined incompetence, whose purpose was to have the accidents and bear the injuries the middle classes would then be fit to avoid." Goodman, *Shifting the Blame: Literature, Law, and the Theory of Accidents in Nineteenth Century America* (New York: Routledge, 1999), 119.

521. In fact, scrupulous detail has been paid by manufacturers to every detail of the cigarette: the characteristics and flavorings of tobacco; the composition of tipping, plug wrap, and cigarette papers; the use of perforations in the paper; the quality of adhesives and printing inks; the addition of filters in the 1950s, some of which contained asbestos; and the decades-long search for the "safe" cigarette, abandoned in the 1970s for fear of litigation. In addition to menthol, hundreds of additives have been experimented with, including ammonia and petchuli oil, as well as a series of products duplicitously advertised on the B&W Web site as "FDA approved," such as beet juice and beeswax.

522. Russell Banks, *The Sweet Hereafter* (New York: HarperCollins, 1991), pp. 90–91.

523. Abel, "The Real Tort Crisis."

524. Banks, *The Sweet Hereafter*, 187.

525. Ibid., 239.

526. Ibid., 32–33.

527. See Klinenberg, *Heat Wave*, for an analysis of the complicated politics of this so-called natural disaster that led to several hundred deaths. Factors in the deaths ranged from highly contested air-conditioning regulation to the politics of single elderly Americans living alone.

528. Mary Ann Doane, "Information, Crisis, Catastrophe," in *Logics of Television: Essays in Cultural Criticism*, ed. Patricia Mellencamp (Bloomington: Indiana University Press, 1990).

529. Banks, *The Sweet Hereafter*, 74.

530. Oliver Wendell Holmes, "Early Forms of Liability," in *Common Law*, ed. Mark DeWolfe Howe (Boston: Little, Brown, 1963), 31. Noted legal historian Morton Horwitz argues that by the late nineteenth century, the law had ceased to be "protective, regulative, paternalistic and above all a paramount expression of the moral sense of the community" and had "come to be thought of as facilitative of individual desires and as simply reflective of the existing organization of economic and political power" (cited in Goodman, *Shifting the Blame*). Goodman discusses the nineteenth-century struggle to keep the law "and its unavoidable morality under the exclusive control of the middle classes" (105).

531. Judge Andrews wrote succinctly of the meaning of proximate cause for the dissent in the New York Court of Appeals opinion of *Pulsgraf* in 1928: " '[B]ecause of convenience, of public policy, of a rough sense of justice, the law arbitrarily declines to trace a series of events beyond a certain point.' " Quoted in Kaufman, *Cardozo*, 297.

532. Scarry, *Bodies in Pain*, 298–99.

533. Ibid., 298.

534. But if the law is an obligitory passage point, the place where people have to go to have injuries recognized and compensated for, it is also mutated by what goes through it. On the one hand we have the "dangerous instrumentality" doctrine, a promising way of coding dangerous objects as lost by the 1930s. But four decades later, a new category, "toxic torts," emerged to try to account for the long-term dangers of our toxic exposures. This is precisely what makes law such an endlessly interesting area of study—and what makes it so open to political manipulation through judicial appointments. Sheila Jasa-

noff has traced the changes in court systems in dealing with these new mass class action suits in "Science and the Statistical Victim."

535. Alain Pottage, "Our Original Inheritance," in *Law, Anthropology, and the Constitution of the Social: Making Persons and Things*, ed. Alain Pottage and Martha Mundy (New York: Cambridge University Press, 2004), 253.

536. See Post, *Prejudicial Appearances*.

537. Holmes, *Common Law*, 65.

Index